Bauwelt Fundamente 178

I0869389

edited by

Elisabeth Blum
Jesko Fezer
Günther Fischer
Kaye Geipel
Angelika Schnell

Edited by Luisa Lorenza Corna and Mark Crinson

Struggles in the Concrete
Architecture and the Marxist Tradition

Bauverlag
Gütersloh · Berlin

Birkhäuser
Basel

The Bauwelt Fundamente series was founded in 1963 by Ulrich Conrads; it was edited from the early 1980s to 2015 jointly with Peter Neitzke.
Supervising editor of this volume: Jesko Fezer

Layout since 2017: Matthias Görlich

Front cover: Rouge Plant Construction, Architects Albert Kahn Associates, photographer unknown, 1918.
Back cover: From the Ground Up, Viollet-le-Duc, 1873.

Library of Congress Control Number: 2025933520

Bibliographic information published by the German National Library
The German National Library lists this publication in the Deutsche Nationalbibliografie; detailed bibliographic data are available on the Internet at http://dnb.dnb.de.

This work is subject to copyright. All rights are reserved, whether the whole or part of the material is concerned, specifically the rights of translation, reprinting, reuse of illustrations, recitation, broadcasting, reproduction on microfilms or in other ways, and storage in databases. For any kind of use, permission of the copyright owner must be obtained.

This publication is also available as an e-book (ISBN PDF 978-3-0356-2894-4)

© 2025 Birkhäuser Verlag GmbH, Basel
P.O. Box 44, 4009 Basel, Switzerland
Part of Walter de Gruyter GmbH, Berlin/Boston and Bauverlag BV GmbH, Gütersloh, Berlin

bau verlag

Printed in Germany

ISBN 978-3-0356-2893-7

9 8 7 6 5 4 3 2 1
www.birkhauser.com

FSC www.fsc.org
MIX
Papier | Fördert gute Waldnutzung
FSC® C089473

Contents

Introduction

Mark Crinson and Luisa Lorenza Corna

An extraordinary diagram appeared in the final stages of the public inquiry into the tragedy of Grenfell Tower, the high-rise social housing block in west London whose raging inferno in 2017 resulted in the deaths of seventy-two people. In the 'Grenfell Web of Blame', the counsel to the inquiry attempted to show the complex entanglements of responsibility for the disaster.[1] If the diagram cannot indicate the reasons for this interdependence of deniability – historically, they go back at least as far as the bonfire of regulations in the neoliberal 1980s – it does show how buck-passing is systemic, allowing building contractors and subcontractors, suppliers, testing authorities, landlords, politicians, and fire inspectors, all to slip free in an ever-shifting and rigged totality. Architects are also part of this entanglement, indeed crucial to the failures that ensued. Specifically, here, the 'Web of Blame' indicates the position of Studio E, the practice that oversaw the 2015 refurbishment of the tower block. The old idea of the sovereign architect, a figure raised above quotidian matters of building construction but somehow also able to hold them together – as master of design and material knowledge, as overseer of procurement, as the disinterested vehicle of the client's needs – was a figure established in the early modern period and then given academic and professional status in the eighteenth and nineteenth centuries. But in the 'Web of Blame' that figure is, at best, a frayed simulacrum of an already eroded myth. The sovereign architect (now the 'lead consultant') in the form of Studio E, was unable to understand building regulations, made fundamental errors in the design of cladding, and passed blame to subcontractors. Shirking responsibility, the architect was unable but also unwilling to reign, reduced to just another node, another thread in the tangled web.

Beyond architects, events like Grenfell (which we will return to later in this Introduction) also serve as a wake-up call for architectural historians, urging

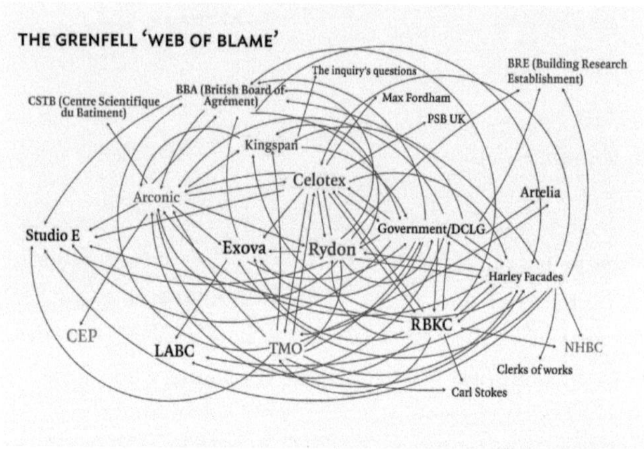

The Grenfell 'Web of Blame', counsel to the Grenfell Inquiry, 2024.

a more profound understanding of architecture's role within contemporary capitalist totality. The direction in which one might look for this is in Marxist critique, the theme explored by this book. However, by opening our edited collection with a reference to a recent catastrophe, we also aim to challenge the notion of intellectual or Marxist critique as detached and to call for a form of historical analysis alert to the brutal realities of contemporary capitalism and its necropolitical logics, to the sight of Grenfell's charred remains and the loss of those who didn't escape the flames.

And yet it would seem at first sight that there are only shaky foundations for a Marxist approach to architectural history: no broad historiographic base, no firm tradition in itself.[2] Perhaps this impression originates in the reluctance of the first wave of major Marxist thinkers to consider the built environment in its material forms. Certainly, despite the undoubted significance in the later twentieth century of, say, Henri Lefebvre's elaboration of the 'production of space' including the abstraction of everyday space, and Manfredo Tafuri's critique of the avant-garde and his exemplifications of how to do architectural history sensitive to ideology and dialectics, and even despite Marxist work in what should be closely related disciplines such as urban sociology (see Nick Beech's chapter later in this book), history of art, and social history, there is no deeply rooted and continuous body of Marxist architectural writing.

Indeed, in certain broad contexts – notably Anglophone architectural writing, but also in many continental European academic cultures – Marxist architectural critique has until very recently been seen as at best a moment which had its brief time before postmodernism of the 1980s, and at worst a mismatched collection of fragmentary and aborted endeavours from whose failure only a few scraps can be redeemed by theoretical speculation.

Architecture and Marxism

The depth and breadth of Marxist work on other aspects of culture makes the relative intermittency of Marxist architectural thinking in itself worth some consideration. After all, it's not as if Marx and Engels failed to consider the architecture of capitalism. Engels's *The Condition of the Working Class in England* (1845) is a veritable catalogue of the kinds of spaces (sometimes in plan or through maps) that capitalism had created, mounting an impassioned and often sardonic critique of the dynamic of concealment and exploitation behind the layout of the industrial city, as well as of how it produces a monadic humanity both confined by its 'limited space' and jolted by its turmoil.[3] Engels showed how poverty was intimately bound up with the sordid spaces remaindered from the pre-industrial city or jerry-built by speculative builders and then commodified by landlords; these were as much the *condition* of the working classes as their working day, their food and clothes, their wages, or their factory disciplines. At the same time, Engels pitched his description of this urban architecture in part as an alternative to the intrusive genre of reports on the industrial city written by social reformers. The devices of the picturesque (the prospect and the view) were thrust jarringly into scenes of urban squalor, parodically transposing landscape devices onto the city. Rather than the paradigms of mapping and observation used by social reformers to navigate areas of the city lived in by the poor, Engels used the metaphor of the labyrinth, playing, satirically again, with mapping and guidebook codes while baulking the reader in seemingly impenetrable spaces, indicating by contrast the local knowledge of the poor who lived in these areas.[4]

He would never return to this rich vein of urban description; his later book *The Housing Question* (1872, 1877) tied the housing crisis of contemporary Germany not to a housing shortage but to the conditions of existing housing, and not to the epi-phenomena of migration from rural areas but to the logic of capitalist development that had created the need for that migration.

Engels's emphasis on the problematic of how to represent the poor and their spaces, how to place them as central to any account of the making and using of the city and its architecture, has resonances with much Marxist work over recent decades, even if it has not been taken up within architectural history and criticism. It's an issue that, of course, goes to the heart both of how architecture is made and how its history is written – the latter so often mirroring the class interests (capital, professional status, property) that produces the former. As Jacques Rancière has explained what he calls the 'speech of the poor' – which we might transpose as the 'architecture of the poor' or even the absence of 'the poor' from architecture – there is a kind of 'suspended truth' as history, in Walter Benjamin's words, turns in a 'secret heliotropism' towards the rulers or victors.[5] Or, as Manfredo Tafuri posed the question, how is the housing of the working class, even when manifesting 'good design', necessarily related to political reform if that class is not to be fully represented in politics itself (specifically here, the management of their own homes)?[6] But while one struggle may be for representation – to be in the actual space, to have it created with the poor in mind, to have their creation as part of it and not confined as the inevitable figure of the other – it is not to mimic the forms of surveillance that all too readily exposed 'slum conditions' or some such, where the seeing of the poor is also the not-seeing of them in favour of some operative rationality. Architecture is thus, structurally and historically, a normative discourse of the victors and disinclined towards these kinds of considerations. All of this entails that accounts of architecture, and thus of the making of its history, have divested themselves of the same class-based differentiations, leading instead to descriptions of the splendours of style or the chronicling of proper names rather than analysis of the material conditions shaping how space is created and the question of its determinations. And too often, when the architecture of the poor is central to architectural writing it comes under the optic of the 'vernacular' which, like the master-slave dialectic, is a projection of architecture's position – western, post-capitalist revolution (agrarian and industrial) – onto its other as merely the product of function, need and mentality.

None of this is to say that a Marxist architectural history should not analyse how power is realised and how it reproduces itself in architecture under capitalism; far from it. Perhaps Marx, with his apparent lack of interest in architecture and urbanism, was to blame. But if, unlike Engels, he never wrote directly about the subject, his work everywhere has implications for how it might be understood. The salient issue here is labour and its relation to class struggle (the struggle of the formation of class as much as between classes), and just as Marx places labour (and its remuneration, its value, its conditions, its social reproduction, its whole anthropology, even its pleasures)[7] as central to the working of capital and thus the making of history, so it is central to the making of architecture, in direct as well as displaced forms: in the relations of production manifested in the building site (as Katie Lloyd Thomas and Silke Kapp explore later in this book), in the creation today of a precariat among the formerly professional labour of architectural offices (given historical resonance in Tom Wilkinson's chapter), and in the relation between exploitation and expropriation in local and global forms of building labour and the consequent racial regimes of modernity. In all these forms of labour there is architecture being made and architecture being used (indeed, the 'ideology of labour' was, Tafuri suggested, perhaps most assimilated by the institution of architecture).[8] In a way the term 'architecture' already had baked into it the sense not only of a particular kind of object but also of an activity led by architects focused on design as a capacity separated from manual work and, as such, one of the techniques identified with the emerging social forms of early modern capitalism. Labour is also central, of course, to the utopian versions of these relations of production, even though their explicit architectures, whether in the form of an alleged autonomy from capitalism or of more pointed difference from it, may have been less of concern to Marx.

Architecture was thus implicit in, or at least it can be seen behind, Marx's discussion of the value-form, of the commodity form (it is almost a cliché now to talk of how housing has become commodified), of mediation, of totality, of the working day and capitalist temporality more generally, of global relations of production (to be explored later in Mark Crinson's chapter), and of course of ideology, and many other classic Marxist issues, all of them with resonance for the understanding and analysis of architecture.[9] In fact, almost everywhere you look in *Capital* architecture is implied: from the division of labour and development of machinery in the 'vast automaton' of the factory,[10] to the great final section on 'So-Called Primitive Accumulation'. In the latter, sardonically likened by Marx to a 'process of natural history', [11] he explains the rationale behind the enclosure movement and thus the agrarian revolution. The whole development of the great eighteenth-century estates and their country houses should be understood in this light, including the infrastructure of new roads and the terraforming of the land both for purposes of surplus-value, for controlling restrictive access, and for the management of the newly proletarianised wage labourer. Indeed, as well as his attention to the value of form,[12] there is more than a smattering of architecture metaphors in Marx's writing. These include most obviously the base-superstructure model (although this was much less used by Marx and Engels than in the mechanistic formulations of some of their followers), and the famous comparison between a bee and an architect (or master builder) which, rather than essentialising human-animal differences, is really about the abstracting effects and the subordination or instrumentalisation of labour to the will of design ('many a human architect [is put] to shame by the construction of [the bee's] honeycomb cells ... [but] the architect builds the cell in his mind before he constructs it in wax').[13]

A historiographic excursus

How to explain the relation between these rich analytical frames and metaphors, these close descriptive aetiologies so suggestive for architectural writing, and the issue of the intermittency of Marxist-influenced work by architectural historians? We may of course conclude that what was instrumental here was the absence of theoretical work directly on the subject by the major early figures, or at least its presence only as something intimated, that is at least until Frankfurt School writers like Siegfried Kracauer, Max Horkheimer and Walter Benjamin.[14] But that would be to avoid explaining what it is about architecture and the specialised writing of its history and criticism – what conditions pervade these – that has entailed the weak intermittency of Marxist writing, both about architecture by Marxists and in the discipline itself.

To take a particular yet illustrative example of this, we might ask how Marxism was and was not part of architectural writing in the Anglophone academy. Let us imagine the contributors to a symposium held in London around 1946 on Marxist-related approaches to architecture and its history. Of course, it would not have the word 'Marxist' anywhere near its title, but nevertheless the scenario offers a snapshot of actual and potential historiography. One contributor might be John Summerson, whose recently published *Georgian London* claimed the centrality of the 'trade cycle … the land speculator and the adventuring builder'.[15] Another might be Anthony Blunt, yet to abandon the influence of the Hungarian Marxist art historian Frederick Antal, certain elements of which were still to be found in his 1941 book on François Mansart.[16] In both cases their private interest in what Marxism might bring to historical work was not followed through into what they published.[17] Suppose Meyer Schapiro had flown over from New York, fresh from his recent articles on the 'critical correlation of the forms and meanings … with historical conditions of the same period and region'.[18] Our imagined symposium might also include the Hungarian Marxists displaced to Britain in the 1930s – Antal himself, Johannes Wilde and Arnold Hauser – each of whom, though art historians, also worked on architecture. We might now be uncomfortable with the importance such writers attributed to the category of style as the focus of social and materialist analysis – a central feature of Vienna School art history – but these matters of style (and form) were, at the same time, what made the connection between architecture and art history possible (thereby, as a side effect, giving architectural history greater visibility in the academy).[19] Beyond style, their fellow central European Marxist Francis

Klingender was then writing what is still one of the standard textbooks on the visual culture and environments of industrial capitalism, *Art and the Industrial Revolution* (1947).

The symposium is a fantasy, of course, but it shows that there were, just after the war, the ingredients of a *tradition* of Marxist architectural history that drew upon pre-war continental developments in German-speaking art history as well as currents of Marxist thought from central Europe, especially the Hungarian circle around Georg Lukács. They would never come together or be sustained, never form that coherent utopian and political action that makes a tradition (indeed, whose prospect activates a certain project of architecture).[20] Instead there was an 'ideological retreat' in art history at this time.[21] The disinclination to make Marxist ideas explicit, even to write as if struggle was something relevant to architecture, had some of the usual reasons and some specific to the discipline. Echoes of McCarthyite anti-Communism in Britain clearly played a role,[22] and there was all that '1956' stood for. More parochially, there was the abandonment of the fusion between art and architectural history that was a consequence of two otherwise unrelated tendencies: a deep suspicion of the Nazi-tainted formalist tradition of German art history, and the new modernist claims for the autonomy of media.[23] Isolated from Marxist historians, architectural history became severed from its links to art history, especially its more radical developments, at the same time as it was marginalised in the now-modernist architectural schools. In the 1950s and 1960s a generation of young architectural critics and historians left for the USA, where any possibility of Marxist architectural analysis was stifled in the long Thermidor of US academic anti-Marxism. Meanwhile, architectural history in Britain became wedded to a theory-averse empiricism and a connoisseurial formalism, both focused on the proclivities or 'agency' of the great and the reproduction of their attributes and protocols. The work of Lefebvre, David Harvey, Fredric Jameson or Tafuri barely penetrated the empiricist wall in Britain; the claim that Marxism was the cultural 'master-code' through which to write architectural criticism was not taken up.[24] And when theory did finally penetrate the wall, it was via Michel Foucault and other post-structuralists.

Architectural history was a 'discipline of propriety',[25] its subject buildings as isolated objects arranged either in diachronic order or within the city as *musée imaginaire*. The 'social' was background at best. All of this in a world where architecture's history was bordered in the same way as the nation, regardless of imperialisms and the extensiveness of colonial rule. On the one hand, the discipline directed its activism through the rising conservation movement; on the other, it practised a forelock-tugging to the pre-industrial class idyll of the country house and its outliers, the National Trust and the journal *Country Life*. Alongside this, the main objections to Marxist approaches were around a set of enduring caricatures: a perceived determinism or reflectionism between an economic base and a cultural superstructure; a perceived lack of interest in analysis of architecture itself in favour of some other thing, some context; the idea that Marxism would act as a hermeneutics of suspicion labelled 'critique'; and, linked to these, that Marxism would demand a purposive not to say utilitarian judgement of effectiveness. There was little or no notion of a realism in architecture or indeed – until the 1980s – of a political critique of avant-gardism along Tafuri's lines, nor of the Lefebvrian 'production of space' as the always socially constituted and contested practice of space making, nor of Jameson's cognitive mapping and its implications for a non-normative understanding of different categories of architecture across space. There was equally, it should be said, little or no interest in colonialism and race, and their imbrications with capitalism, until at least Anthony D. King's work of the late 1970s and then this was immediately marginalised. (Even a critical relation to the imperial archive – reflected upon in Onyeka Igwe's chapter later in this book – has only recently been introduced to architecture). Eventually architectural history, after the hegemony of the empiricists, reached its own form of happy (if barely coexisting) pluralism, one already reached in art history. If this was a new architectural history, more prepared to break beyond mere empiricism, then it was still poorly prepared to treat the social as more than decorative 'context', always behind or beyond the architecture, or to treat history as anything but ever-present cause.

To be fair, even though Marxist architectural writing may lack a solid historiographical base and tradition, the interest in applying the tools provided by Marx to analyse the built environment, as well as its relation to nature and ecology (explored in both Rujana Rebernjak's and Alistair Cartwright's essays later in this book) have shown signs of significant revival in recent architectural history and theory.[26] This interest may not always be visible as a continuous line of inquiry, but it resurfaces at intervals, when the conditions become more severe (one thinks particularly of housing crisis and precarity of work, but also of rising ethnocentrism and neo-fascism, of the renewed onslaughts of settler colonialism, and so on). If we examine the architectural criticism and history of the past decade, we can see a number of researchers committed to recovering forgotten attempts at reshaping architectural history and practice from a materialist perspective: either by exploring pre-modern and modern architecture through Marxist categories and lenses (of labour, abstraction, and alienation) that have yet to receive sufficient attention;[27] by beginning to open up the structural conjunctions between race, capitalism and architecture;[28] by investigating Marxism and architectural theory in the old 'second' and 'third' worlds;[29] or by analysing how contemporary architecture aligns with the dictates of our neoliberal society.[30] The list above is certainly not comprehensive, but it is meant to provide evidence of a return of Marxist-inflected research.

Worth more attention is an area thus far untouched in our mapping: the relationship between Marxism and feminism in architecture. This nexus is complex to address, as the historiographical foundation is not just shaky but almost non-existent (though see Luisa Lorenza Corna's chapter later). One notable exception to this general neglect is the new edition of the 1984 book *Making Space, Women and the Man-Made Environment* by the British group Matrix. Matrix was a feminist cooperative of architects which evolved from the New Architecture Movement (NAM), a socialist coalition dedicated to unionising architectural work and rethinking the profession, placing users at its centre. Yet, if the link to socialism and Marxist theory is somehow inscribed in the history of the collective, their book is hesitant about making Marxist affiliation explicit. Matrix, as with many other feminist collectives of the 1970s–80s came out of a split with broader socialist organisations perceived as led by men, and as such was perhaps cautious in using 'the masters' tools'.

That said, as highlighted by Katie Lloyd Thomas and Karen Burns in their brief introduction to the book's re-edition, the ideas and methods of Matrix were decisively materialist.[31] The group's work started from the premise that women are products of social structures and, as such, have different experiences and needs in relation to the built environment which are rarely expressed. This wasn't a thesis found in architectural writing at the time, as there was virtually none on the subject, but a conclusion the members of Matrix reached by combining socialist readings with their first-hand experience of marginalisation as women professionals and mothers. Yet this realisation was only the beginning – a plan for action, so to speak. As they themselves declared, understanding how women were 'placed' in the 'man-made' environment served the purpose of subverting that order. Their political force was remarkable, but our aim here is not to celebrate their practice. Instead, our book focuses on excavations like those conducted by Thomas and Burns, as they exemplify an approach to architectural history that traces Marxism on the fringes. In other words, it engages with theories and practices – praxis, more precisely – that identify new forms of oppression and struggle without explicitly relying on the Marxian lexicon.

A different conception of the resources of Marxist criticism was generated by the internal debate in US architecture schools about the supposed 'post-critical' condition and its implications for architectural critique, as well as asking again the Tafurian question 'can architecture be an emancipatory project under capitalism?'. The result was series of books edited by Nadir Lahiji, and gathering many critics of the separation of academic discourse from political critiques of capitalism.[32] Much of this focuses on rightly criticising the idea of a post-political environment, and instead rethinking the relation between architecture and politics deploying critical dispositions cultivated by the Frankfurt School and revived in recent work by Slavoj Žižek, Jacques Rancière and others. The most powerful arguments anathematise the way that post-critical discourses, often

peppered with French post-structural terms, have coincided with neoliberal politics and a 'postmodern management of capitalism'.[33] But the project can feel as if it still cleaves to parameters shared by its targets – the view from the architectural studio, an elevated notion of 'theory' divorced from praxis, the idea of disciplinary autonomy, and debates *within* architectural culture (or, specifically, the culture of US architecture schools) – and thus is limited by its aim of 'reclaiming the abandoned radical project *in* the discipline' (our italics).[34]
Another line of research, initiated by Pier Vittorio Aureli and the researchers formerly affiliated with his PhD programme 'The City as a Project', revisits the history of architecture from antiquity to the twentieth century with a focus on the category of labour. Their analysis draws particularly on Mario Tronti's so-called 'Copernican revolution', a heterodox move of Italian 1960s Marxism which reversed the traditional understanding of the relationship between capital and labour.[35] For Tronti and his 'workerist' comrades, it is class struggle that compels capitalism to adapt and evolve by creating new forms to suppress workers' insubordination, not the other way around as established readings of capital posited. Through this lens, Aureli and Francesco Marullo challenge the common interpretation of modernist architecture as the result of aesthetic and ethical imperatives, shedding light on its ties to economic and political necessities. Aureli illustrates this point with reference to Le Corbusier's Maison Dom-Ino, explaining how the architect's decision to leave the completion of the building to its future inhabitants was not so much an effort to include or empower the underprivileged, but a strategy to stir a desire for ownership among the working class, thereby keeping class conflict in check.[36] Marullo, on the other hand, turns his attention to early twentieth-century industrial architecture in the USA, correlating the introduction of new production methods with changes in the spatial configuration of factories, as reflected in architectural plans. His research liberates technical drawings from their confined architectural meaning, and suggests a reading of simplified, generic forms in certain factory plans as evidence of industrial capitalism's need to concentrate large masses of indistinct workers, with the aim of integrating and subsuming their cooperative labour 'as lymph for progress'.[37] (A different take on this is the subject of Claire Zimmerman's chapter in this book).

Whereas the above research has positioned the category of labour at the core of what happens in architectural history, another recent strand of Marxist-leaning analysis focuses on the labour of architects in the present. More sociological in its approach, this body of work examines how architects' roles have been reshaped by contemporary capitalism and digital technologies. The nonprofit organisation Architecture Lobby, for example, has explored these transformations through surveys of both practitioners and theorists, using the collected data to propose guidelines for regulating the profession. These guidelines include advocating laws prohibiting unpaid internships and suggesting the abrogation of fee structures based on construction percentages. In the Architecture Lobby's efforts there is a clear echo of Manfredo Tafuri's 1970s concerns about the proletarianisation of architects.[38] Building on his critique, the organisation challenges the architectural profession's often misleading self-perception, urging architects to see themselves as part of a broader labour force, subject to the same economic forces as other workers.[39]
While the Architecture Lobby's work primarily focuses on the designer's labour, the research of Katie Lloyd Thomas, Tilo Amhoff, and Nick Beech broadens the scope to address the architectural industry in its entirety. Their work, culminating in the 2014 conference *Industries of Architecture* and its subsequent publication, explores the various sites of production and the interrelations that shape architectural projects.[40] This research also relates to what Howard Davis calls the 'culture of building' in architectural history – the systems of knowledge, rules, procedures and habits practised by all actors involved in architectural production.[41] While the focus on labour aligns this work with other recent Marxist-leaning scholars, what sets it apart is the attempt to dislodge the architect from centre-stage of the industry and direct attention to materials and processes often overlooked in traditional architectural history.[42]

Contemporary struggles (and failures) in the concrete

Struggles in the Concrete is a deliberately allusive title for this book. It lodges perhaps the most fundamental of Marxist concepts, class struggle, into the heart of architectural thinking. Here, 'concrete' is both materialism in the sense of the multifarious and complexly mediated material realities of the world in which life is made, and it is the facticity or matter of architecture which takes natural or synthetic substances, shaping and framing that life as part of a societal order, including what is enabled and allowed to flourish, what is guided or directed, and what is dominated and oppressed. To think of struggles in architecture is to think of an architectural-historical materialism, of architecture as coextensive with material life. But it is also to think of architecture – by which is meant all the human built environment – as one of the most coherent and significant aspects of material life, as both the expression and the framework for social and historical experience. Marxist approaches to architecture, then, are at one level simply attempts to approximate a reality that is already 'Marxist in its structure'.[43]

The choice of the term 'concrete' must be further stressed. In the history of twentieth-century architecture, concrete stands out as a material like no other. Although its origins date back thousands of years, the introduction of reinforced concrete – a combination of cement and steel – enabled large spans without the need for arches, revolutionising both building methods and architectural aesthetics. In the post-1945 period its unfinished form, the iconic *béton brut*, became symbolic of an abstract expressionism in architecture and gave its name to brutalism, perhaps the last international movement to merge style with ethos, with a commitment to embracing the intrinsic qualities of building materials. For Alison and Peter Smithson, brutalism's essence wasn't an obsession with cement or functional forms, but the ability to 'see materials for what they were: the woodness of wood; the sandiness of sand', and, we might add, the concreteness of concrete.[44]

An understanding of architecture as material literacy offers, we argue, another possible Marxist approach to the discipline, and one that demands urgent attention, given the central role of materials in some of the most catastrophic failures of the last decade, with the Grenfell Tower tragedy standing as a key tipping point. To be clear, we are not assigning sole responsibility for such events to architects' ignorance about building materials. The responsibility, as the intricate diagram discussed earlier on suggests, is shared among

Grenfell Tower in west London, eleven months after the fire, May 2018.

companies, testing authorities, politicians, and architects – essentially, the various public and private actors that make up the contemporary construction industry. Moreover, the root cause lies not so much in genuine inexperience about material performance but in the deliberate cover-up of both systemic and individual inadequacy, as seen in the rigged testing of insulation boards and cladding panels by the companies Celotex and Arconic. Still, whether unintentional, calculated, or a combination of both, the question remains: how have the contemporary architecture and building industries become so numb to materials, their performances and their effects that they allowed, as someone put it, the equivalent of 'adding the fuel power of a 19,000-litre oil tanker to the walls of a building'?[45] The answer lies in their unbridled neoliberalism, marked by deregulation, the erosion of standards, and the increasing division of labour and fragmentation of responsibility. These shifts have weakened oversight and accountability, allowing profit-driven decisions to override safety and materially informed considerations.

What we are signalling here is a dangerous reversal of the Smithsons' lesson. By making this comparison, however, we are not attempting to pit the 'glorious' achievements of postwar architecture against the failures of today's vulture or cannibal capitalism[46] – the widespread exposure of modernism's shortcomings prevents any uncritical celebration. The Smithsons' principle of material integrity allows us to emphasise the consequences of disregarding such considerations among manufacturers, architects, and testing authorities, going beyond what the British architects may have originally envisioned. The risk extends not only to the impoverishment of architectural practice but also to the potential maiming or destruction of the lives of building inhabitants. A Marxist approach to architecture must therefore learn from the Smithsons' ethical attention to materials – what they enable or hinder – while also maintaining a macroscopic perspective that considers the building in (or as) its social context, and how and by whom these materials will be used and abused.

Moreover, as the long-awaited second part of the Grenfell Report revealed, everyone was aware of the vulnerabilities of the demographic typically occupying such buildings.[47] Yet, this awareness did not translate into consideration; rather, it allowed the actors involved to lower their threshold of attention or turn a blind eye to the failings that could – and did – cause harm. The report exposed the link between managed decline, class indifference, and structural racism, implicating not only political representatives but also the building and architectural industries that shape our cities. In light of this failure to build and maintain dwellings for those excluded by the speculative real estate market, it seems relevant to ask Tafuri's question again (explored later in this book by Nick Thoburn) – *what is class architecture?* For Tafuri, such an architecture was impossible without a class-based criticism,[48] a thesis that resonates with the statement of a relative of a victim of the Grenfell fire: 'The system isn't broken', he said, 'it was built this way.'[49]

Events like Grenfell and the subsequent inquiries are a warning to architects, often too focused on the pristine images of their newly completed projects than on their long-term performance. Questions about how buildings age and require maintenance rarely appear to top the contemporary architectural agenda, preoccupied as it is with capturing the present moment through striking forms and novel ideas. In recent years, particularly in the wake of the COVID-19 pandemic and the mounting challenges posed by climate change, political theorists and activists have turned their attention to the 'crisis of care'.[50] This term refers to a widespread yet unevenly distributed breakdown in the ability to maintain social, ecological, and political systems: social reproduction as a 'major site of capitalist crisis'.[51] In response, various actions, manifestos, and academic texts have called for a politics that places care at the heart of the state, the economy, and grassroots activism, recognising that while care may be a source of critique its exploitation also makes it part of capital accumulation. Far from being a departure from traditional materialism and class politics, as orthodox Marxists may at first sight perceive, on closer inspection 'care' is just a more expanded understanding of the term labour, one that considers the invisible intermingling of emotional and practical work through which society is sustained and thrives and which extends through displacing and offloading reproductive work onto migrant workers from poor regions through 'global care chains'.[52] We want to suggest here that a Marxist approach to architecture, in line with the stakes of our times, should make the concept of 'care' its own. In the context of architecture, care translates into maintenance, meaning a design approach that prioritises use value, and involves relinquishing the modernist notion of authorship, rethinking architectural practice as the act of upkeeping buildings already in place and protecting the communities that inhabit them.

Overview

The edited collection that follows brings together substantial historical and theoretical work by both architectural historians and theorists dealing with the variety of analytical categories and concepts that belong to the Marxist tradition. As already argued, we are interested to widen out that tradition in terms of how it relates to architecture, to juxtapose the concerns of Marxism and the concerns of architectural analysis, as well as to relate Marxist writing about architecture to some of the pressing issues of our present moment. The book, therefore, has two main aims. The first is to re-examine overlooked figures whose work links architecture with Marxism and to recontextualise those whose contributions have lapsed into obscurity: hence figures such as Marta Lonzi, Sérgio Ferro and Anthony D. King. As part of this aim the book also engages with major figures such as Siegfried Kracauer, Manfredo Tafuri, Stuart Hall, and even the very-non-Marxist Eugène Emmanuel Viollet-le-Duc, and it comes at their work from previously unexplored perspectives.

The second aim is to reorient architectural thinking, via Marxism, to the pressing concerns of the contemporary world and of the role of architecture within it. This is most obviously flagged up in the titles of the four thematic sections of the book: 'Labour and its Histories'; 'Infrastructure and Environment'; 'Ideological Formations'; and 'Building the Racial Regime of Modernity'. In the first section, the precarity of work is discussed through the 'proletarianised' or precarious conditions of the architectural profession as well as its relation to architectural labour more widely, most especially the organisation of the building site. This initial section also looks at the classic site of modern labour, the factory, and especially its organisation around the assembly line. In the second section, we ask how concepts of environment and infrastructure have been understood in three contexts: the late welfare state in western Europe and residents' perception of housing; Communist Yugoslavia with its distinctive policies of self-management; and, finally, through notions of nature and ecology, as well as labour and race, in the thinking of Viollet-le-Duc. The third section addresses various 'ideological formations' that have shaped – and continue to shape – architectural historiography. One of these is the call for planetary accounts of architecture and its history, which are counterposed with critical concepts of the global, including Marxist notions of totality and of combined and uneven development. A second, less-discussed ideological construct examined here is the figure of the architect, and the way it has served as an umbrella for reactionary forms of gender relations. In the final section, abstracted discourses on the 'urban' are questioned not by using urban protest as symptomatic but through a re-examination of the material forms of such protest and its repression; relatedly, the section also asks in what ways a Marxist critique of the racial regime of modernity, through an encounter with its archival formations, can be extended to the imbrication of race within forms of architectural production.

Notes

1 See https://prodgti.s3.eu-west-2.amazonaws.com/Grenfell%20Web%20of%20Blame.pdf?VersionId=u4UrBx.EEpbYUh0w7ussLrNu5LoSp4pu (accessed 21/10/24).

2 Luisa Lorenza Corna highlights the lack of a solid historiographical foundation in architectural Marxism and attempts to retrace the connections between the two fields in her 'Architecture', in Bev Skeggs, Sara Farris, Alberto Toscano, Svenja Bromberg (eds.), *The Sage Handbook of Marxism* (London: Sage, 2021).

3 Friedrich Engels, *The Condition of the Working Class in England* (1845) (Harmondsworth: Penguin, 1987), 68–9.

4 See for instance, the 'view' from Ducie Bridge in Manchester, closely followed by Long Millgate where the visitor 'has lost all clue, and knows not whither to turn': Engels, *Condition of the Working Class*, 89–90.

5 Jacques Rancière, *The Names of History*, trans. Hassan Melehy (Minneapolis: University of Minnesota Press, 1994), 51; Jacques Rancière, *Dissenting Words: Interviews with Jacques Rancière*, ed. and trans. by Emiliano Battista (London: Bloomsbury, 2017), 100, 128, 154.

6 Gail Day, 'Manfredo Tafuri, Fredric Jameson and the Contestations of Political Memory', *Historical Materialism*, vol. 20, no. 1 (2012), 31–77.

7 Caroline Arscott, 'William Morris, Decoration and Materialism', in Andrew Hemingway (ed.), *Marxism and the History of Art from William Morris to the New Left* (London: Pluto, 2006), 9–27; Stewart Martin, 'Approaching Marx's Aesthetic: Or, What is Sensuous Practice?', in Warren Carter, Barnaby Haran, and Frederic J. Schwarz (eds), *Renew Marxist Art History* (London: Art Books, 2013), 78–93.

8 Manfredo Tafuri, 'Note to the Second (Italian) Edition', in *Theories and Histories of Architecture* (London: Granada, 1980), unpaginated.

9 On time, for instance, see David Harvey, 'Money, Time, Space, and the City', in *Consciousness and the Urban Experience: Studies in the History and Theory of Capitalist Urbanization* (Baltimore: John Hopkins University Press, 1985), 1–35.

10 Karl Marx, *Capital – A Critique of Political Economy Volume 1*, trans. by Ben Fowkes (Harmondsworth: Penguin, 1976), 502.

11 This is from the first preface of 1867 to Marx, *Capital*, 92. See also Marx's interest in the London property speculator Nicholas Barbon: Ibid., 127, 226, 242.

12 Anna Kornbluh, *The Order of Forms: Realism, Formalism, and Social Space* (Chicago IL and London: University of Chicago Press, 2019), 17.

13 Marx, *Capital*, 284.

14 Also worth mentioning in Western Marxism is Georg Lukács's recently translated *The Specificity of the Aesthetic* (1951) volume 1, ed. Tyrus Miller (Chicago: Haymarket, 2024), and especially volume 2 (to be published in 2026).

15 John Summerson, *Georgian London* (1945), revised edition (London: Peregrine Books, 1978), 26.

16 For Antal and Blunt see Matthew Critchley, 'Mannerism and Method: Class and Artistic Agency in the Writing of Anthony Blunt, 1934 to 1949', *Architectural Theory Review*, vol. 24, no. 2 (2020), 164–181.

17 Elizabeth McKellar. 'Summerson's Marxist Moment: Georgian London and Historical Materialism', paper given at the 'Struggles in the Concrete' conference, Birkbeck, April 2023.

18 Meyer Schapiro, 'From Mozarabic to Romanesque in Silos', *Art Bulletin*, vol. 21, no. 4 (December 1939), 313. For Schapiro and Marxism see Andrew Hemingway, 'Meyer Schapiro: Marxism, Science and Art', in Hemingway (ed.), *Marxism*, 123–142; Otto Karl Werckmeister, 'Jugglers in a Monastery', *Oxford Art Journal*, vol. 17, no. 1 (1994), 60–4.

19 On Antal see Paul Stirton, 'Frederick Antal', in Hemingway (ed.), *Marxism*, 45–66.

20 Fredric Jameson, 'Architecture and the Critique of Ideology', in Joan Ockman ed., *Architecture, Criticism, and Ideology* (Princeton: Princeton Architectural Press, 1985), 72–3.

21 John Roberts, 'Arnold Hauser', in Hemingway (ed.), *Marxism*, 164.

22 As instanced by the fuss around the International Conference on Regional Planning and Development (1956), five of whose organising committee members were accused of being 'Communists or Communist sympathisers' by *The Spectator*, followed by allegations made by the Home and Foreign Offices: Edinburgh University Archives, Percy Johnson-Marshall Papers, GB0237/PJM/ICRPD/1.

23 Mark Crinson and Richard J. Williams, *The Architecture of Art History – A Historiography* (London: Bloomsbury, 2018).

24 Leo Robson, 'Jameson After Post Critique', *New Left Review* no. 144 (Nov/Dec 2023), 114.

25 Hayden White, 'Foreword: Rancière's Revisionism', in Rancière, *The Names of History*, trans. Hassan Melehy, x.

26 The recent rediscovery of Marx and Engels's writing on ecology and metabolic rift has inspired important work that is beginning to seep through into architectural history: see John Bellamy Foster, *Marx's Ecology: Materialism and Nature* (New York: Monthly Review Press, 2000); John Bellamy Foster, *The Return of Nature: Socialism and Ecology* (New York: Monthly Review Press, 2020); Andreas Malm, *Fossil Capital: The Rise of Steam Power and the Roots of Global Warming* (London: Verso, 2016). On architectural history see, for instance, Mark Crinson, *Shock City: Image and Architecture in Industrial Manchester* (London: Paul Mellon Centre for Studies in British Art, 2022), 137–163; Reinhold Martin, 'On the Fence: Media, Ecology, Marx', *Critical Inquiry*, vol. 49, no. 3 (Spring 2023), 359–383.

27 Pier Vittorio Aureli, *Architecture and Abstraction* (Cambridge, MA, and London: MIT Press, 2023), vii-xxv.

28 See Ginger Nolan, *Savage Mind to Savage Machine: Racial Science and Twentieth-Century Design* (Minneapolis: University of Minnesota Press, 2021). If not explicitly Marxist, see also Irene Cheng, Charles L. Davis II, and Mabel O. Wilson (eds.), *Race and Modern Architecture* (Pittsburgh: University of Pittsburgh Press, 2020).

29 See the special issue of *Architectural Histories* ed. Hilde Heynen and Sebastiaan Loosen, on 'Marxism and Architectural History Across the East-West Divide', vol. 6, no. 1 (2018).

30 Douglas Spencer, *The Architecture of Neoliberalism* (London: Bloomsbury, 2016); Douglas Spencer, *Critique of Architecture: Essays on Theory, Autonomy, and Political Economy* (Basel: Birkhäuser, 2021); Katie Lloyd Thomas, Tilo Amhoff, and Nick Beech (eds.), *Industries of Architecture* (London and New York: Routledge, 2016).

31 See the Preface by Karen Burns and Katie Lloyd Thomas in Matrix, *Making Space: Women and the Man-Made Environment* (1984) (London: Verso: 2022); Karen Burns, and Lori Brown, 'Telling Transnational Histories of Women in Architecture, 1960–2015'. *Architectural Histories*, vol. 8, no. 1 (2020), 15.

32 Nadir Z. Lahiji (ed.), *Architecture Against the Post-Political: Essays in Reclaiming the Critical Project* (London: Routledge, 2014); Nadir Z. Lahiji (ed.), *Can Architecture be an Emancipatory Project?* (Winchester: Zero Books, 2016). See also Spencer, *The Architecture of Neoliberalism*.

33 Lahiji 'Introduction' in Lahiji (ed.), *Architecture Against*, 6.

34 Ibid., 1.

35 Pier Vittorio Aureli, *The Project of Autonomy* (New York: Temple Hoyne Buell Center, 2008), 38.

36 Pier Vittorio Aureli, 'Introduction. Means to an End: The Rise and Fall of the Architectural Project of the City', and Francesco Marullo, 'Architecture and Revolution. The Typical Plan as Index of Generic', both in Pier Vittorio Aureli (ed.), *The City as a Project* (Berlin: Ruby Press, 2013).

37 Marullo, 'Architecture and Revolution'.

38 This is a recurring theme in Manfredo Tafuri's work. His initial reference to the 'proletarianization of the architect' appears in his seminal essay 'Toward a Critique of Architectural Ideology', *Contropiano* 1 (January/April 1969), later included in Manfredo Tafuri, *Architecture and Utopia* trans. Barbara Luigia La Penta (Cambridge, Mass and London: MIT Press, 1979).

39 See the Architecture Lobby's website https://architecture-lobby.org; and Peggy Deamer (ed.), *The Architect as Worker: Immaterial Labor, the Creative Class, and the Politics of Design* (London: Bloomsbury, 2015).

40 Lloyd Thomas, Amhoff, and Beech (eds.), *Industries of Architecture*.

41 Howard Davis, *The Culture of Building* (New York: Oxford University Press, 2006).

42 Marxist critique of algorithmic architecture should also be mentioned: see Spencer, *The Architecture of Neoliberalism*.

43 Fredric Jameson, *Inventions of a Present – The Novel in Its Crisis of Globalization* (London: Verso, 2024), 27.

44 Alison and Peter Smithson, 'The "As Found" and the "Found",' in David Robbins (ed.), *The Independent Group: Postwar Britain and the Aesthetics of Plenty* (Cambridge, Mass and London: MIT Press, 1990), 201–202.

45 *Inside Housing* (10 March 2021), https://www.insidehousing.co.uk/news/grenfell-cladding-firm-considered-possibility-of-fire-killing-60-or-70-people-in-2007-69946 (accessed 23 October 2024).

46 Nancy Fraser, *Cannibal Capitalism* (London: Verso, 2023).

47 This was released in September 2024: https://www.grenfelltowerinquiry.org.uk/phase-2-report (accessed 23 October 2024).

48 Tafuri, 'Note', unpaginated. This is opposed by him to 'sugary official "Marxism".'

49 *Inside Housing* (14 March 2022): https://www.insidehousing.co.uk/insight/grenfell-tower-inquiry-diary-week-72-the-system-isnt-broken-it-was-built-this-way-75128 (accessed 23 October 2024)

50 See Emma Dowling, *The Care Crisis: What Caused It and How Can We End It?* (London: Verso, 2021); The Care Collective, *The Care Manifesto: The Politics of Interdependence* (London: Verso, 2020).

51 Fraser, *Cannibal Capitalism*, 53–74.

52 Nancy Fraser and Rahel Jaeggi, *Capitalism – A Conversation in Critical Theory* (London: Polity, 2018), 86–7.

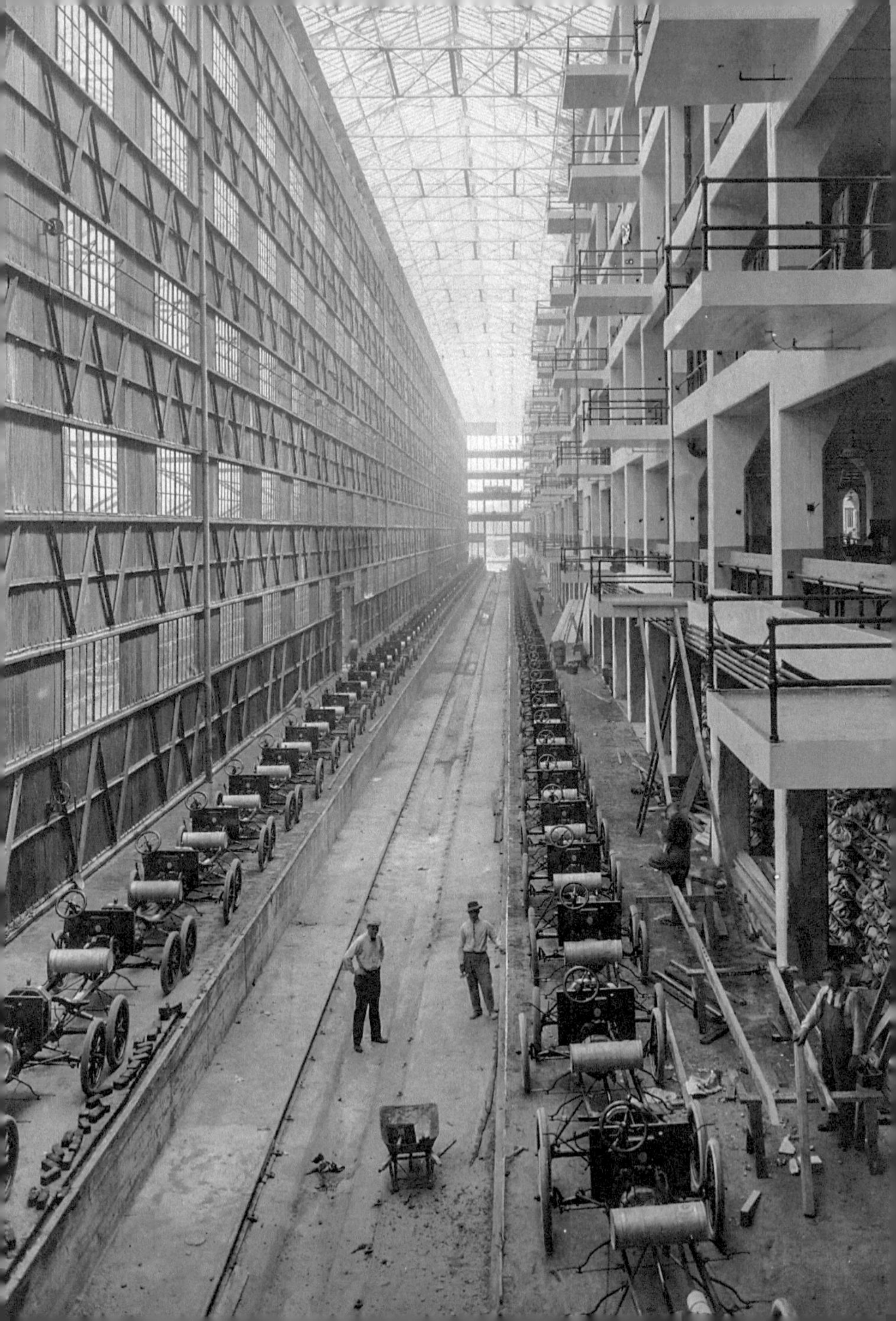

Section 1
Labour and its Histories

Chapter 1
Siegfried Kracauer, Architectural Employee

Tom Wilkinson

> 'The second nature, the nature of man-made structures ...
> is a charnel house of long-dead interiorities.'
> (Georg Lukács, *The Theory of the Novel*, 1920)

'I hate the mindless work. I am constantly counting down the hours until we finish': this was how Siegfried Kracauer recorded his feelings about the internship he was then undertaking on a building site as part of his first year of architectural studies in 1907.[1] An inauspicious start to a career in design, one might think, and for Kracauer the profession did not improve much with acquaintance. Fourteen years later, he gave up architecture for a job at the *Frankfurter Zeitung*, and today he is primarily known for the cultural criticism that he produced in this capacity.

Nevertheless, several of Kracauer's better-known writings concern architectural subjects, among them cinemas, city plans, hotel lobbies and shopping arcades, and it has frequently been remarked that many of his ostensibly non-architectural texts bear the marks of his training, too.[2] These remarks have largely focused on his essay 'The Mass Ornament' (1927), whereas in what follows I will turn to another of Kracauer's most significant mid-career works, his 1930 book on Weimar's new middle classes, *Die Angestellten* (translated as 'The Salaried Masses').[3] Alongside 'The Mass Ornament' and his 1928 novel *Ginster* (to which I shall return), *Die Angestellten* is the most elaborated expression of Kracauer's materialist turn, which followed his reading of Marx's early writings in 1925; prior to this, his theoretical interests had primarily been formed by intensive engagement with the work of Georg Simmel and Max Scheler. However, rather than seeking the origins of his materialist critique in his early sociological speculation, or in the architectural *knowl-*

edge gleaned in the course of his training – without denying the significance of these factors – I will reflect instead on the question of how his *experience* as an architectural worker relates to his later ideas.
This question has been asked before. Recently, Carsten Ruhl has argued that,

> Kracauer's general criticism of modern society [...] is largely based on the experiences Kracauer made as a practising architect. For as an employed architect, he himself did not only belong to the new class of clerks [...] but also directly experienced the paradoxes and dysfunctionalities of the growing planning bureaucracy and the general impact this had on architectural practice.[4]

This illuminating observation, one of many in Ruhl's essay, makes the strongest claim yet regarding the significance of his professional experience, and clarifies what is at stake: Kracauer was the only member of the Frankfurt School circle to have trained as an architect (indeed, he is one of the few socialist theorists to have been a designer, William Morris being the other obvious example), or, for that matter, to have worked as an employee. However, Ruhl uses this insight to once again shed light on Kracauer's adherence to the ornamental – specifically, as he puts it in his title, 'the ornamental nature of the new capitalist order'. While this topic is undoubtedly of central importance to the critic's thought, my interests lie elsewhere.

•

After the decade of wage suppression that followed the crisis of 2007–8, the tightening of the labour market and the inflationary crisis caused by the Covid pandemic unleashed a wave of industrial action not seen since the 1970s. Architecture has not been untouched by this phenomenon. Already in 2013, an organisation named The Architecture Lobby was founded in the USA by Peggy Deamer in order to foster unionisation within the profession, while in the UK, a new union of architectural workers, UVW-SAW (United Voices of the World – Section of Architectural Workers), was formed in 2019.[5] Long hours, low pay, uncertain prospects and abusive management practices have spurred a generation of architectural workers to collective action.[6] These are not proletarians, however, and unlike their bosses, the owners of practices, they are not traditional petites bourgeoises either (or, in the case of very large concerns, bourgeoises); rather, they are the *new* petite bourgeoisie – 'wage-earning employees who do not belong to the working class but are themselves exploited by capital', to follow the classic definition of Nicos Poulantzas.[7]

In the face of these recent developments, the question of the class structure of the architectural profession, and the political implications thereof, have taken on a fresh significance. Hence my appeal to Kracauer: as an expert theorist (that is, one with knowledge derived from praxis) of alienated architectural labour, and of the new middle classes in general. This may seem somewhat perverse, as Kracauer himself was sceptical of the expert.[8] In 1931, he wrote that 'from craftsmen to political economists and scholars, experts are unable to understand the current situation in a way that would be necessary, under the prevailing circumstances, to carry out even their purely professional duties.'[9] He attributed this to the increasing specialisation of their training, combined with a residual idealism in the German universities, both of which prevented any comprehension of the social totality. Today, the architect-expert still seems inadequate to the intractable situation – appears, in fact, to be more or less irrelevant – and so Kracauer's prescribed remedy might still have some efficacy: 'He has, especially in times of crisis, to confront the requirements that arise from the enclave in which he works with the more comprehensive ones of society.'[10]

Despite his scepticism regarding this possibility, Kracauer's expert view of the situation, derived from his own experience as a disenchanted professional, arguably attained a relationship to the totality in *Die Angestellten.* This first appeared as a series of articles in the *Frankfurter Zeitung* at the end of 1929 before being published as a book early the next year. The topic of his study – the white-collared, urban masses, clerks and shop workers, low-ranking civil servants, and so on – were however not quite 'unknown territory', as Kracauer titles the first chapter. There had been substantial debate regarding this stratum in the years preceding his investigations, and he refers to some of this literature.[11] Indeed, the crucial insight that this group has been proletarianised without being able to divorce their sympathies from the bourgeoisie is derived from the work of economist Emil Lederer.[12]

Kracauer's approach is distinguished from this growing literature by its method and its angle of approach. By the latter, I mean that he did not focus exclusively on the working conditions and political allegiances of his subjects, but rather placed them in a wider context, 'the imperceptible dreadfulness of normal existence'.[13] This encompassed their cultural pursuits, a provocative topic given that the petite bourgeoisie was widely seen as being culture-less, or possessed of only the shoddiest commercial ersatz for such a thing. While he took this matter seriously, in *Die Angestellten* Kracauer moved on from the cautious, Simmelian optimism of his earlier writings on the products of the culture industry, particularly film, replacing this with a deeply pessimistic view of their ideological function. Kracauer situated the leisure of the *Angestellten* in a functional continuum with their work: 'At the same moment in which firms are rationalised, these establishments rationalise the pleasures of the salary-earning armies ... binding employees by enchantment to the place the ruling stratum desires, and diverting them from critical questions.'[14] Architecture did not escape this judgement unscathed.

The method of the study reflects its focus: it is a kind of 'sociological literature',[15] which Kracauer likened in the introduction to a mosaic, as opposed to a report or photograph, forms associated with the *neue Sachlichkleit.* Kracauer attributed this fashion to the 'hunger for directness that is undoubtedly a consequence of the malnutrition caused by German idealism', but, he said, 'a hundred reports from a factory do not add up to the reality of the factory.' Instead: 'Reality is a construction ... it is to be found solely in the mosaic that is assembled from single observations on the basis of comprehension of their meaning.'[16] The pieces of this mosaic or montage are taken from interviews conducted by Kracauer with workers, managers and union functionaries, as well as snippets from internal company documents and professional journals, and advertisements from illustrated magazines. The image that emerges from this collection of fragments corresponds to the fragmentary consciousness of its subject, which is made up of these incoherent elements, and it will not resolve until the latter's social position is resolved: this is the 'meaning' according to which the mosaic is organised, and this is carried through at a microscopic scale, at the level of language itself.

The frustrated aspirations of the new middle classes, who had experienced a decline in conditions, status and pay since the stabilisation of the economy in 1924, were partially satiated with daytrips, organised sport, and nightclubs. Kracauer famously described these phenomena as 'shelters for the homeless'.[17] In a seemingly perverse move, he borrows the notion of transcendental homelessness from Georg Lukács, the pre-Marxist Lukács of his 1920 essay, *The Theory of the Novel*, while rejecting his more recent Marxism as idealist. In a letter to Ernst Bloch of 1926, he criticised Lukács in no uncertain terms: 'Instead of permeating Marxism with realia [*mit Realien zu durchdringen*], he introduces the spirit and metaphysics of exhausted idealism and along the way he forgets about the materialist categories that should have been interpreted ... Philosophically, he is – I would not say so publicly – a reactionary.'[18] Instead, Kracauer performs his own marxisation of the early Lukács. He stands the latter's Hegelian metaphor on its feet, materialising it – for the spiritually homeless are accommodated in 'shelters in the literal sense', real buildings such as cinemas and the 'pleasure barracks' of Haus Vaterland, a Berlin nightclub complex with numerous themed bars and restaurants.[19] We see here the traces of his architectural training, which he applies to language itself by constructing metaphors which are not just metaphors but real structures.[20] In the real abstraction of Kracauer's language, where thought is radically *durchdrungen* with *Realien*, we find the product of his continued architectural labours; despite his scepticism of its built works, there is a discernible kinship to architectural modernism – if we follow Giedion's view that *Durchdringung*, interpenetration, is one of its key characteristics.[21]

But can it be said that Kracauer's architectural experiences radicalised him, leading to his materialist turn? To trace the connections between his two careers we need to sketch a portrait of the architect as an employee. In doing so, we are reliant on his surviving diaries and letters, and also on *Ginster*. The novel covers the years around the First World War, when its protagonist – like its author – was setting out in his profession. But it is fiction, and, furthermore, it was written after Kracauer's materialist turn, adding to the difficulty

Design for a war memorial cemetery, Frankfurt am Main, architect Siegfried Kracauer, 1916.

of using it as a source to uncover the roots of that development. Before turning to this slippery account, I will outline his curriculum vitae.[22]

Kracauer was born in Frankfurt in 1889, to a petit bourgeois Jewish family – his father was a travelling salesman who dealt in textiles, without resounding success. He began studying architecture in nearby Darmstadt in 1907, then transferred to Berlin that winter, where he first heard Simmel lecture. From 1909 to 1912 he studied with Theodor Fischer at Munich, where he passed his diploma. He then began working at a local firm while writing his doctoral thesis. He was often miserable and lonely during these early years, and he wrote impassioned, Nietzschean poetry while working on competition entries.

In 1914 he volunteered but was found unfit to serve, and he spent the war years working for the firm of Max Seckbach, who built predominantly for the Jewish community, including a number of synagogues. Kracauer's designs won the firm a competition to design a Jewish war cemetery for Frankfurt, which still stands. He was finally called up in 1917, albeit briefly, being found unfit once more. After being sent home, he worked for the municipal planning department at Osnabrück, a small city in western Germany, and designed an estate for workers there. He also continued working on competitions for Seckbach. During this period Simmel, with whom he was in correspondence, encouraged him to devote his energies to more intellectual pursuits. In any case, he struggled to find a permanent position in the economic turmoil following the war; he got periodic work from Seckbach and turned down a job in Amsterdam because of the low pay. In 1921, aged 32, Kracauer gave up on the profession to become a journalist.

He had spent the first fourteen years of his adult life working on and in architecture, a career that he found tedious and depressing. And that is a compelling enough reason to focus on this apparently insignificant aspect of Kracauer's life and work: it has an unmistakable flavour of *actualité* for anyone who knows young architects and indeed for anyone employed in precarious white-collar professions. In 1920, he wrote to his friend Margarete Susman: 'I am already over thirty-one, in other words ancient, this eternally provisional existence wears me down, all of my contemporaries have long since overtaken me, really fate should at long last satisfy the modest demands that I place on life.'[23]

What precisely did Kracauer dislike about architectural work? It was not simply the difficulty of finding any – his reaction came earlier than this. During the summer internship mentioned at the beginning of this chapter he decided that the site was not the place for him. During breaks from working on the roof he was reading Dostoevsky, Nietzsche and Kant, so these are in part the complaints of an intellectually inclined young man forced into a type of work that he did not enjoy. But there was something about the particular conditions of architecture that were unsatisfactory. Architecture is, after all, an indeterminate profession, and has been since its inauguration in the Renaissance: somewhere between a trade and an intellectual pursuit. As part of his training Kracauer acquired practical experience on building sites and learned about geometry and construction, but he also studied aesthetics and philosophy, and wrote a doctoral thesis on the historical development of style and technique. Kracauer, as an architect, was a divided personality: half *Bildungsbürger*, educated middle class, and half *Angestellter*. In the former capacity, architecture was not unstimulating to him, but as an architectural *Angestellter*, his working life was full of frustrations. During his studies, he complained that 'the work is no fun at all. I regard it as a waste of time. It makes me tired and incapable of more serious work and creative production.'[24] As Gerwin Zohlen notes, Kracauer distinguishes here between *Arbeit* and *Schaffen*, work and creativity, putting his finger on the point of tension in the role of architect. Tellingly, in his classic work on the division between intellectual and manual labour, Alfred Sohn-Rethel turns to a passage from Marx on architecture in order to clarify the development of this split: 'What distinguishes the worst of architects from the best of bees is that the architect builds the cell in his mind before he constructs it in wax.' Sohn-Rethel adds, 'but for us the essential question is: in whose head is the intended result of the labour process anticipated?'[25] While architects had successfully extracted themselves from the building site during the Renaissance, as practice was elaborated into ever larger and more bureaucratically convoluted concerns – something occurring in these years in the private offices of Erich Mendelsohn in Germany and Albert Kahn in the USA, and in the Neue Frankfurt of Ernst May – a new level was excavated beneath the architect-scholar, that of the architect-clerk. The latter bore neither hod nor idea.

Ginster, published in 1928, presents a panorama of this disenchanted profession across several episodes. At the book's opening, the protagonist is working directly for a private client named Herr Allinger, a *Kunstgewerbler* or applied artist who designs ceramics. This bourgeois dabbler, who has engaged Ginster to design a swimming pool – which he is developing with a ceramics firm with which he has a professional relationship – seems intended to represent the kind of reformers who populated organisations such as the Werkbund at the time. Despite his artistic inclinations, their relationship is one of mutual incomprehension. While Ginster, with a kind of primitive class analysis, asserts that 'the entrance and foyer should be entirely inconspicuous … Most of the people who make use of it are accustomed to climbing the service stairs', his client has an altogether more grandiose vision, related no doubt to his commercial entanglements in the scheme.[26] However, as these ideas are being elaborated, they hear news of the first mobilisation: 'Nothing will come of the swimming pool', says Allinger. The crossed wires, whimsical demands and wasted effort in this brief episode typify the frustrations of working for a private client.

Later, the protagonist goes to work for a small practice owned by a Herr Valentin, who shares certain biographical details with Kracauer's employer Seckbach. Valentin is a typical example of this petit bourgeois type:

> a deputy of the city building department and a chairman of the architects' association. These honorary positions didn't bring any money in, they could only lead to practically utilisable relationships. It was more important to Herr Valentin that, as occupant of such posts, he raised himself to the status of a public person, who could command trust.[27]

These pretences are not matched by his circumstances, however: his office is in a room of his house from which it feels a bed has just been removed, the drawing table and rolls of paper having 'merely selected it as a lair'.[28] There, Valentin works on minor shop conversions, demonstrating the paucity of design work during the war. One happy exception is a competition for a war cemetery 'announced by the city for the benefit of dead soldiers and needy architects'.[29] As mentioned earlier, Kracauer had produced a similar design; Ginster likewise wins the commission for the firm, and then has the unnerving but far from unique experience of seeing his boss take the credit for the proposal.

In these straitened circumstances, the architect is engaged in endless battles with craftsmen and trades. Kracauer also describes Valentin's rivalries with other architects, one of whom, his nemesis, wins a contract from under his nose, and so he sends him an insulting letter addressed not to *Herr Architekt* but to *Herr Bautechniker*, Mr Site Engineer (Kracauer adds in an acid aside, 'incidentally, neither of them had graduated from a technical university').[30] This status anxiety is one that had been troubling German architects since before the war. In 1903, the Bund Deutscher Architeken (Association of German Architects) was established to promote and protect the status of the profession. In their founding manifesto, 'What we want!', they argued:

> The cultivation of the art of building [*Baukunst*] as the herald of contemporary thought lies predominantly in our hands, as independent, artistically creative architects … We see the greatest danger to our artistic life,

> the worst opponent of our own efforts, in the ruthless entrepreneurs, who, without ideals and ruled only by the profit motive, exploit the freedom of trade, which is otherwise so beneficial.[31]

The preceding years had seen a massive building boom in German cities, especially Berlin, which expanded rapidly as speculative developments were erected on its outskirts. Anyone could call themselves an architect and could set to work covering Germany with what their more highly trained brethren saw as trash. The BDA also feared and envied the position of official architects, the *Stadtbauräte* with their coveted civil servant status.

Finally, after the war Ginster goes to work for the municipal architects' department in a small town referred to as 'Q', designing workers' housing. This mirrors Kracauer's experience in Osnabrück, where he came up with a project that somewhat resembled Richard Riemerschmid's housing at the garden city Hellerau in Dresden. In other words, Kracauer's architectural work was quite conservative by 1919, and in *Ginster* the protagonist refers to his work as *niedlich* (twee): he 'wondered over the deliberate tweeness even more, given that the *Stadtbaurat* had described the workers as a rabble. First they were shot and then they were planted in a garden – he couldn't grasp the connection, it was because his boss wanted the workers to flourish so that they would be fresh to be used again in the next war.'[32]

Kracauer had thus experienced the three main types of architectural employment available at the time: working as an independent architect directly for a client, a frustrating relationship which comes to nothing; the private firm with its constant scrabble for commissions and its exploitation of its workers; and the municipal architects' department with its contemptuous relationship to those it built for. The disenchantment of the profession seemed total and, as inflation heightened, its precarity became intolerable. These were the years of *Die Not der geistigen Arbeiter*, as Alfred Weber put it in 1923, the distress of the intellectual workers. The political and economic chaos of the postwar years undermined *Bildungsbürgertum* and *Angestellten* alike, as salaries, savings and income from rents and investments evaporated. This experience radicalised many of the newly impoverished middle classes; some, like

Kracauer, Benjamin and Adorno turned to the left, many more turned to the right. A regular job in journalism – as another form of *Angestellter*, it should be noted – no doubt seemed like a relatively safe haven compared with the struggle of architecture.

Faced by these conditions, some architects sought a radical reorganisation of their profession. The Arbeitsrat für Kunst ('workers council for art') was established in the council or soviet period of the 1918–19 German revolution, probably by Bruno Taut. Its founding programme was that the arts were to be united under architecture. Influenced by developments in revolutionary Russia, the Arbeitsrat was certainly opposed to private enterprise, but it was also against state paternalism – it hoped instead for new forms of democratic patronage, in which commissions would come via the workers' councils.[33] There is no evidence that Kracauer had any interest in such radical experiments in socialisation, despite this being a widespread demand at the time, not just in architecture. It was a short-lived moment in any case, even in the AfK. Taut resigned as its head in 1919, disillusioned by the development of parliamentary democracy and the SDP's lack of interest. He was replaced by Gropius, who returned to traditional sources of patronage in the face of economic crisis – but he still wanted to involve lay people in architecture. The AfK's first show, Ausstellung für unbekannte Architekten, in Berlin in 1919, solicited anonymous submissions. In this regard, its aims ran counter to the professionalisation that motivated the Association of German Architects.

The aims of the latter were shared by Kracauer, who wrote an article in 1921 supporting their demands: 'German architects are so involved in the preservation and creation of our cultural assets that for this reason alone the difficult struggle they are currently waging for their existence and recognition under public law deserves general attention.'[34] His main argument is for the statutory regulation of the architect's title, but he also makes a claim for the importance of private firms:

> Quite apart from the distress in which most private architects find themselves at the moment, the state and municipalities, which will probably be the main building contractors in Germany for a long time to come,

> can count on significant savings if they entrust more of the design and implementation of their building commissions to freelance artists than before … The image offered by the majority of our German cities shows vividly enough where it leads us when the planning and processing of all public building tasks lies exclusively in the hands of an anonymous bureaucracy.[35]

This *cri de coeur* of professional *amour-propre* might make us think of Kracauer as a curious realist indeed, as Adorno would later call him, and a true petit bourgeois. It is important to remember that this is the voice of Kracauer between architecture and Marx, however; in *Die Angestellten*, he dedicates a section to unravelling such bourgeois mythology, which sounds almost like a criticism of his earlier position: 'the indispensable precondition for private economy is the autonomous entrepreneur, so the defence of his sovereignty is the central issue.'[36]

To return to my earlier question about the connections between his experience as an architect and his turn to materialism: he had clearly not been radicalised immediately by his work experiences. In any case, he was far from being alone in his moderation at the time, even among the avant-gardists. In his essay on the socialisation of architecture in Weimar, Manfredo Tafuri says

> to enter the city will only be possible by recognising that concrete results will be produced only by disenchanted professions … the avant-gardes are called upon to betray themselves, to come to an end, to dissolve out of extreme fidelity to their own premises … infiltration into the institutions, management of a vast network of alternative institutions, management of precisely defined economic sectors, diverse tactics that require diverse techniques, forcing intellectual work into specialisation, into entering the forest of bureaucracy.[37]

Tafuri's key case study is Martin Wagner, the Stadtbaurat of Berlin from 1925. Already during the war Wagner had been advocating the socialisation of the building industry, and in 1919 he published a significant article on this topic.

The idea of socialisation proposed here is a surprising one, perhaps: he does not call for nationalisation or even municipalisation of the building trades. 'It would be an error of the gravest kind to force the entry into a bureaucratic machinery, regulated by pure administrative work, a system of businesses that is built upon personal responsibilities, on the capacity for individual action, on the freedom of decisions, and on personal powers.'[38] He sounds rather like Kracauer here – or perhaps, vice versa. Instead, Wagner argues for the revival of the medieval *Bauhütte*, a kind of primitive guild of masons, and asks that the architect should insert himself into these rather than insisting on his artistic autonomy: 'at his drawing table, he gives way completely to his ideals. This office work trains him unilaterally in aesthetics, unreality, and overspending.'[39]

Kracauer would not have gone so far as this in the early 1920s. His writings on architecture from that moment were an object lesson in the key problem described in *Die Angestellten*: the failure of consciousness to keep up with material conditions. However, as time passed his identification with the profession declined. When he came to write *Ginster* and *Die Angestellten*, he had a new lens through which to view architecture, portraying it in these books respectively as exploiting its workers and those who used its end products, even in their most supposedly radical form. Nevertheless, his architectural experiences, if not the proximate cause of his materialist turn, arguably laid its foundations – would he have chosen to excavate the false consciousness of the *Angestellten* if he had not recently dug himself out from it? They certainly influenced the form of his later works, those concrete metaphors and the *Durchdringung* with realia. This concretion, in fact, shows us that for Kracauer form is not to be distinguished from thought, and that he has carried over the split personality of the architect – *Bildungsbürger/Angestellter* – into the realm of theory. Adorno would later say that this is the most important lesson Kracauer taught him: 'the fissures and flaws in a philosophy are more essential to it that the continuity of its meaning.'[40] It is possible that only Kracauer – the only one of Adorno's interlocutors to have worked in architectural practice – could have taught him this.

•

Despite the achievements of Kracauer's work of the late 1920s he could not be said to offer a cogent programme in response to the situation that he diagnosed with such devastating acuity. As Mülder-Bach says, his hope in the power of enlightenment is gestural and forlorn.[41] And although there are clear parallels between Kracauer's experiences and the situation of architects today, this hope seems even more gestural. All the while, the alienation he diagnosed has intensified. Pier Vittorio Aureli has recently written that 'the extreme commodification of architecture now undermines the role of architects, reserving for them the same fate as builders at the dawn of modernity'.[42] While the ranks of architectural employees have certainly swollen, their conditions have worsened, and the nature of their work become even more alienated, I would not agree that they have been proletarianised. Rather, they remain *Angestellten*, with all of the same epistemological problems that Kracauer attributed to that social position.[43] As for the possibilities of collective action, Kracauer was far from optimistic on this topic, describing the unions as a 'repair shop' helping to keep capitalism running.[44] This was of course a very different moment in the history of organised labour, and whether the Weimar settlement can be compared to the grassroots organising happening in workplaces today is questionable. Nevertheless, the lack of success of organisations like the Architecture Lobby, which is perhaps related to the absence of class analysis in their work, and the failure of the present, union-backed president of the Royal Institute of British Architects to effect any improvements to working conditions, suggests that some things have not changed.[45] In any case, it seems likely that Kracauer would have preferred to stand to one side, as usual, and patiently wait.

The last piece of architecture to appear in *Ginster*, in a final chapter set five years after the war's end (that is, at the time of stabilisation in Germany that is the focus of *Die Angestellten*) is a ruined patrician house in Marseille. Perhaps this is identical to the erstwhile dwelling of those homeless white-collared masses: 'the house of bourgeois ideas and feelings in which they used to live has collapsed, its foundation eroded by economic development.'[46] But, while in Berlin the new petite bourgeoisie fled to shelters for the homeless, in Marseille, 'the façade, once so distinguished, grows together with the walls of the neighbouring household into an indistinguishable mishmash.'[47] Adorno persuaded Kracauer to cut this chapter when the novel was republished in 1963, perhaps because even this extremely limited optimism did not correspond to the received wisdom regarding the fate of the *Angestellten*: that is, their turn to the right. But this is a sociological fiction – they did not actually vote en bloc for the Nazis, unlike the bourgeoisie to which Adorno himself belonged – and in their ultimate decay the *Angestellten* would collapse instead into their neighbours.[48]

Notes

1 I would like to thank all the architects who have ever complained to me about their work; this essay is dedicated to them. Ingrid Belke and Irina Renz (eds.), *Siegfried Kracauer 1889–1966* (Marbach am Neckar: Deutsche Schillergesellschaft, 1994), 9.

2 Gerwin Zohlen, 'Schmugglerpfad. Siegfried Kracauer, Architekt und Schriftsteller', in Michael Kessler and Thomas Y. Levin (eds.), *Siegfried Kracauer: Neue Interpretationen* (Tübingen: Stauffenburg Verlag, 1990), 325–344.

3 For example, Claire Zimmerman, 'Siegfried Kracauer's Architectures', in *Culture in the Anteroom: The Legacies of Siegfried Kracauer,* edited by Gerd Gemünden and Johannes von Moltke (Ann Arbor, MI: University of Michigan Press, 2012), 149–65.

4 Carsten Ruhl, *Kracauer's Architecture: The Ornamental Nature of the New Capitalist Order* (Weimar: M Books, 2022), 54.

5 https://architecture-lobby.org/ and https://uvw-saw.org.uk/. Anjulie Rao, 'Tuning the Choir: Ten Years of the Architecture Lobby', *New York Review of Architecture*, 3.7.23. https://nyra.nyc/articles/tuning-the-choir.

6 On these conditions, see (for instance) Marco Biraghi, 'L'architettura come lavoro concreto', *Gizmo* (6.12.2016), https://www.gizmoweb.org/2016/12/larchitettura-come-lavoro-concreto/.

7 Nicos Poulantzas, *Classes in Contemporary Capitalism*, trans. David Fernbach (London: NLB, 1975), 251. The social class of the architect per se has not to my knowledge been addressed in any detail, despite the professional status of the architect being a long-standing concern of historiography.

8 The expert was a contested figure in Germany in this period, a controversy sparked by a series of lectures given by Sergei Tretyakov in 1931. On this debate, see Frederic J. Schwartz, *Blind Spots: Critical Theory and the History of Art in Twentieth-Century Germany* (New Haven: Yale, 2005), 86–101; Schwartz argues that Benjamin's later texts 'The Author as Producer' and 'The Work of Art in the Age of its Technological Reproducibility' are in part a riposte to Kracauer's sceptical position on this subject.

9 Kracauer, 'Der Fachmann', in *Schriften* vol. 5, no. 2, ed. Inka Mülder-Bach (Frankfurt: Suhrkamp, 1990), 402.

10 Ibid., 404.

11 Val Burris, 'The Discovery of the New Middle Class', *Theory and Society* vol. 15, no. 3 (May 1986), 317–49.

12 Emil Lederer, 'The Restructuring of the Proletariat', *Neue Rundschau*, August 1929. Cited by Kracauer in *The Salaried Masses: Duty and Distraction in Weimar Germany*, trans. Quintin Hoare (London: Verso, 1998), 81.

13 Kracauer, *Salaried Masses*, 101.

14 Kracauer, *Salaried Masses*, 91–94.

15 Kracauer, 'Reisen, nüchtern', *Frankfurter Zeitung* 10.7.32, in *Schriften* vol. 5, no. 3, 88. Inka Mülder-Bach points out the aptness of this description for his own work: Inka Mülder-Bach, *Siegfried Kracauer – Grenzgänger zwischen Theorie und Literatur. Seine frühen Schriften 1913–1933* (Stuttgart: Springer-Verlag, 1985), 116.

16 Kracauer, *Salaried Masses*, 32.

17 This is the title of the section of the *Salaried Masses* in which Kracauer discusses the leisure pursuits of the *Angestellten*.

18 Kracauer to Bloch, 27.5.1926, in Ernst Bloch, *Briefe, 1903–1975* vol. 1, ed. Karola Bloch et al. (Frankfurt: Suhrkamp, 1985), 272–273, 273.

19 Kracauer, *Salaried Masses*, 91.

20 Kracauer's architectural metaphors have frequently been noted, e.g. by Zohlen, 'Schmugglerpfad', 339–40. However, in Zohlen's view, this is a 'metaphorization of architecture' – not vice versa. Adorno criticised this metaphorisation as a form of fetishism. Theodor Adorno, 'The Curious Realist: On Siegfried Kracauer', trans. Shierry Weber Nicholsen, *New German Critique* no. 54 (1991), 159–77. This view has been rebuffed in turn, e.g. by Mülder-Bach, *Siegfried Kracauer*, 132.

21 This is a central concept of Sigfried Giedion's early work, especially *Bauen in Frankreich, Bauen in Eisen, Bauen in Eisenbeton* (Leipzig: Klinkhardt & Biermann, 1928). On Kracauer's attitude towards the neues Bauen, see Hans-Georg van Arburg, 'The Last Dwelling Before the Last: Siegfried Kracauer's Critical Contribution to the Modernist Housing Debate in Weimar Germany', *New German Critique* vol. 47, no. 3 (November 2020), 99–140.

22 This account is derived from Belke and Renz, *Siegfried Kracauer*, and Jörg Später, *Kracauer: A Biography,* trans. Daniel Steuer (London: Polity, 2020).

23 Belke and Renz, *Siegfried Kracauer*, 34.
24 Zohlen, 'Schmugglerpfad', 325.
25 Alfred Sohn-Rethel, *Intellectual and Manual Labour: A Critique of Epistemology* (London: Macmillan, 1978), 85.
26 Siegfried Kracauer, *Ginster* (1928) (Frankfurt: Suhrkamp, 2019), 14–15.
27 Kracauer, *Ginster*, 79.
28 Ibid., 77.
29 Ibid., 140.
30 Ibid., 80–81.
31 'Was wir wollen! Proklamation des BDA, veröffentlicht bei der Gründung im Jahr 1903', in Bernhard Gaber, *Die Entwicklung des Berufsstandes des freischaffenden Architekten* (Essen: Verlag Richard Bacht, 1966), 223–224.
32 Kracauer, *Ginster,* 280.
33 Marcel Bois, '"The Art! – That's one Thing! When it's there" On the History of the Arbeitsrat für Kunst in the Early Weimar Republic', *Bauhaus Imaginista*, https://www.bauhaus-imaginista.org/articles/3207/the-art-that-s-one-thing-when-it-s-there.
34 Kracauer, 'Standesfragen der Architektenschaft', *Frankfurter Zeitung*, 4/5/1921, in *Werke* vol. 5, no. 1, 193.
35 Kracauer, 'Standesfragen', 195–6.
36 Kracauer, *Salaried Masses*, 96.
37 Manfredo Tafuri, 'Sozialpolitik and the City in Weimar Germany', *The Sphere and the Labyrinth*, trans. Pellegrino d'Acierno and Robert Connolly (Cambridge, Mass. and London: MIT Press, 1987), 197–233, 198.
38 Martin Wagner, 'The Socialization of the Construction Industry', in Tafuri, *The Sphere and the Labyrinth*, 235–63, 42.
39 Wagner, 'The Socialization of the Construction Industry', 244.
40 Adorno, 'The Curious Realist', 160.
41 Mülder-Bach, *Siegfried Kracauer*, 120.
42 Pier Vittorio Aureli, *Architecture and Abstraction* (Cambridge Mass and London: MIT Press, 2023), xxv. Aureli proposes a solution derived from the pedagogy of Hannes Meyer at the Bauhaus, i.e. the repositioning of students as workers: Aureli, *Architecture and Abstraction*, 255–59.
43 For a recent account of this class in Britain, see Dan Evans, *A Nation of Shopkeepers: The Unstoppable Rise of the Petty Bourgeoisie* (London: Repeater, 2023).
44 This is the title of the section on unions in *The Salaried Masses*.
45 Tom Ravenscroft, 'Architectural workers union calls out RIBA president's "immediate U-turn" on campaign pledge', *Dezeen* (15.09.2023), https://www.dezeen.com/2023/09/15/riba-president-muyiwa-oki-pledge-u-turn/.
46 Kracauer, *Salaried Masses*, 88.
47 Kracauer, *Ginster*, 332. On this image, see Von Arburg, 'The Last Dwelling Before the Last', 127–128.
48 Burris, 'The Discovery of the New Middle Class', 340–341.

Chapter 2
Down Below, Disqualification: How to Design the Formal Subsumption of Labour

Silke Kapp and Katie Lloyd Thomas

Approaches to architecture and its history with a Marxian lens have been largely explored during the twentieth century. If there is anything they agree on, it is the relevance of *production*. Without production, there would be no capitalist circulation, distribution, culture, or everyday life to criticise and to combat. The interesting question here is what exactly theorists and historians understand by *architectural production*. If we assume that architecture equals design, as a realm separated from 'actual' construction, any critique will remain focused on the production of design itself: its ideological representations of power, the constraints that it imposes on people, the lack of participation in design processes, the working conditions in architectural firms, and so on. In contrast, understanding architecture as the whole of *design and construction*, and placing it in the larger picture of political economy leads to a different kind of critique. This is precisely the approach that the French-Brazilian architect, painter and theorist Sérgio Ferro has been developing since the 1960s.[1]

A key point in Ferro's historical analysis is that construction was one of the first branches of production to be organised as a capitalist manufacture. He discloses the separation between design and the building site as a process mobilised by capital, showing how design became a tool of command and has changed in step with the historical conditions of capitalist building production. This distinguishes his approach from that of other critical authors, who focus either on architectural labour or on construction labour, but do not address the contradictory relationships between them. Manfredo Tafuri's approach stands as an example at one end of this spectrum.[2] He considers architecture mainly as part of the 'superstructure', that is, as artistic or intellectual labour. He hardly acknowledges the fact that art engages with capital mostly through the sphere of circulation (attracting value that has already been produced elsewhere), while architectural design is indispensable for a sector of productive capital (extracting value from wage-labour). Linda Clarke's history of the construction of London in the late eighteenth to nineteenth centuries, *Building Capitalism* (1992) is an example at the other end of this spectrum. She emphasises construction labour: she recognises the changing professional role of architects in the transition to capitalist building production, but without interrogating the part played by design and related architectural techniques in reorganising social relations of production during this transition.[3]

Our aim here is to first set out Ferro's approach and then to expand it within a concrete historical context. We begin by explaining some of Ferro's central arguments based on the Marxian concepts of *manufacture*, and *real* and *formal subsumption*. The second section outlines how Ferro reads classical design, from the Renaissance until the nineteenth century, as a device of economic and social devaluation of labour. Complementing rather than opposing Ferro's interpretation, our third section delves into the context of eighteenth-century London. There we show that not only design as such, but also the practice of specification emerged as a tool to subordinate construction labour. In other words, we argue that the symbolic devaluation and deskilling of building workers, as well as the breaking up of their co-operation were – and still are – mobilised at both ends of architectural practice: the highly celebrated practice of design and the rather underestimated 'technical' practice of specification.

Formal subsumption on the building site

The concept of *manufacture* is central to Ferro's discussion of the relationship between architectural design and (the disqualification of) construction labour. Manufacture, in Marx's terms, means the organisation of production under capital before or without large-scale machinery. Craftspeople become wage-labourers, selling their labour-power instead of the products of their labour and having their tasks more and more divided in a no longer self-organised scheme of production. Nevertheless, the labour process as such relies on the same technologies and skills. As Marx says, 'capital took over an *available, established labour process* [...]. The work may become more intensive, its duration may be extended, it may become more continuous or orderly under the eye of the interested capitalist, but in themselves these changes do not affect the character of the actual labour process, the actual mode of working'.[4]

Historically, manufacture characterises the period in which capitalist relations are first established, 'roughly speaking, from the middle of the sixteenth century to the last third of the eighteenth century'.[5] However, manufacture persists even in advanced capitalist economies. Why is that? If the source of value is human labour, the amount of surplus-value produced in a capitalist society correlates to the amount of labour-power that goes into production. For any particular business, using more machinery and less labour-power may increase profits, but for the economy as a whole, less labour-power reduces the mass of surplus-value and thus the average rate of profit. Labour-intensive branches of the economy are needed because the mass of surplus-value that they produce is distributed across the economy via the market mechanism of *equalisation*, in some ways comparable to the behaviour of water in communicating vessels – no matter where the water is poured in, it raises the overall level.

With this in mind, Ferro states that construction has retained the form of manufacture – labour-intensive, with a relatively low degree of mechanisation – and that capitalism could hardly do without the mass of surplus-value 'poured' into the economy by construction labour.[6] The common idea that the construction industry is somewhat backward but creates many jobs expresses the same fact, only without acknowledging, as Ferro does, that this is a structural function in the system, not an accident.

One could argue that construction has ultimately developed into a modern industry. However, the fully mechanised building site is more of a dream of architects and building contractors than a reality. A vivid illustration comes from a collection of postcards produced by Jean-Marc Côté and other artists

***En l'an 2000: Chantier de construction électrique*, engraving drawn c.1900 presumably by Jean-Marc Côté. Paris: Lithographie Villemard et fils, 1910.**

for the 1900 World Exposition in Paris, depicting 'the year 2000' with the expected technological advances. The card title *Chantier de construction électrique* shows a male architect with his drawings sitting in a small cabin and pressing buttons to activate robotic arms, which carry out the building process directly, without any other workers. While this has hardly ever happened outside research labs, actual 'progress' since 1900 seems to be in site management and devices to better instruct and monitor each of the worker's moves. Andrés Mella and Matthew Savage, using data from the International Labour Organization, calculated that in 2014 building sites 'accounted for more than 273 million jobs worldwide, constituting an estimated 8.6 per cent of the total global employment'.[7] We consider that this sufficiently substantiates Ferro's argument: construction is still labour-intensive, and it is still a manufacture in Marx's sense.

Management, domination or, as Marx says, *subsumption* of labour is crucial for manufacture. Since 'handicraft skill is the foundation of manufacture, and since the mechanism of manufacture as a whole possesses no objective framework which would be independent of the workers themselves, capital is constantly compelled to wrestle with the insubordination of the workers'.[8] Marx calls the subordination of labour typical for manufacture *formal* subsumption, in contrast to the *real* subsumption, which sets in with industrial machinery. Formal subsumption means that the knowledge and know-how needed for the labour process belongs to the workers, so that the command carried out by capital is not based in any technical reasoning. Workers who are 'just' formally subsumed would be able to execute the same labour process by themselves, without the external command. Thus, from capital's point of view, formal subsumption is risky and fragile. No material condition guarantees its authority over labour. Under real subsumption this is no longer the case, as the labour process or 'actual way of working' is determined by the machinery.

Ferro uses Marx's concept of formal subsumption to understand how construction becomes a capitalist manufacture. He stresses that capital's means of 'wrestling' with insubordination are often blatantly violent – time and again, working conditions on construction sites around the world are denounced – but that recognising and combating such violence is not enough. He shows that there is also a history of more subtle architectural means of subsumption which demands critical attention.

In the following two sections we explore two of these architectural means. The first is classical architecture in the Renaissance and the path leading to it, which Ferro analyses in detail in *Construction of Classical Design*. Here we summarise his train of thought.[9] The second is architectural specification, which Ferro only hints at in his discussion of 'prescriptions' and where our own contribution to the history of the subsumption of construction labour sets in. Although at first sight classical design and specification seem disparate realms in the architectural universe, we argue that both are tools in the effort to achieve a level of control over labour.

Compare the central rose window of Laon Cathedral, built in the twelfth century, with the central rose window of Strasbourg Cathedral, built about a century later. In the first case the ornaments follow the logic of the craft and its tools. If we regard design as being the concept or idea behind what is materially carried out, it seems that whoever conceived these shapes did it with knowledge of the craft. There might have been a real-scale drawing traced on a stone floor, or a timber mould, but these were part of the building activity. On the other hand, the intricate circles of the facade of Strasbourg Cathedral have certainly not been designed with large-scale dividers, but with a small hand-held compass. Instead of measuring and marking shapes directly on to the stonework, the proposed design has been drawn at reduced scale. The design here operates in a medium other than building itself, and follows another logic.[10] Panofsky has famously associated this other logic with 'scholasticism'.[11] We may believe him or not, but the question is what motivates this separation or why design distances itself from the logic of construction as such? Ferro states that predefining the product according to a rationale that does not belong to the activity and knowledge of construction workers is the first step to their subordination. The drawing changes the rules of the game. For those in charge of the site, the drawing is a tool to exert and legitimate authority. Formal subsumption in construction starts literally with the subordination to a form.

The problem is that taking this form or shape from a realm completely unrelated to construction seems arbitrary and not very convincing in the long run. More than just being different from construction, design had to achieve a kind of opposition to it. Note that *difference* means a non-essential relation, or a relation whose elements do not depend on each other (like oak trees and pine trees), while *opposition* is an essential relation (like day and night): each of the opposing elements exists only because the other exists. Ferro argues that the design separate from the building site had to establish a relation in which design itself appears indispensable.

According to Ferro's interpretation, this is precisely where the repertoire of classical orders and ornaments allegedly 'reborn' from Antiquity comes into play: it belongs to a building tradition, but not to the one that a central European building worker of the late Middle Ages would be familiar with. It seems to follow a building logic but, again, not one that is in any way real. More than the philosophical reasons often given to explain the take up of classical design (such as new humanism), Ferro argues that these forms enable architectural design as a device to organise the building activity top-down and make it profitable.

Classical design was the main device to put the knowledge and know-how of skilled craftspeople under a heteronomous control. Where Romanesque capitals are works of craftspeople who were at the same time artists and 'ordinary' workers, classical design in contrast, means a practice whose outcome is prescribed and standardised. It devalues the knowledge and know-how that sustains the building practice as such, and it allows for a hierarchy between skilled and unskilled workers and their wages. Furthermore, it introduces a difference between the practices of sculptors or painters, who create in the material medium on which they themselves are working, and that of architects, who create in the abstract medium of drawing or modelling, and then instruct others, who in turn are not allowed any creative freedom. Ferro shows this difference in Michelangelo's Medici Chapel: as an architect, Michelangelo defines the result in advance and expects his workers to follow his instructions precisely, leaving no trace of their working process; as a sculptor, he creates while executing and makes the process itself visible by leaving some parts unpolished, unfinished, *non finito.*[12]

We are especially interested in a later period when the classical repertoire becomes common knowledge among construction craftspeople, while, at the same time, ordinary buildings become part of capitalist production. In France around 1700 architects still succeeded in protecting their practice through mystification. For instance, Claude Perrault failed in his attempt to simplify the incredibly complicated proportions that François Blondel's *Cours d'Architecture* (1675–83) had established.[13] Architects defended them as 'natural' or 'human', while also knowing that dispensing with classical design as specialised knowledge would undermine their trade, just as contractors knew that it would undermine the authority of capital over labour on site, that is, formal subsumption. A century later, however, it became impossible to prevent unorthodox uses of classical orders.[14] The sheer volume of buildings produced as commodities in European cities and the fact that craftspeople had by then acquired enough experience with classical design made it less and less effective as a tool of domination.

Here, a gap appears in Ferro's account. It will be more than a century before the next means he identifies emerges – the use of reinforced concrete to empower so-called intellectual labour and, once again, devalue workers' knowledge and know-how. Were other means mobilised for the formal subsumption of labour during this interim period? Our hypothesis is that a distinctive form of specification organised around the building trades comes into the picture at precisely this point. It is true that the use of the specification and other text-based documents far predates the use of architectural drawings for setting out buildings in advance,[15] which only developed as typical practice together with classical design. But by examining a specific transition in the history of these documents, we can understand how the specification in the particular form of the trades-based document is enlisted as a tool of domination.

Tracing a critical history of architectural relations of production (and their accessories) under capitalism requires jumping from general considerations to particular ones and back again, as well as from one place to another, depending on where certain moves appear more clearly. Leaving general developments in Central Europe, we now turn to Britain to show the emergence of the trades-based specification. Ferro states that despite 'regional and chronological differences', there are 'structural tonics [which] determine the expansion of productive capitalism in construction'.[16] Yet he also acknowledges that 'they do not obviously correspond to any historical sequence occurring in the same region'.

The differences in scale between macrohistory and microhistory entail some difficulty concerning formulation. *Design*, in macrohistorical discourse, can include complements, specifications or subsidiary documents of various kinds, the distinction between which only matters for microhistory. We all know that the fifteenth-century Italian *disegno* is not the seventeenth-century French *dessin*.[17]

Classical design in its general sense prevails up to the twentieth century, but it seems that over time the drawing loses its power as its particular accessory. To indicate how specifications take the place of classical design drawings we move to a context that Ferro does not address, namely to London at the end of the eighteenth century. The analysis of documents produced there shows that the form of the specification underwent a substantial change, from what was basically a list with almost nothing to say about building processes, to a series of 'work orders' structured around the building trades. We speculate that this form of specification is one of the new techniques that step in to subordinate building labour as classical design ceases to be effective.

How to use specifications

In his analysis of separated design Ferro repeatedly insists that drawings produced offsite to instruct building are not the only means which capital enlists to subordinate building workers. A whole range of text-based documents such as memoranda, schedules and specifications perform this function. Because of their entanglement in the work process, these documents, often referred to as *prescrições* (or 'prescriptions') by Ferro, provide another lens on the development of means of domination.[18]

On the building site, plans and memoranda – made by architects, engineers, 'multidisciplinary teams', or whoever it may be – decoded by masters and communicated as work orders, are what command the divided labour.[19] This 'writing work' of architects is usually seen as 'merely' technical or legal, as if supplementary or of another (lower) order to the elevated making of drawings.[20] Ferro's use of the term 'pre-scription' draws attention to the status of all these documents as prior instructions, both for the object building and for the bodies who will build it. In insisting that all these documents – written or drawn – are in fact tools of command and domination Ferro does more than *add* the specification to a discussion of the drawing. In showing us that the drawing – despite its resemblance to an artwork – is in fact of the same order as the specification, he inverts our understanding. Both specification *and* drawing are architecture's weapons in the disqualification and division of labour in an industry which must structurally remain a manufacture.

Ferro is most explicit about the significance of prescriptions in his essay 'Concrete as Weapon' (2018) where he explores the widespread take up of reinforced concrete in France in the late nineteenth and early twentieth centuries. The use of reinforced concrete, Ferro argues, disqualified (or diminished the power and value of) masons and carpenters – the 'aristocracy of construction' – who were also key figures in the workers' movements, which were strong at the time. In construction, as a production process that had remained substantially unchanged in technical and material terms even while other industries were mechanising, the mobilisation of concrete and iron construction marked a move away from formal subsumption towards real subsumption – or as Ferro puts it 'an ersatz'[21] or 'substitution of real subsumption'.[22] The pace of labour is not yet determined by machinery but it is dictated by a new kind of management, that directly interferes with the labour process itself. If reinforced concrete acts as a replacement for the machine in this quasi-real subsumption, important for us is that 'comprehensive prescriptions' also play a central role:

> The general economic purpose of this transformation [...] in Karl Marx's terms, from formal to real subsumption, was the increase of relative surplus value by higher labour productivity through the introduction of machinery *and comprehensive prescriptions.*[23]

One means to disqualify labour is: 'industrial management through the centralization of knowledge and through authoritative, meticulous prescription.'[24] With the use of reinforced concrete, calculations and specifications for reinforcement and concrete mixes moved to the engineer's office where they were set out in detailed, quasi-scientific instructions, external to and overriding the know-how of the building worker. As when drawing moves from the building site to the tracing room or architect's office there is a transfer from the embodied knowledge of the building worker to the paperwork of prescriptive documents. As Ferro puts it: 'There was something of a rush to import the workers' know-how (aided by the emerging areas of materials science and structural analysis) and translate it into service orders, with the distant prospect on the horizon of dismissing, once and for all, this same know-how.'[25]

In terms of the form and content of these 'service orders', Ferro observes that during this period 'design specifications became more demanding, precise and comprehensive,' and that there was an 'inflation of these prescriptions'.[26] Like the few other architectural commentators who show any interest in these documents, such as John Summerson in *Georgian London*[27] and Howard Davis in *The Culture of Building*[28] Ferro picks up on the increase in their detail and length. Summerson and Davis make similar observations regarding the increase in detail of specifications produced in London more than a century earlier, just as the building industry was transitioning to a full-blown capitalist model. However, close analysis of documents produced in the London area reveals a more fundamental change than greater precision to the structure and content of the specification in this period. The emergence of a new form of a document – the trades-based specification – in fact affirms and is explained by Ferro's hypotheses more directly than the prescriptive documents he refers to in 'Concrete as Weapon'.

Typical of specifications before this transformation, the 'Articles of Agreement for a townhouse at St. James's Square, London' from 1734 to 36 takes the form of a medieval indenture or contract.[29] It is written out twice in ink on parchment by a scribe acting for a notary. That there are no spaces between words indicates that the document was intended for legal purposes rather than to be read for information. The specification is signed by carpenter Benjamin Timbrell who ran the contract on site (and went on to work as an architect), by the client William Heathcote and by his architect Henry Flitcroft (himself a former carpenter). Once signed, it was cut in two, one version for the client and the other for the contractor. The wavy line of the cut at the top of the document demonstrated materially the two fragments' original unity for perpetuity. The text describes the building as an object – it moves floor by floor from the lowest to the highest storey – 'A plan of the lower storey'; 'A plan of the hall and parlour floor'; 'A plan of the chamber floor'; 'A plan of the attick storey' (and then to the outbuildings) – similar to a drawn section.

Chimneys

William Heathcote

Articles of Agreement for a town house for Sir William Heathcote at St. James's Square, 1734–6.

Some materials (oak, deal, teak, fir) are named but, like a drawing, the document comprises mostly a series of dimensions, except that they are given in words, for example:

> No.3 Plan of the Chamber floor The same to be thirteen foot six inches high in the clear when finished the teaked flooring framed of sound and good fir timber Beams fourteen inches by twelve the ceiling joysts a little below the Girder to preserve the Ceilings from cracking the upper joyst not less than neine inches by two and an half to be floored with clean deal dowelled except the landing of the two staircases.[30]

No instructions are provided about building processes. The specification outlines in skeleton form what the contractor has committed to execute and assumes quality of work on trust.

In contrast, the specification for Newgate Gaol and the Sessions House at the Old Bailey (also in London) produced only a few decades later, in 1769, by

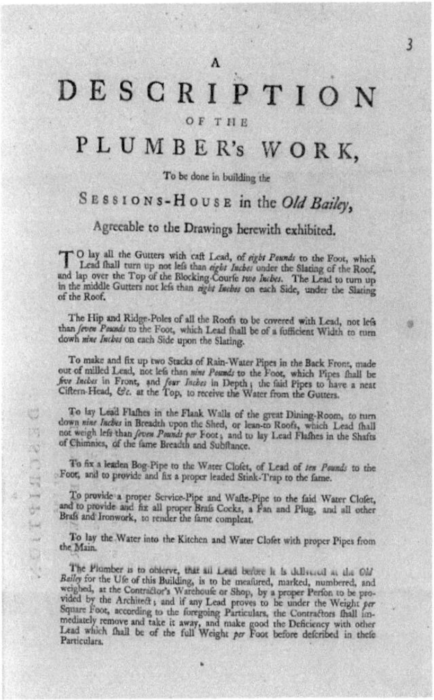

3

A

DESCRIPTION

OF THE

PLUMBER's WORK,

To be done in building the

SESSIONS-HOUSE in the *Old Bailey*,

Agreeable to the Drawings herewith exhibited.

TO lay all the Gutters with caſt Lead, of *eight Pounds* to the Foot, which Lead ſhall turn up not leſs than *eight Inches* under the Slating of the Roof, and lap over the Top of the Blocking-Courſe *two Inches*. The Lead to turn up in the middle Gutters not leſs than *eight Inches* on each Side, under the Slating of the Roof.

The Hip and Ridge-Poles of all the Roofs to be covered with Lead, not leſs than *ſeven Pounds* to the Foot, which Lead ſhall be of a ſufficient Width to turn dowh *nine Inches* on each Side upon the Slating.

To make and fix up two Stacks of Rain-Water Pipes in the Back Front, made out of milled Lead, not leſs than *nine Pounds* to the Foot, which Pipes ſhall be *five Inches* in Front, and *four Inches* in Depth; the ſaid Pipes to have a neat Ciſtern-Head, &c. at the Top, to receive the Water from the Gutters.

To lay Lead Flaſhes in the Flank Walls of the great Dining-Room, to turn down *nine Inches* in Breadth upon the Shed, or lean-to Roofs, which Lead ſhall not weigh leſs than *ſeven Pounds per* Foot; and to lay Lead Flaſhes in the Shafts of Chimnies, of the ſame Breadth and Subſtance.

To fix a leaden Bog-Pipe to the Water Cloſet, of Lead of *ten Pounds* to the Foot, and to provide and fix a proper leaded Stink-Trap to the ſame.

To provide a proper Service-Pipe and Waſte-Pipe to the ſaid Water Cloſet, and to provide and fix all proper Braſs Cocks, a Fan and Plug, and all other Braſs and Ironwork, to render the ſame compleat.

To lay the Water into the Kitchen and Water Cloſet with proper Pipes from the Main.

The Plumber is to obſerve, that all Lead before it is delivered at the *Old Bailey* for the Uſe of this Building, is to be meaſured, marked, numbered, and weighed, at the Contractor's Warehouſe or Shop, by a proper Perſon to be provided by the Architect; and if any Lead proves to be under the Weight *per* Square Foot, according to the foregoing Particulars, the Contractors ſhall immediately remove and take it away, and make good the Deficiency with other Lead which ſhall be of the full Weight *per* Foot before deſcribed in theſe Particulars.

A Description of the Plumber's Work, Specification for Newgate Gaol and the Sessions-House at the Old Bailey (1769).

the practice of architect George Dance the Younger, has a radically different form.[31] It is no longer organised around the structure of the building but around the structure of the trades. Indeed, this document allocates a separate printed pamphlet to each of the eight trades involved: 'A Description of the Plumber's Work', 'A Description of the Painter's Work', and so on. In comparison to the single page of the St. James's Square document, the trade pamphlets are four to eight pages long, and each one includes detailed descriptions of the manner and methods of work the builder is to use (bricklayer; carpenter; glazier; mason; painter; 'plaisterer'; plumber; smith/ironmonger). Thus, it is both divided by trades, and prescribes the work to be carried out by them. In this case the contract was overseen by the architect,[32] but by the nineteenth century it would become the typical form of contract used when a general contractor oversaw the work.

One way to understand the new format of the trades-based specification concerns the method of payment. The older dimensions-based type was set up to allow for payment 'by measure' after work is completed on site. The trades-based specification accommodated the newer practice of letting out the contract and paying for work in advance.[33] However, Ferro's arguments about the importance of formal subsumption in the development of building work provides a more precise understanding of this new form of specification. He identifies the splintering of trades with Marx's arguments about the division of labour from labour in manufacture:

> [...] the co-operation of wage-labourers is entirely brought about by the capital that employs them. Their unification into one single productive body, and the establishment of a connection between their individual functions, lies outside their competence. These things are not their own act, but the act of the capital that brings them together and maintains them in that situation. Hence the interconnection between their various labours confronts them, in the realm of ideas, as a plan drawn up by the capitalist, and, in practice, as his authority, as the powerful will of a being outside them, who subjects their activity to his purpose.[34]

For Ferro, when building remains a form of capitalist manufacture the trades maintain their own specialisms and know-how but their capacity to coordinate and cooperate with each other gets taken away, in order that they can be organised externally 'by the capital that employs them'. This bringing together of the now 'scattered activities' of the skilled workers is given over to the work of the drawings and prescriptions – which are in general produced by the architect:

> These plans and memoranda constitute the only close links, in effect, between the scattered activities of carpenters, painters, plumbers, masons, and so on, during material production. They designate the to-do [...] subjecting the splintered production to the paths others have determined for it, and restoring, but deformedly, what was taken from it. The role these paper rolls play is clear: they bring together labour with labour, labour with tool, and an activity that is carried out mindlessly with a functional end.[35]

There is more to the parcellated specifications from Newgate Gaol than the evidence that several trades were working on site and that each was now subcontracted. With Ferro's analysis in mind, we see that the documents are themselves tools in breaking up one trade from another. The pamphlet system gave each subcontractor a description of only their own part of the work. Labour has been divided by trade, but what now brings the 'collective worker' together under capital is the paper document, the architect who writes it and the contractor who mobilises it in the building process.

Ferro's arguments also draw attention to a second aspect of the trades-based specification – the emergence of the description of work processes in the clauses of the specification. In contrast to the dimensions-led specification for the house at St James's Square, process-based clauses describe in varying detail the work to be carried out by each trade. They specify not the finished object but the methods by which to achieve it. The paint clause from the Newgate Gaol specification is an example:

> Description of the Painter's Work
> To paint all the outside Wood and Iron-Works, in every Part of this Building, four Times in Oil, and to paint all the inside Wood and Iron Works, in every Part of this Building, three Times in Oil, of such plain colours *as shall be directed.*[36]

Note that in addition to specifying details of the paintwork which in the older specification were assumed on trust, this clause also refers to the direction of the architect whose job it is to oversee work on site and give further instructions.

The practice of process-based specification emerges at different times in other building cultures. In Britain it continued for the next two hundred years. The most detailed clauses are for the making up of mortars on site, as for example in this early nineteenth-century specification for a workshop, which was transcribed into a collection of exemplar documents from his practice by the prolific London-based architect David Mocatta:

> One Bushel of well burnt unslacked lime made from Dorking of Mersham grey chalk or Halling Lime to Three Bushels of clean Thames sand to be

> taken from the river between Fulham and London Bridge. The lime and sand to be mixed together during the suspension of slacking by wetting the lime and then covering it with its due proportion of sand. The proportion of each to be duly measured. It is then to be passed thro' a fine screen of no less than 35 units at equal distance in breadth of every foot. It is then to be sufficiently beat or passed through a proper mill.[37]

Variations of this clause can be seen throughout nineteenth-century specifications, but what does the writing down of the 'how' by the architect achieve when it appears in the specification? Explicitly it acts as setting a standard for the quality of the work, but actually it transfers the decision of how to build something away from the building worker to the designer and facilitates the disqualification of the builder.

Not all building processes lend themselves as well to process-based description. Little detail of method is ever given for the work of the mason and the carpenter, while the making of 'matterised' homogeneous materials like mortar, and later concrete are especially susceptible to process-based description.[38] Indeed, some of the most detailed sections of twentieth-century specifications are those describing how to prepare formwork, mix concrete, pour it and finish the cast pieces. The 'Concretor' section of the specification for Egypt End in Buckinghamshire, one of the earliest modernist houses in Britain to be built using perfectly smooth reinforced concrete in 1934–35, takes up a quarter of the document's length.[39] The 1961 specification for the board-marked concrete of the Elfrida Rathbone School for the Educationally Subnormal in South London runs to sixteen pages of prose, despite the fact that only two assembly hall roofs were made out of the material.[40]

The trades-based specification with its process-based clauses intensifies in detail throughout the nineteenth and twentieth centuries. The division of trades in the documents (and of labour) separates into ever smaller and more specialist units – as can be seen in the 1898 table of contents from the first edition of *Specification*, an annual publication providing best practice which lists over thirty-eight trades including 'Well-Sinker', 'Terra Cotta Worker', 'Thatcher', 'Art Metal Worker' and 'Paperhanger'.[41] (Each section is actually called a

'Division'!) The trades-based specification remains the dominant form right up to the 1970s when it is reconceived in more 'scientific' and commodity-based terms – though retaining in fact a similar order based on the logic of what happens first on site. Of course, this change does not mean that the disqualification of the worker for capital comes to an end! Only, we might argue, that once again, as with the mobilisation of classical design, the potency of trades-based specification as a technique fades and is replaced by other means.

For a history of separated design

Examining the trades-based specification, which comes into use with the emergence of the full-blown capitalist building industry, enables us to see explicitly the transfer of skill from building workers to 'the capital that employs them'. At the same time, it is an instrument in that process. The trades-based specification is organised around – and organises – an increasingly parcellated division of labour among building workers, and in turn takes on the role of overseeing and totalising or re-unifying work on site. Not simply more precise or detailed, it is a distinctive form of the 'comprehensive prescriptions' Ferro identifies that operates as another 'weapon' in the real or quasi-real subsumption of labour. But it emerges much earlier than the calculations and paperwork involved in the specification of reinforced concrete and arrives only once classical design has lost its potency as a tool of domination.
Ferro shows that the separation of design from the building site was a primary means in the formal subsumption of building labour. It may not be so surprising that management and contractual documents like the trades-based specification would be instruments in capital's re-organisation of work on site. More surprising is Ferro's inclusion of the architectural drawing in his category of prescriptive instruments. By understanding the drawing (and the design) in terms of the specification, rather than as distinct from it, we better recognise the extent to which both forms of prescription – directly or not – specify not only the building object but also the labour that produces it.
That the drawing seems to have a special status with respect to other design

instruments like the specification is itself an effect of separated design and the ideological need to raise the activity of design and architects above the work of building and building workers. Further, we suggest that the persuasive power of this separation leads historians – even those taking a Marxian approach – to look either to design *or* the building site as separate spheres, without considering their necessary relation under capitalist production. In the light of Ferro's arguments, the relation itself between design and the building site becomes the object of study, telling new stories about architecture where the principles of classical design, the compass-drawn elevation of a cathedral, and the clauses of a specification are all means of the formal and quasi-real subsumption of building labour.

Notes

1 Sérgio Ferro was born in Curitiba (Brazil) in 1938, and studied at the University of São Paulo's Faculty of Architecture and Urbanism from 1957 to 1961. With Rodrigo Lefèvre and Flávio Império, he formed the collective Arquitetura Nova (1962–1970). Due to persecution by the military dictatorship which took over the Brazilian State in 1964, he moved to France, working as a professor at the École Nationale Supérieure d'Architecture de Grenoble from 1972 to 2003. There he founded and directed the laboratory Dessin/Chantier. In 1992 he was made Chevalier de l'Ordre des Arts et des Lettres. Ferro's seminal text *'O canteiro e o desenho'* was first published in 1976, followed by a number of exhibitions, papers and books, in Portuguese and French. Part of his writings was recently translated into English through the research project 'Translating Ferro / Transforming Knowledges of Architecture, Design and Labour for the New Field of Production Studies' (TF/TK), and is now being published: Sérgio Ferro, *Architecture from Below: An Anthology*, eds. Silke Kapp and Mariana Moura, trans. Ellen Heyward and Ana Naomi de Sousa (London: Mack, 2024); Sérgio Ferro, *Design and the Building Site, and Complementary Essays*, eds. Silke Kapp and Mariana Moura, trans. Ana Naomi de Sousa and Ellen Heyward (Mack, forthcoming 2025), as yet unpaginated; and Sérgio Ferro, *Construction of Classical Design*, eds. Silke Kapp and Mariana Moura, trans. Ellen Heyward and Ana Naomi de Sousa (Mack, forthcoming 2025). Our arguments here are based on these three volumes.

2 See Manfredo Tafuri, 'Toward a Critique of Architectural Ideology', trans. Stephen Sartarelli, in K. Michael Hays (ed.), *Architecture Theory since 1968* (Cambridge, Mass and London: MIT Press, [1969] 2000), 6–35; *Theories and History of Architecture*, trans. Giorgio Verrecchia (New York: Harper & Row, [1976] 1980).

3 Linda Clarke, *Building Capitalism: Historical Change and the Labour Process in the Production of the Built Environment* (London: Routledge, 1992), 12–13.

4 Karl Marx, 'Results of the Immediate Process of Production' [1861- 1863], in Karl Marx, *Capital: A Critique of Political Economy*, vol. I, trans. Ben Fowkes (London: Penguin; New Left Review, 1976), 1021.

5 Marx, *Capital*, 455.

6 See Sérgio Ferro, 'Dessin/Chantier: An Introduction for Newcastle' [2014], trans. Ricardo Agarez and Silke Kapp, in Sérgio Ferro, *Architecture from Below: An Anthology* (London: Mack, 2024), 25–27; 'Concrete as Weapon' [2018], trans. Alice Fiuza and Silke Kapp in Ferro, *Architecture from Below*, 196–7.

7 Andrés Mella and Matthew Savage, *Construction Sector Employment in Low Income Countries* (London: Infrastructure and Cities for Economic Development, UK Department for International Development, 2018), 9.

8 Marx, *Capital*, vol. I, 489–490.

9 See Ferro, *Construction of Classical Design*.

10 Ferro is of course not the only commentator to note that architectural drawing produces a distance from the building site. In *The Alphabet and the Algorithm* (Cambridge, Mass: MIT Press, 2011), Mario Carpo proposes that Alberti was the 'inventor' of notation as design; Jonathan Hill has explored the significance of 'disegno' and the drawing out of ideas for the establishment of the architect, see 'Drawing Research' in *Journal of Architecture*, vol. 11, no. 3 (2006), 329–333. Alberto Pérez-Gómez's detailed studies of drawing practices on site and off in *Architecture and the Crisis of Modern Science* (Cambridge, Mass: MIT Press, 1985) and his and Louise Pelletier's *Architectural Representation and the Perspective Hinge* (Cambridge, Mass: MIT Press, 2000), both lament the loss of meaning this shift entailed. However, in these analyses separated design is identified with the Renaissance, and of interest more for marking the beginning of the architect, than for its effects on relations of production.

11 Erwin Panofsky, *Gothic Architecture and Scholasticism* (New York: Meridian Books, 1957 [1951]).

12 Sérgio Ferro, *Michel-Ange, architecte et sculpteur de la chapelle Medicis* (Lyon: Plan Fixe, 1998).

13 See Antoine Picon, *French Architects and Engineers in the Age of Enlightenment*, trans. Martin Thom (Cambridge and New York: Cambridge University Press, 1992), 26–34.

14 See, for instance, A. W. N. Pugin's 'Illustration of the Practice of Architecture in the Nineteenth Century on New Improved and Cheap Principles', in

Contrasts: or a Parallel Between the Noble Edifices of the Fourteenth and Fifteenth Centuries (London: James Moyes, 1836).

15 John Gelder, *Specifying Architecture: A Guide to Professional Practice* (Milsons Point: Construction Information Systems, Australia, 2001).

16 Ferro, *Construction of Classical Design*.

17 Ibid., subchapter 'Ancillaries to Drawing'.

18 For more on the use of 'prescription' in relation to the architectural specification see Katie Lloyd Thomas, *Building Materials: Material Theory and the Architectural Specification* (London: Routledge, 2022), 132–133.

19 Sérgio Ferro, 'Design and the Building Site' [1976], in *Design and the Building Site; Construction of Classical Design*.

20 Katie Lloyd Thomas and Tilo Amhoff, 'Writing Work: Changing Practices of Architectural Specification', in Peggy Deamer (ed.), *The Architect as Worker* (London: Bloomsbury, 2015), 121–143.

21 Ferro, 'Concrete as Weapon', 191.

22 Ibid., 200.

23 Ibid., 177.

24 Ibid., 197.

25 Ibid., 210.

26 Ibid., 188.

27 John Summerson, *Georgian London* (London: Pleiades Books, 1945).

28 Howard Davis, *The Culture of Building* (Oxford: Oxford University Press, 2006).

29 Articles of Agreement for a town house for Sir William Heathcote at St. James's Square (1734–6), RIBA Archives, HeW/1/1/2.

30 Articles of Agreement for a town house for Sir William Heathcote at St. James's Square (1734–6), RIBA Archives, HeW/1/1/2.

31 Specification for Newgate Gaol and the Sessions-House at the Old Bailey (1769), RIBA Archives, EW no. 790.

32 Dorothy Stroud, *George Dance, Architect 1745–1825* (London: Faber and Faber, 1971).

33 See Lloyd Thomas and Amhoff, 'Writing Work'.

34 Marx, *Capital*, vol. I, 449–450, cited in Ferro, *Design and the Building Site*.

35 Ferro, *Design and the Building Site*.

36 Specification for Newgate Gaol, our emphasis.

37 Specification for a Workshop, in David Mocatta, *Specifications* (1833–43,) RIBA Archives, MoD/1/1.

38 Katie Lloyd Thomas has coined the term 'matterization' to describe the rendering homogeneous of variegated materials in *Building Materials: Material Theory and the Architectural Specification* (London: Routledge, 2022), 103–106.

39 Specification of Works for a House at Farnham Common, Bucks (1934), RIBA Archives, SaG/17/3.

40 Specification for the Works at Elfrida Rathbone School of the Educationally Subnormal, Camberwell (1961), RIBA Archives, LCC/AD/1.

41 *Specification*, 1898.

Chapter 3
'Capitalist Sorcery' and the Daylight Auto Factory

Claire Zimmerman

This chapter has two goals. First, to consider industrial architecture within a spectrum that relates buildings to the economic forces that produce them, and the social relations that unfold within them. Second, to analyse industrial buildings as sites where the social relations of capitalism took form through material and spatial arrangements that were carefully planned and remain legible. Industrial architecture is often examined by architects or architectural historians as a kind of architectural countermodel; a reductive, functional, vernacular way of building that occasionally offers formally persuasive models for high culture to borrow from, adapt, or appropriate; or challenges architects to craft new 'symbolic forms' for industrial society.[1] Such approaches neglect a vast body of construction occupied by thousands of people.

My claim here is that industrial architecture is not merely the doppelgänger of culturally elite architecture (which has long dominated architectural history) but rather a crucial diagnostic device in its own right, and the site of still-unfamiliar material and spatial inventions that merit further study. Factories' highly optimised construction marks a kind of limit condition for building within capitalism, similar to infrastructural forms like highways, bridges and large machines. But unlike such infrastructure, industrial architecture largely evolved in dialogue with automation. The factories of US Midwest automobile production, for example, saw a surge in automation between 1905 and 1915 that was at least as transformative as that of the English textile industry between 1765 and 1785.[2] These dramatic changes mean factory buildings and their uses can disclose relationships between political economy, the state and architecture perhaps more effectively than their close cousins, high rise office buildings (factories for white collar workers). What we learn from studying this 'null-sum architecture' (the phrase is Reyner Banham's) bears on all sorts of buildings.

Highland Park Ford Plant, Michigan, after 1914.

The chapter focuses on daylight factories, defined as buildings framed in concrete or steel that maximise the penetration of natural light through wider column spans and higher ceilings than their brick and timber frame predecessors allowed. The daylight factory helped transform North American workplaces, providing safer and more accommodating workplaces for the manufacture of large assemblies like cars, trucks and tractors. I explore how daylight factories participated in and developed industrial capitalism, keeping in mind the rapid increase in automobiles, the extensive network of roads built to run them on, and the fuel needed to power them. But the chapter also focuses on the introduction of the moving assembly line and what it meant for work in these factories. Daylight factories also functioned without moving lines (not all companies automated as fully as Henry Ford, and not all processes were automated). So, although daylight factories and moving lines have often been seen as coordinated innovations, each dependent upon the other, they represent two contradictory stages of industrial manufacture, jammed together in time. Both occurred within the nexus of so-called 'welfare capitalism' – to be explained below – of early twentieth-century North America: the first appeared in Detroit in 1905; the second by early 1914.[3]

Throughout 1913–14, the moving assembly line for automobile manufacture developed inside a daylight factory: the Highland Park, Michigan, plant of the Ford Motor Company. The moving line, in contrast to the building that housed it, transformed daylight factories from good workspaces into highly productive machine-buildings. The introduction of the line to newly minted daylight factories in concrete or steel transformed a building type that was meant to improve working conditions into an environmental apparatus that made them notoriously worse. To the soft power of architectural design as rendered in better factory workplaces, the assembly line added mass coercion – the proverbial iron fist of high-volume mass production nested discretely inside the velvet glove of buildings that were purported to provide better working conditions, greater amenities and clearer organisation.

'Industrial architecture' does not just designate a set of building types dedicated to making things. Rather, this kind of building concretises a disparate array of technical processes of which the moving line is one. The buildings that arise around industrial uses change, sometimes as frequently as technical processes. Daylight factories evolved from instance to instance, in line with changes in manufacturing; floor-to-ceiling heights, column and beam design, column span – all changed over time. The design of assembly-line production, likewise, adapted around regularly changing processes after the system was invented and implemented. Thus, I consider two architectural-technological inventions here, both also subject to regular technical 'upshifts' during the period of industrial acceleration that characterised the growth of the auto industry.

The daylight factory and the moving line are interpreted here as two forces within the broader intermingling of technology, social life, production and 'mental conception' that Marx identified in Chapter XV of *Capital* volume 1, the chapter on machinery and large-scale industry.[4] They were not isolated inventions or building innovations; they were embedded in a web of relationships. Sometimes rapid, sometimes episodic, changes to manufacturing are closely linked to socio-economic life: when the Model T was replaced by the Model A in 1927, for example, Ford Motor Company shut down its entire operation, throwing thousands out of work for months, and stopping the flow of profit to the company. A dramatic example of change in the use of factory buildings, perhaps, this example echoes throughout the history of industrial architecture more generally. If part of the point here is to disentangle two technical inventions that worked at cross purposes, it is also to note that both were dedicated to the subsumption of labour as described by Marx: the daylight factory, in its configuration in Highland Park's 'Old Shop', to the formal subsumption of labour in already existing practices of automobile making based on manufacture at stations on the factory floor; the moving assembly line, through its increase in speed, scale of production and its unique way of lashing human beings to each other and to machinery, to Marx's 'real' subsumption of labour.[5]

In examining the moving assembly line and the daylight factory, the chapter refers to 'capitalist sorcery' as a way to characterise how modern industrial built environments adapted so well to change and mutation. The term comes from the book of the same title by Philippe Pignarre and Isabelle Stengers. who diagnose near-diabolical shape-shifting in the conditions of capitalism, the ways in which an economic system has adapted to any effort to counter it by continuously taking new forms that perpetuate acceleration and growth.[6] Here, I follow the *pas de deux* between two architectural elements, the daylight factory and the moving assembly line, as their relationship changed incrementally, while industrialists sought lower prices and higher profits in the intensely competitive environment of 'boomtown Detroit'. Whether the situation analysed here still pertains in industrial environments today will determine whether the 'sounder of the depths' that Pignarre and Stengers call for might still do any good.[7]

A spectrum of building

Architectural history has tended to adopt a hierarchy of building, in which the term 'architecture' has been used to frame and analyse buildings as understood within elite culture. Museums and other cultural institutions, civic or state buildings, large commercial institutions, high-end residential skyscrapers and bespoke houses typically qualify as architecture and occupy space in historical accounts. They sit at one end of a spectrum of building. Commercial vernacular includes a huge volume of building from skyscraper office buildings to smaller-scale retail; this kind of architecture occupies a broad strip on the spectrum of building activity understood in terms of economic function, sometimes high (i.e. expensive), sometimes low end. Mass housing occupies a category of its own, recently a focus for historians (as in much of the UK's postwar state-funded mass housing). Factories are another kind of utilitarian vernacular, and 'certainly not architecture.' Factories and mass housing sit at the opposite end of the spectrum from art museums and bespoke villas. Yet despite the implicit 'grading' of the built environment sketched here, organised by the cost that underpins built environments, the significance of economic function is seldom discussed relationally, across the spectrum of different building types.

If factories, like mass housing, sit at one extreme of the spectrum, as buildings for which costs of construction are carefully monitored and controlled in relation to functional requirements, this is because they enhance profit for their makers in ways that many buildings do not. Housing can be made more economically productive by retrofitting dwellings for more occupants, or simply packing more residents into the same amount of space. Such practices are often irregular and widespread, if not illegal. Factories, however, are sites where relative surplus value is meant to increase over time, as innovations in production processes accrue and productivity yields rise. At the other extreme of our spectrum of building are what we might refer to as *sumptuary buildings*, made with the profits deriving from industry, much like the Carnegie libraries deployed the surplus profits of the Carnegie Corporation, or Rockefeller Center those of Standard Oil, or a luxurious villa those of the industrialist who commissioned it. In between these two extremes are buildings that balance input and outflow; where cost is monitored but where other agendas determine budgets and representational functions, like a public library, a civic building, or a fast-food franchise. There are various images conjured by this scheme, but what is the utility of such a yardstick of economic building?

That factories occupy the extreme edge of a spectrum of building considered in relation to the economics of architecture suggests their diagnostic utility in understanding architecture as a distributor of class relations and opportunities. Their qualities are determined in relation to quantities, and they are considered by their owners and makers as primarily and overtly economic instruments. In the context of this chapter, the industrial-architectural inventions of second wave industrialisation in North America are seen to concretise economic function in the first decades of the twentieth century. This is not to suggest that such buildings have no 'architecture'. It is to suggest that their achievements as architecture – as buildings that improve the experience of users over that which came before – can be especially impressive when considered in relation to the stringencies of their design. Since industrial buildings are also collectively designed (by architects, plant engineers, clients and workmen), decisions made by designers must be justified in terms with which plant engineers (who work directly for the client) will agree. Their most crucial documents are process schedules and routine diagrams, followed by plans, sections, elevations and perspectives that thereby acquire a different relationship to the buildings they describe. Potential changes to the production process mean that architectural envelopes must be loose and baggy in relation to what lies within. While it may be small wonder, then, that they have not formed a central part of the history of architecture as authored art form, their stringencies of design and execution suggest that studying them carefully now may yield useful results. Such buildings used available resources efficiently, they didn't waste, and they were judged successful by how well they did the job assigned to them. And although they performed the tasks of industrial capitalism with brutal efficiency after construction, those that survive generally no longer do so today.

Detroit

The story begins in Detroit, Michigan. The concrete- and steel-framed manufacturing campuses that began to appear there around 1905 were located in the heart of the city, like the fields of single-family dwellings that surrounded them. The urban pattern of Detroit grew up around 20-foot house fronts sited in roughly 34-foot lots. This same increment echoed in the bays of the concrete factory that typically spanned from 20 to 32 feet, creating a spatial correlation that gave the city mat-like regularity when viewed from the air. For the first half of the twentieth century, factory campuses were integrated into, and formed a crucial part of Detroit, but also of Hamtramck, Highland Park, Flint, Pontiac and other midwestern industrial cities in which the auto industry took hold. Pedestrian access was important in 1910s Detroit; the single-family house and residential neighbourhood were the housing standard. The 'Motor City' was a worker's walking and streetcar city.

The daylight factory was introduced to Detroit by December 1905, with the famous Packard Building #10 and other concrete-framed daylight buildings announcing its arrival. Michael G. Smith has documented the construction of three of these buildings in close succession; all using a proprietary concrete technology that came to be known as 'Trussed Concrete' or 'the Kahn System', attributed to the engineer Julius Kahn and his architect brother and partner Albert.[8] These buildings were heralded for their wide spans, tall ceilings and generous fenestration, but also because they were fire-proof. Top floors might be skylit; but lower floors also had much larger windows than the timber framed brick and stone buildings that they replaced. As the building type developed, other amenities were added to daylight factories to make them better workplaces – generous sanitary facilities, health clinics, canteens. But at least one major adaptation to daylight factories had the opposite effect. As becomes quickly apparent from an examination of these buildings' use, changes that made them more easily adaptable to new manufacturing processes took precedence over changes that improved working conditions.

The daylight factory is closely associated with that other invention of late nineteenth or early twentieth-century industry: the moving assembly line.

Observed in Cincinnati and Chicago meatpacking plants in the nineteenth century, the moving assembly line was used for the efficient dismemberment of livestock after slaughter. Sigfried Giedion accounts for its development in *Mechanization takes Command*, beginning with the Archimedean screw and the automation experiments of Oliver Evans.[9] In the context of Ford Motor Company, the moving assembly line resulted from constant tinkering in the Highland Park plant throughout 1913, to optimise subassemblies at first, and then to extend the concept to the full car.[10] These two inventions, both of which characterise second wave industrialisation, however, could hardly differ more. One represents the architectural version of welfare capitalism, with architectural amenities like large windows and generous service spaces; the other, just the opposite – a machine consisting of a mobile armature (a chain, a conveyor belt, an overhead suspension rail) that transports components of car motor, chassis and body as they are slowly built, one that can be installed in many different versions and configurations to maximise surplus profit production with little regard for the comfort or convenience of factory workers.[11]

In addition, both the building and the machine are tied to a network of production, one that leads from the rail sidings that extend deep inside the buildings to the freight lines that connect both coasts of North America to international markets, forging a tie between a national transport infrastructure and an architectural instance. Industrial campuses are typically striped with rails, some even dating to the period of construction itself, when materials were brought into sites in trolleys or railcars. Rail lines penetrated deep into building interiors, bringing in raw materials and taking away finished products.[12] The CIAM map of Detroit showed graphically how this worked; Robert Fishman has expanded the image by convincingly showing that 'linear urbanism' resulted from the transport basis of industrial manufacture.[13] Lindy Biggs relates a mode of movement through factory campuses to notions of 'throughput' or 'flow', and theorists of capitalism remind us of the importance of constant movement to capitalism itself.[14] The factory was the nexus between extraction, production and transportation, the concrete appearance of an expansive system. The changes to the automobile industry that followed the sit-down strikes of the 1930s, the frequent strikes of the wartime years, and the postwar 'Treaty of Detroit' are linked to the decline of auto production in the US, as manufacturers moved factories to the non-unionised US south, destroying the 'innovative milieu' of Detroit and the Midwest. In the process, some argue, automakers cut off their noses to spite their face.[15] Here, the linkage between strikes and architecture is considered with a view to the role that architecture played both in advancing and showing the movement of industrial capitalism in this instance.

The Daylight Factory

The daylight factory is so named because it increased the quantity of natural light for manufacturing, even though electricity still supplemented daylight and lengthened working hours in the northern hemisphere's winter months. Since earlier timber-framed mill buildings were also generously fenestrated, albeit within the limits of brick wall construction, the increase in daylight in the new plants was striking enough to generate the name.[16] In the daylight factory, a regular structural system in reinforced concrete or steel simultaneously held up the building and subdivided it into equal increments. Large operable windows let in natural light supplemented by skylights and clerestories, all of which provided ventilation and air exchange. The regularity of the architecture often related to possible expansion in different directions, both horizontally and vertically. As industry grew, factories might also grow.

In the case of manufacturing buildings in concrete, a complex system of attachments or inserts could be embedded within concrete columns and beams or bolted and screwed into the structure, as they were in their steel-framed cousins. Electrical outlets, conduits, shafts and hangers of different kinds provided either construction system with electric power, flexible use, central heating and fire protection in the form of sprinklers. Power to operate machinery came from turbines generally housed in a separate powerhouse. In the early daylight factories, power supplied belts and shafts that ran along ceilings, like those of the earliest water-powered mills in New or old England. As the building type developed, electrical circuits powered individual machines or groups of machines. Gradually, each workstation became independent of the others.[17]

Expandable steel or concrete buildings were designed to maximise workers' productivity by better accommodating their needs and attending to their comfort through spatial design, the architectural response to welfare capitalism. Such buildings developed differently from the motorised assembly lines that later traversed them – the advance guard of a new relation between capital and labour to which I return below. Welfare capitalism as it developed out of the Progressive Era in the United States (in reaction to the excesses of the Gilded Age), prioritised the mutual benefit of industrialist and industrial worker. The idea that a rising tide lifts all boats underpinned investments in architecture that demonstrably improved working conditions. The enlarged size of the factories, in comparison to earlier manufacturing buildings, was associated with higher volume production. Amenities like natural light, sanitary installations, locker rooms, canteens and cafeterias, and first-aid stations offered potential improvements in social relations as well as productivity gains. The Burroughs plant in Plymouth, Michigan (completed 1938), for example, was equipped with a gym and bleachers and an auditorium. The industrialist had a vested interest in keeping workers happy and comfortable.

After its 1905 introduction by the Packard and Cadillac Motor Companies, the reinforced-concrete daylight factory became an industry staple. When Henry Ford needed larger spaces, he commissioned a new building in Highland Park, Michigan, from the Kahn brothers. This 'Crystal Palace' was to become a manifesto building, celebrated in architectural literature for years to come. Ford's infamous moving assembly line, introduced here four years after the building was completed, became associated with the long linear form of the building, as if the building concretely represented the line within. In fact, Ford had wanted a very large open floor plan to enable experimentation; Highland Park was initially laid out with workstations, much like its predecessor on Piquette Avenue. Whether the assembly line was somehow envisioned or anticipated by Ford and his engineers is difficult to determine. It was not yet in existence when the building was built.

The assembly line

If the moving assembly line for automotive manufacturing did not exist in 1910, many precedents did. According to David Nye, however, there was no plan to invent or install the moving line when Highland Park was built.[18] A pair of photographs taken in 1913 show a putative before and after: in the first, women make metal coils for the flywheel magneto, the first component of the Ford engine placed on a moving line; in the second, we see the early iteration of the magneto assembly line.

'The assembly line' is even something of a misnomer. Auto factories had multiple moving lines in their early days, all slowly converging on the chassis of the automobile, like tributaries flowing to the sea of cars gathered in vast parking lots outside the plant's walls. William Klann recounted the slow evolution of assembly line production at Highland Park: 'The first was the magneto coil assembly in 1912. Then came the motor assembly. Next was the transmission assembly of putting the gears together ... the next one was assembling the magneto to the flywheel. That was fourth in the series ... The first belt conveyor we had was for assembling magneto coils.'[19] At Highland Park or its successor plant at River Rouge, different iterations of the assembly line appear as a linked chain bolted to the concrete floor of the factory along its length, or as a set of rolling conveyors at knee or waist height, or as a track circling along the ceiling plane. These suspended racks and hooks snake through the space over the workers' heads, bringing wheels, tyres or other parts to the line from above.

Assembly-line production, however, grew to be highly systematised at Highland Park and River Rouge. In principle, each assembly line required five ingredients: the subdivision of labour; interchangeable parts; single-function machines; the sequential ordering of machines; and the moving line itself. These components differed among the many versions of the line that were

Women workers assembling magnetos at the Highland Park Plant, Michigan, c. 1913.

developed experimentally in the Highland Park building. The design of the system has been attributed to Ford manager Clarence W. Avery; Klann recalled his own part in its development in 1955. Like Giedion, he had seen the meatpacking houses: 'With going to Chicago and seeing this slaughterhouse, I got the idea that I could put a lot of jobs on these conveyors ... The first one I started to work out was on the motor assembly putting the crankshaft in.'[20] In this oral history, Klann had already acknowledged that the first moving assembly line was that for the assembly of the magneto, so he was not claiming authorship of the idea of a moving line. Like others at FMC, he acknowledged the group effort that its invention reflected. But after the moving line had been introduced to most manufacturing processes at Highland Park over the course of 1913, it was only a matter of time until other auto

Magneto assembly line at Ford Motor Company Highland Park Plant, Michigan, 1913.

manufacturers adopted the technique in their own factories.[21] Nye notes that competing claims to the invention of Ford's assembly line underscore the fact that it was the work of many.[22]

Klann's reference to the assembly-line slaughterhouses in Chicago, reminds us that the work was backbreaking and potentially dangerous, as in the hazards encountered at Highland Park: '… on the second day one of the men by the name of Langlois forgot to tighten his clamp, and when he turned over the crankshaft with the three-foot long bar, he threw the cylinder block off the bench and the cylinder block hit his leg … They found his leg was broken above the knee.[23] Klann recalls elsewhere how workers did not want assembly-line jobs as they were being invented throughout 1913. Anxiety about the moving line was fuelled by the experience of workers like Langlois, the fear of speedup, and the monotony of repetitive work. The subsequent increase in worker wages to five dollars a day was intended to reduce turnover at the plant after the introduction of the moving line. But the effects of the assembly line as described by German visitor Arthur Zeidler in 1929 include the impact of a line that was controlled mechanically rather than by human effort:

> The conveyor started as a simple means of carrying articles, but became a tyrant dominating the workers. When the conveyor is speeded up the workers are forced to follow its dictates, and to hurry with their jobs accordingly. The conveyor's speed invariably determines the worker's speed … The conveyor is the master. If the management in a factory decides to increase its speed by ten per cent … tens of thousands of hands … must work ten per cent faster. The workers are bound to the conveyor the way the galley slaves were bound to the vessel.[24]

Similarly, on the subject of worker and machine relations in the context of Detroit, Lindy Biggs has written: 'In the new system of constantly repeated routine movements [the motions of workers] began to merge with those of the machine.'[25] Thus the introduction of the moving assembly line to US workers constituted a sea change in the social relations of industrial production in Detroit and other automotive manufacturing centres. Such descriptions recall the conditions of production that Marx observed in English factories in the nineteenth century, when automatic spinning and weaving replaced handwork. What happened in Detroit is familiar to any readers of *Capital* or the earlier fragment on machines in the *Grundrisse*.[26] But was the moving line just another version of the mule jenny or the automated loom?

Nye interprets the assembly line 'not as a rigid system … but rather as a moment of synthesis for a still evolving processing technology.'[27] In other words, the moving line, the conveyor belt, the suspended motorised tracks – all these were highly flexible and mutable inventions. They could also be combined into integrated systems within the Ford plants. Nye celebrates the ingenuity of Klann, Avery and others in inventing this highly orchestrated, carefully tailored technology, without reflecting unduly on this stage of capitalism or its consequences for jobs in Motor City going forward. For Henry Ford, the processing technology worked for ever greater optimisation and efficiency of operation. His skilled and highly creative workers (Klann and many others) invented and fabricated moving assembly lines in their first iterations. They were evidently designing themselves and their fellow workers out of challenging and difficult jobs, perhaps with the idea that better ones would follow. In this moment of synthesis, the mechanised assembly line shifted gears for another stage in the evolving relationship between human and machine operators, where the labour of humans was again determined by the requirements of machines. This is the shift from formal to real subsumption of labour; that is, the stage where capitalism constitutes a 'real revolution' in Marx's words, and labour is determined by acceleration and expansion, main goals of the moving line.[28]

The demise of the daylight factory

The need to move things vertically at Highland Park constituted a flaw in the assembly-line process, but the consequences of this shortcoming could only be fully understood once moving assembly had been fully integrated into production at the plant. This occurred over the course of 1913. It took some time before 'all the kinks were worked out', as Klann recalled.[29] Highland Park had grown quickly, and the array of processes that had to be designed to fit moving lines meant that FMC had built an enormous campus – adding the vast six-storey New Shop to the four-storey 'Old Shop' of the Crystal Palace along Woodward Avenue – before it became apparent that vertical stacking of floors was an inherently inefficient building form for assembly-line buildings.
Horizontal assembly determined the physical layout of the much larger plant at River Rouge from 1917. After 1927 the Rouge became the centre of Ford production. Although the multi-storey plant in Detroit was less efficient than the single level manufacturing plant at the Rouge, it was just one of many multistorey concrete factories built by 1927. What proportion of midwestern industrial installations went on in these 'obsolete' buildings from the 1920s until

Craneway at the Ford Highland Park Plant, Michigan, 1914.

they were abandoned in the decade or two after the Second World War? In Detroit and Flint alone, manufacturers Hudson, Packard, Ford, Dodge, General Motors' Buick and Chevrolet, and their many subcontractors (Fisher Body, Budd Wheel, and others) had built multi-storey plants; Ford's widely spread assembly plants, advertised in a company booklet in 1915, were all multi-storey. These buildings could not just be abandoned. As substantial capital investments, they remained in use for decades, recovering their initial cost from the surpluses provided by wage labour and economies of scale. But they could accommodate moving assembly with workarounds like those at Highland Park, and they did so for decades. Their obsolescence no doubt facilitated the postwar exodus of auto production from midwestern cities. New plants were indisputably needed; their location was a function of their potential profitability.

While the building technology of multi-storey construction may have been technically obsolete by the First World War, there were also other reasons for the demise of the daylight factory. Labour unions successfully challenged automobile manufacturers thirty years after the first appearance of the type. As many have noted, protests could surround these buildings, invade them, and occupy them, effecting significant changes to labour relations in the walkouts of 1933 and a crucial sit-down strike in Flint in the winter of 1936–37. Daylight factories saw the emergence of collective action in the auto industry after years of simmering labour unrest and suppression. It was the strike itself, however, that produced labour solidarity: the chance to strategise together, to keep watch, to organise meals, to play chequers and guitars, to rest on the cushioned seats of future Chevrolets that acted as a spatial condenser in which class solidarity emerged.[30] The real subsumption of labour to capital paused for a brief spell; in that pause, new relations emerged, long after the buildings that housed them were built. These relations provided a strong base for the United Auto Workers union, one that endured for decades, and was only undone by the next round of capitalist sorcery.

The daylight factories had aged along with the automobile industry. The plethora of auto producers in Detroit before the Second World War gradually shrank to three after the war: Ford, General Motors and Chrysler. At the same time, the daylight factories had realised the costs invested in their original construction over thirty or forty years of operation. Their obsolescence was an increasing liability. Two architectural developments of the postwar period are especially notable. First, an entirely new building type replaced the old daylight factories, whether in the industrial Midwest, or in the American South, where the obsolescence of the old plants provided yet another pretext for new plants in new places. New manufacturing facilities in Detroit and surrounds were single- or dual-level manufacturing buildings without windows. They were no longer embedded in city neighbourhoods with pedestrian street front access; instead, they were placed in the centre of their building plots with broad buffer zones and earth berms between perimeter fencing and building entry. Entry to the plant grounds was controlled by gates. It was impossible to go on strike in such buildings; indeed, building design had solved the problem presented to industry by the sitdown.

The second architectural development is found in buildings that remained, mostly steel-framed daylight factories. These buildings were covered in enamelled metal panelling similar to that used on the exteriors of the new fenced manufacturing sites. Old daylight buildings are still recognisable today through their siting alongside streets and close to neighbourhoods. These survivors were often owned by smaller companies associated with automobile production, companies that lacked the means to rebuild in the declining economy of the postwar period; or they were acquired by new owners with less capital to invest in physical plant improvement. Among the most striking of these metal-clad glass buildings is one known as Detroit Seamless Steel Tubes in Dearborn, made famous in its earliest iteration when it was published in the architectural treatise, *The Modern Functional Building* by German critic Adolf Behne in 1926. Detroit Seamless Steel Tubes was covered in the mid-1970s in response to the oil crisis, in a bid to decrease its energy consumption by increasing its insulating capacity.

These two developments illustrate opposed trends: in the first, architecture moves in lock step with capitalist sorcery, as industry designs out inefficiencies such as labour action. In this trend, industry's social character is ignored or overlooked; only its economic impact matters. In the second, buildings persist when profits are low through a form of benign neglect. If they cannot be replaced or properly repaired, they can at least be covered up, reducing their maintenance and masking their age in a city where industrial investment has vanished. As the metal panels begin to spall off fifty years later, glass-clad daylight buildings appear beneath. They constitute one of the last surviving links to a radically dynamic manufacturing system that changed human history forever, a system that naturalised automobility and that saw the appearance of an architectural amenity (the daylight factory), its seeming alter ego (the moving assembly line for automobile production), and the countless automobiles that dominate global transit today. In fact, as we have seen, all three were part of the accelerated effects of capitalism itself.

Notes

1 The best-known examples of the former include Karl Friedrich Schinkel's Bauakademie in Berlin (1836), and Walter Gropius and Adolf Meyer's Bauhaus Dessau (1925–26); of the latter, Peter Behrens' AEG Turbine Hall in Berlin (1909).

2 Four crucial inventions that automated British textile production were the water frame (Richard Arkwright, 1765), the Boulton and Watt steam engine (1765), the spinning mule (Samuel Crompton, 1779), and the power loom (Edward Cartwright, 1785). Note that all bear the names of their inventors, even though each was a product of incremental, collective work: 'A critical history of technology would show how little any of the inventions of the eighteenth century are the work of a single individual': Karl Marx, *Capital – A Critique of Political Economy Volume 1*, trans. by Ben Fowkes (Harmondsworth: Penguin, 1976), 493.

3 On 'welfare capitalism' see Stuart D. Brandes, *American Welfare Capitalism 1880–1940* (Chicago: University of Chicago Press, 1970); Daniel Nelson, 'The Rise of Welfare Work', in *Managers and Workers: Origins of Twentieth-Century Factory System in the United States, 1880–1920* (Madison: University of Wisconsin Press, 1995), 99–118; David Brody, 'The Rise and Decline of Welfare Capitalism', in *Workers in Industrial America: Essays on the Twentieth-Century Struggle* (Oxford: Oxford University Press, 1993), 48–81.

4 Marx, *Capital*, 493–494. Also see David Harvey, *A Companion to Marx's Capital* (London: Verso, 2018), 191–203.

5 See Marx, *Capital,* 1019–1025.

6 Pignarre and Stengers craft memorable images of anti-capitalist work in the wake of Seattle's 1999 protests. They adopt the term 'sounders of the depths,' for intellectuals, as those who 'cannot announce directions nor choose them.' They ask, rather, 'can one pass through here, and how?' Such figures speak clearly in words that others can understand, because their warnings need to be heard immediately and with urgency. Stengers and Pignarre model a contemporary anti-capitalism that recognises Marx's insistence on the social basis of capitalism, on the pathology of economy 'transformed into a *politics that kills politics'*. They repeat the cry 'another world is possible' throughout the book, which reads today as an inspiring, if romantic, cry for a post-Seattle revolution that remains elusive in 2024. See Philippe Pignarre and Isabelle Stengers, *Capitalist Sorcery: Breaking the Spell* (Basingstoke and New York: Palgrave Macmillan, 2011), 8–9.

7 I differ slightly with Pignarre and Stengers' seeming desubjectivisation – even reification, perhaps – of capitalism. You can't have capitalism without capitalists.

8 Michael G. Smith, 'The First Concrete Auto Factory: An Error in the Historical Record', *Journal of the Society of Architectural Historians* vol. 78, no. 4 (December 2019), 442–53.

9 Sigfried Giedion, *Mechanization takes Command: A Contribution to Anonymous History* (Oxford: Oxford University Press, 1948), 77–128.

10 David E. Nye, *America's Assembly Line* (Cambridge, Mass: MIT Press, 2013), 13. Also see David E. Nye, *Electrifying America: Social Meanings of a New Technology, 1880–1940* (Cambridge, Mass: MIT Press, 1990); Lindy Biggs, *The Rational Factory: Architecture, Technology, and Work in America's Age of Mass Production* (Baltimore: Johns Hopkins University Press, 1996).

11 'The machine, therefore, is a mechanism that, after being set in motion, performs with its tools the same operations as the worker formerly did with similar tools ... From the moment that the tool proper is taken from man and fitted into a mechanism, a machine takes the place of a mere implement.' Marx, *Capital*, 495.

12 See Luis Pancorbo Crespo and Inés Martín Robles, 'Architecture as Technical Object: Industrial Architecture of Albert Kahn', *VLC arquitectura,* vol. 1, no. 2 (2014,: 1–31; Luis Pancorbo Crespo and Inés Martín Robles, 'Linajes férreos: Uso tipológico de precedentes ferroviarios en Albert Kahn', *Cuaderno de Notas*, no. 17 (2016), 78–103.

13 Robert Fishman, 'Detroit: Linear City', in *Mapping Detroit: Land, Community, and Shaping a City*, edited by June Manning Thomas and Henco Bekkering (Detroit, 2015), 77–100.

14 Lindy Biggs, *The Rational Factory: Architecture, Technology, and Work in America's Age of Mass Production* (Baltimore: Johns Hopkins University Press, 1996).

15 Joshua Murray and Michael Schwartz, *Wrecked: How the American Automobile Industry Destroyed*

Its Capacity to Compete (New York: Russell Sage Foundation, 2019); Sidney Fine, *Sit-Down: The General Motors Strike of 1936–1937* (Ann Arbor, MI: University of Michigan Press, 2020).

16 *The American Architect* published a regular feature,'Daylighting the Factory', from c. 1916 to 1918 inclusive. For one example see vol. 109 (March 1916), 184–186. Also see Miron Mislin, 'Die Tageslichtfabrik – the Daylight Factory', in *Architektur Stadt Raum/ kunstexte.de* no. 1(2017), 1–7.

17 See Thomas A. Markus, *Buildings and Power: Freedom and Control in the Origin of Modern Building Types* (London: Routledge, 1993).

18 David E. Nye, *America's Assembly Line* (Cambridge, Mass: MIT Press, 2013), 13. Also see Nye, *Electrifying America: Social Meanings of a New Technology, 1880–1940* (Cambridge, Mass: MIT Press, 1990); Daniel Nelson, *Managers and Workers: Origins of the Twentieth-Century Factory System in the United States, 1880–1920* (Madison: University of Wisconsin Press, 1995).

19 William C. Klann, 'The Reminiscences of Mr. William C. Klann', Sept. 1955, Dearborn: Benson Ford Research Center, 23–25.

20 Ibid., 23–25.

21 Nye details the components of assembly-line production that preceded Henry Ford's combination of them and provides a long history of assembly-line manufacturing dating as far back as Han China. See Nye, *America's Assembly Line,* 14–18.

22 Ibid., 21.

23 Klann 'Reminiscences', 25–43.

24 Quoted in Robert W. Dunn, *Labor and Automobiles* (NY: International Press, 1929), 85.

25 Lindy Biggs, *The Rational Factory: Architecture, Technology, and Work in America's Age of Mass Production* (Baltimore: Johns Hopkins University Press, 1996), 121. Biggs cites similar language from Andrew Ure's 1835 *Philosophy of Manufacture*: Biggs, *Rational Factory*, 4. Indeed, the theme is well-represented in industrial literature from both sides. Compare Marx's 'All work at a machine requires the worker to be taught from childhood upwards, in order that he may learn to adapt his own movements to the uniform and unceasing motion of an automaton': Marx, *Capital,* 546.

26 Marx, *Capital*, Chapter XV.

27 Nye, *America's Assembly Line,* 38.

28 Marx, *Capital*, 1034–1038.

29 Klann, 'Reminiscences', 43.

30 The term 'social condenser' was coined by revolutionary Soviet architects and theorists for workers' clubs (many by Konstantin Melnikov) and the Narkomfin residential apartment building in Moscow, among others. The concept derives in part from earlier precedents such as Charles Fourier's Phalanstery, partially executed in Jean-Baptiste Godin's 1849 Familistère in Guise. Henri Lefebvre and Soviet historian Anatole Kopp explored the social condenser at the University of Nantes in the 1970s, describing it as 'both an "image" of a new society and a "mould" which contributes to its creation': Lukasz Stanek, 'Collective Luxury', *Journal of Architecture,* vol. 22, no. 3 (2017), 478–487.

HSBC
HSBC
KPMG

Section 2
Infrastructure and Environment

Chapter 4
Designing the Environment of Self-Management: Marxist Theory and Architectural Discourse in 1960s and 1970s Yugoslavia

Rujana Rebernjak

In 1971, the architect and urbanist Branko Petrović shared the vision of a strange creature from a dystopian future: it had a large head and abnormally large lungs, wide shoulders, atrophied arms and legs, and long, spatula-like fingers. Its whole body, intentionally grotesque if not quite humorous, appeared designed as one large pollution-management system, with detoxification organs hidden under chin rolls and a multi-filter respiratory apparatus in place of its nose. First published in the weekly *Omladinski tjednik*, the creature, named Homo Effluviens, represented a future human body adapted to respond to an increasingly polluted, unwelcoming environment. Reproduced in Petrović's self-initiated study titled 'Systematisation of the Phenomenon of Human Environment', Homo Effluviens captured a growing anxiety about environmental degradation in socialist Yugoslavia.

Over the 1970s, both in the popular press, as well as architectural and design magazines, reflections on the emerging ecological crises came to be framed within the context of state socialism and Yugoslavia's unique system of workers' self-management. Set in opposition to the throwaway culture associated with the capitalist west, debates about the environment were presented as another frontier of the Cold War. As the design theorist Goroslav Keller wrote in 1973: 'It seems to me that it is precisely on the level of the environment that the big opportunity for socialism lies. By planning economic growth, more balanced and steady growth can be achieved in all areas. Of course,' he qualified his argument, such balance could only be attained 'if all efforts are focused on satisfying collective and not individual needs, wants and goals. [...] this presupposes the creation of a new system of socialist

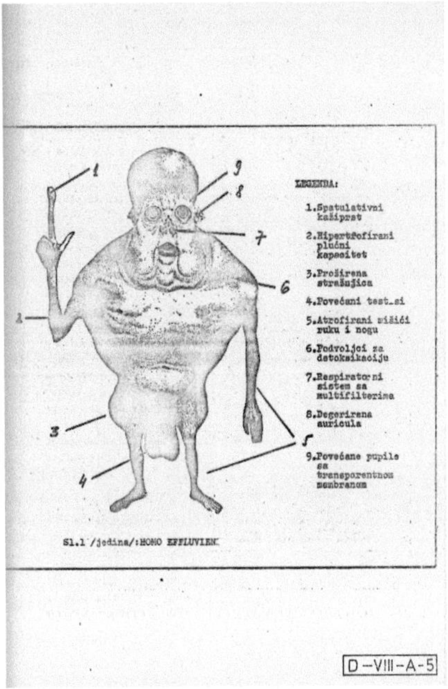

Homo Effluviens from *Sitematizacija fenomena čovjekove okoline*, 1971.

cultural and ethical values that would incorporate new attitudes towards our environment.'[1]

But where would this consciousness and attitude towards the environment emerge from? What kind of ideas would shape it? And how could the need to 'protect' the environment be reconciled with everyday struggles under real-existing socialism? For Yugoslav architects, urbanists, designers and theorists, the problem of the environment became a problem of design. This chapter traces the development of environmental design as a new paradigm of architectural and design production in socialist Yugoslavia between the late 1960s and early 1970s, situating it within the political and social context of workers' self-management – the key tenet of Yugoslavia's third-way socialism. Environmental design emerged out of a critique of postwar urban planning and was shaped by cybernetics as a new way of understanding the relationship between society, nature and the built environment. A growing awareness of environmental degradation and human impact on the environment, culminating in the 1972 UN Habitat conference that led to a change in Yugoslav planning regulations emphasising the role of design in conservation, provided a further impetus for the environmental turn as a way of legitimising architectural practice under state socialism.

In this sense, Yugoslav architects and designers were attuned to similar debates happening across the east-west divide. In the UK, for example, William Holford's emphasis on ecology in reframing architectural practice within the broader sphere of the built environment in the early 1960s, 'could be seen as an effort to locate new means of legitimisation when the tenets of modernist architecture could no longer function as the yardsticks for town planning, design and construction'.[2] In the Soviet Union in the 1970s, on the other hand, the Senezh studio approached urban design through an environmental framework as a way of negotiating the resistance to modernist urban planning. Faced with a 'waning belief in the idea that a reformed socialism might enable a transition to communism', Senezh designers turned towards environmental design as a way of shaping new Soviet values.[3] This was design as a form of critique, as Tom Cubbin writes, expressed through architectural models of idealised Soviet cities, but also design as a form of politics, where the immediate environment, understood as a system of signs, was meant to reshape the consciousness of Soviet citizens.[4]

Similarly, Yugoslav architects and designers mobilised environmental design as a useful, if elusive, concept in their effort to address a wide range of concerns: unregulated urban development; the marginalised role of architects and designers in society; the increasing depletion of the natural environment; the failures of self-management to enact meaningful social change. In their efforts to devise solutions to such complex problems – problems that were both political, ideological and material – Yugoslav designers sought to advocate a new, systemic approach to design practice, one that extended from objects to buildings, from visual communications to organisational forms. In Goroslav Keller's words, 'Resolving the issues of the environment is possible [...] only when addressing the totality of things that make up that same environment.'[5] For Branko Petrović, this project extended even further, encompassing the human subject. As he wrote: 'every [...] manifestation of the phenomenon of the environment, points to the subject as a participant and active agent. Therefore, in every situation and event, the subject must be defined, and, in the bottom line, it must also be created.'[6]

While Yugoslav architects and designers rarely engaged in sophisticated theoretical and ideological debates, their emphasis on totality and the human subject can be read in relation to the work of Praxis philosophers. Between 1964 and 1974, a group of philosophers from Zagreb and Belgrade universities, published the *Praxis* journal and organised a summer school on the island of Korčula. Both became outlets for the exchange of ideas with European philosophers, such as Ernst Bloch, Erich Fromm, Herbert Marcuse, Henri Lefebvre and Jürgen Habermas. Turning to Marx's early writing, and especially his *Economic and Philosophical Manuscripts* of 1844, the Praxis philosophers sought to outline a new ideological underpinning of the Yugoslav state. Rooted in a traumatic period following Yugoslavia's expulsion from the Cominform in 1948, their writing and research sought to offer 'in both theory and practice [...] a genuine reconsideration of all the Stalinist values which had been propagated in the name of Marxism'.[7] In contrast to the Soviet dogma, which in their view 'reified the dialectic into abstract formal method', the Praxis philosophers emphasised the active role of individuals, arguing that history 'is made neither by objective forces nor dialectical laws; it is made instead by people, who act to transform their world within the limits of historically defined possibilities'.[8] The emphasis on individual creative agency was at the core of Praxis's Marxist humanism, upon which they built not only a critique of Stalinism, but also of Yugoslav self-managed socialism. They were, in Darko Suvin's terms, the 'loyal opposition' of the Yugoslav regime.[9] Without attaching their work directly to the Praxis school, for that would have been politically dangerous, it was on these same terms that Yugoslav architects approached a critique of architecture and urbanism as a critique of self-management.

And yet, situating environmental design within this theoretical context poses a problem, for the way it was envisioned, debated and practised in socialist Yugoslavia had more to do with technocratic bureaucracy than individual creative agency. Largely embracing technocratic systems-thinking, Yugoslav architects and designers presented environmental design as a way of addressing wider economic, social and political challenges of the period. By turning to techno-utopianism and borrowing its conceptual underpinnings from their western counterparts, namely the work of Tomás Maldonado at the Ulm School, Yugoslav architects and designers reproduced through environmental design the same tensions and failures that Praxis philosophers identified in workers' self-management. By tracing the genealogy of environmental design in the context of the Cold War, this chapter will seek to evaluate the way Marxist theory might have informed Yugoslav design practice and question whether a distinct conception of environmental design emerged from the theory and practice of socialist self-management.

Critiques of urban planning as critiques of self-management

Self-management was first introduced to Yugoslavia following Tito's split with Stalin in 1948, and the country's resulting expulsion from the Cominform. In a moment of political, economic and ideological uncertainty, Yugoslav political leaders sought to re-evaluate Marxist-Leninist dogma that underpinned the Communist Party's rule as a way of reasserting their legitimacy, both domestically and internationally. As the Yugoslav historian Dušan Bilandžić has written: 'Yugoslav Communists posed to themselves a dilemma: either there exist real Communists and true socialism in the USSR [...] or else socialism there is deformed and Communists are no longer Communists in which case the CPY [Communist Party of Yugoslavia] is the true Marxist Party and Stalin and the CPSU leadership no longer stand on true socialist positions.'[10] It was Milovan Djilas, at the time the Secretary of the Central Committee and minister for propaganda (who later became the most high-profile Yugoslav dissident), who came up with the idea of self-management while re-reading Marx's *Capital* where he 'rediscovered the Marxian principle of social self-management, with its anti-bureaucratic and anti-statist implications'.[11] In Đilas's view, the Yugoslav Communists were now in a position to start rebuilding the country's political, economic and social institutions based on Marx's idea of the free association of producers, thus setting the country apart from Stalinism and its centralised bureaucratic control. This Marxian re-awakening ultimately resulted in the Basic Law on the Management of State Economic Enterprises and Higher Economic Associations by the Work collectives, approved by the National Assembly in June 1950.

The law on self-management meant that the means of production were no longer owned and controlled centrally by the state, but became social property. Workers in each factory or enterprise became 'trustees of the share of this socially owned property committed to their hands in the form of machinery, buildings, etc., exercising their trusteeship through elective organs: workers' councils consisting of between fifteen and one hundred and twenty members [...] and management boards of less than two dozen members, selected by the workers' council and including the director of the enterprise'.[12] While workers were now, nominally, able to exercise their power in managing the enterprise, their power remained limited and merely formal. Instead, the enterprise directors, as party appointees acting on behalf of the state, ultimately held the decision-making power and were required to operate within the constraints of the economic plan.

This discrepancy between Marxist theory and the everyday practice of self-management was reflected in the way Yugoslav citizens and workers themselves interpreted and experienced the system. As the sociologist Sharon Zukin has revealed, Yugoslav citizens held 'a dualistic, perhaps even a contradictory, perception of self-management as both an ideological goal and a set of economic rights', with 'perceptions of socialism [...] related to their standard of living, relative to their previous experience, on the one hand, and, on the other, to the kinds of lives they see their neighbours and relatives enjoying'.[13] This was self-managed socialism measured through western-style consumerism. For Yugoslav workers, as sociologists and historians have shown, the quality of one's home, the objects it was furnished with, the car parked in front of it, as well as educational, cultural, travel or leisure opportunities were all related to their position within the social order charted by self-management, as such goods and services were, both implicitly and explicitly, attained through one's workplace.[14] This emphasis on the 'good life' was imparted through official ideology that equated 'the common good with individual betterment'.[15] As Zukin writes 'Just as individual Yugoslavs tend to describe socialism in terms of a higher standard of living' referring to refrigerators, electric ovens or clothes and trips bought on credit from their enterprise, 'so the official ideology imparts the lesson that "Progress is our most important product".'[16] In this context, modernist housing blocks in New Zagreb or New Belgrade could be seen as the material proof of the successes of self-management.

Embracing Yugoslavia's political project, architects and designers saw themselves as central in constructing self-managed socialism in everyday experience. In contrast to the later conception of 'environment', over the 1950s the architectural and design press mostly referred to *okolina, sredina, prostor* or *ambijent* as the milieu of architectural production.[17] These concepts appeared, somewhat interchangeably, in Yugoslav magazines to refer to the relationship between people and their environment. Central to the idea of space (*prostor*) in the early postwar years was *sinteza,* the modernist ideal of the synthesis of visual arts, architecture and design. Such an approach placed architecture and design at the basis of wider social and cultural reforms envisioning that new, modern living environments would, in turn, produce a new socialist subjectivity.[18] In the first decade after the war, the main focus of architectural and design practice was the development of large housing projects for the growing working class moving from rural areas to rapidly industrialising urban centres. To keep up with the demand for housing, prefabricated systems, such as the well-known JU-60 and JU-61 models, were at the basis of numerous standardised mass housing projects mushrooming across Yugoslavia.[19]

However, this indexical relationship between architecture and self-managed modernity, came under scrutiny over the 1960s, as increasingly critical voices emerged, questioning Yugoslavia's rapid urban development. The critique was twofold: on the one hand, there was a consistent lack of housing for many workers across Yugoslavia's major urban centres that resulted in dire living conditions and led to unregulated construction; secondly, mass housing blocks and fragmented urban development came to be seen as the cause of an increasingly alienated working class. Both issues were seen as a failure of architecture, as well as a failure of workers' self-management. In 1964, the social sciences journal *Naše teme,* a precursor of *Praxis* in its exploration of subjects such as humanism, alienation, self-management and ideology, captured some of that criticism in an issue dedicated to architecture and urbanism under the headline 'Urbanizam mimo socijalizma?' (Urbanism in spite of socialism?).[20]

Featuring articles by prominent Yugoslav politicians, art historians, architects and sociologists, its main argument was that too often urbanism was conflated with quantitative housing development, leaving other vital aspects of life in cities largely unresolved. The art historian Žarko Domljan complained about architecture's 'rationalistic conception of life' and 'blind slavery to the functionalist dogma'.[21] Through a critique of modernist architecture, he outlined broader concerns about fragmentation and alienation that were at the core of the Marxist humanist discourse put forward by the Praxis group. Domljan described the experience of contemporary life in cities as a 'moment of unfreedom', writing that 'things and their masses, their relationships dictate the order and the rhythm [of life] and man is not allowed to change anything, to shape [anything] according to his or her desires'.[22] For Domljan, unless a more radical reform of urban development was brought to the fore that would emphasise individual agency, Yugoslav workers living in cities would be compelled to 'renounce freedom or to look for an escape in alienation'.[23] In the view of Praxis philosophers, alienation was the central animating concept of Marx's writing, uniting his earlier work with *Capital*.[24] Praxis, defined as a 'conscious, goal-oriented social activity in which man realises the optimal potentialities of his being, and which is therefore an end in itself', as opposed to alienation, provided the form of critical action where '[man] purposefully changes his natural surroundings, creates various forms and conditions of social life, and creates himself precisely by changing his environment'.[25] To 'escape alienation', Domljan seemed to suggest, architecture and urbanism needed to shape an environment where praxis would be possible.

It is from this perspective that Praxis philosophers critiqued Yugoslav self-management, for, in their view, it should have been the aim of a self-managed socialist society to shape the preconditions for unalienated labour. For key figures such as Rudi Supek, as Gerson S. Sher has documented, 'the goal of self-management is no less than the transcendence of the alienation of the producer by overcoming the harmful aspects of the division of labour which have been responsible for antagonistic class divisions' of the past.[26] To achieve that, in the mid-1960s, Supek turned to technology. He saw the automation of production as a way of addressing some of the tensions in Yugoslav self-management: the increasing divisions between management and labour; the increasing bureaucratisation of the state; and the integration of self-management into wider spheres of society, outside production. While maintaining a degree of scepticism regarding the impact of technology on the working class, the Praxis authors were part of the wider debate about the role of cybernetics and automation under workers' self-management. Stretching its influence from economics to sociology, from architecture to ecology, cybernetics presented a way of addressing wider economic, social and political challenges of the period. In other words, technology became a substitute for politics. And it is in this techno-utopian discourse that the roots of environmental design need to be located.

The environment as a technological system

Environmental design was first introduced in Yugoslav architectural and design press by design theorist Fedor Kritovac writing in the magazine *Čovjek i prostor* in 1969. Kritovac used the English term 'environment' to set out the key principles of this new design methodology. His definition, borrowed from Tomás Maldonado, described environmental design as an 'integration of three spheres: the object sphere (the artificial world of industrial products), the built or building environment (the sphere of construction – even though in the era of industrial prefabrication we can also be referring to manufactured objects) and the communication environment (the system of communication, in the first instance, visual communication)'.[27]

While Yugoslav designers were well-attuned to wider architectural and design debates of the period, with references to the work of Archigram or Cedric Price and the writing of Reyner Banham, for example, regularly appearing on the pages of local magazines, this understanding of environmental design came to Yugoslavia as part of wider international exchange through New Tendencies. New Tendencies was a neo-avant-garde movement of artists, designers and critics founded in Zagreb that organised five exhibitions and a series of symposia in the period between 1961 and 1973. New Tendencies presented a vision of 'cybernetic socialism', as Armin Medosch wrote, articulated 'first with analog, and then with digital means'.[28] The work of New Tendencies fell under the umbrella of what Umberto Eco, in 1962, called 'programmed art works', seeking to actively involve viewers in the production of work.[29] The viewer was 'expected to find her or his critical agency' within a clearly defined, proto-cybernetic system: modular, systematic artwork that required user input and interaction.[30] The artists, theorists and critics associated with New Tendencies also published a magazine, titled *BIT International,* that formed a platform for debate on the emergence of new media technologies in contemporary art and design practice.[31] Some of the key figures that participated in New Tendencies' exhibitions were Italian artists, designers and theorists, such as Alberto Biasi, Manfredo Massironi, Enzo Mari or Carlo Giulio Argan; figures associated with the Parisian Groupe de Recherche d'Art Visuel (GRAV) such as François Morellet and Julio Le Parc; Swiss designer Karl Gerstner; as well as key figures of the Ulm School, such as Max Bense, Tomás Maldonado and Gui Bonsiepe. New Tendencies thus presented a key vehicle through which international ideas about cybernetics as a way of reconceptualising the role of art and design in society were introduced to Yugoslav architects and designers. The movement also highlights Yugoslavia's unique position on the international stage marked by its openness towards the west.

Yet debates about cybernetics were not confined solely to artistic circles, but became part of a wider public discourse. In 1962, the politician Dušan Čalić called automation and cybernetics 'socialist technologies' that had a central role to play under self-managed socialism. Čalić saw automation as a key instrument in human liberation for it was to 'free man of direct work in the production process and to welcome him, as Marx argued, to the "realm of freedom".'[32] This was a freedom from alienated labour that could result in, as Marxist humanism emphasised, Marx's free development of the individual and the 'complete return of man to himself as a social being'.[33]

Such views became prominent during the 1960s and a focal point of social, economic and political reform to workers' self-management.[34] Due to growing economic challenges, a series of market reforms were introduced between 1961 and 1965, resulting in greater competition between individual enterprises. The need for increased productivity within a market-oriented context introduced by the economic reforms, together with more efficient decision-making processes, became a pressing concern. To this problem, technology was presented as a solution. Over the 1960s, automation and cybernetics were invoked as central to the practice of self-management. As Borislav Bakić succinctly put it, paraphrasing Lefebvre: 'socialism = self-management plus cybernetics'.[35] For Bakić, a Belgrade-based economist, there was a clear alignment between the processes of self-management and cybernetic systems of feedback and control. He wrote: 'Self-managed decision-making constitutes, in essence, the establishment of an optimal regime for the functioning of all parts (subsystems) and all parts of parts (sub-subsystems), in order for the whole system to achieve its established goals.'[36] Therefore, once the 'optimal regime' of the enterprise was set by the workers' council, worker-managers became 'executors' of such a regime, simplifying the cybernetic feedback loop. Further, if self-management was, in its essence, a system premised on the gathering and processing of information through the mechanism of the workers' council meeting, then cybernetics provided a useful model for reimagining the system of workers' self-management.

The Yugoslav understanding of environmental design needs to be seen within these wider tensions and debates about the role of automation and cybernetics under socialism. Environmental design envisioned dynamic mechanisms of feedback and control within complex, interconnected systems that comprised people, objects, spaces and visual media, as well as a move away from an individualistic to a collaborative approach to architectural and design practice.

In Fedor Kritovac's words, writing in the magazine *Arhitektura* in 1969, 'A "classic" understanding of architecture and urbanism where the object is understood to be the spatial-plastic reality determined by given functional constraints as well as "classic" visual-plastic principles, will have to give way to a conception that is being developed independently: the concept of ENVIRONMENT, i.e. AN INTEGRATED DYNAMIC SYSTEM OF A COMMUNICATIVE-OBJECTIVE MILIEU.'[37]

Of course, such reimagining of architectural practice was part of a wider techno-utopian discourse across both sides of the Iron Curtain. Set in the context of the Cold War, new technologies provided the backdrop to everyday life, as Jane Pavitt and David Crowley have argued, 'with terms such as "networks", "feedback", "systems", "software" and "hardware" acquiring broader meaning beyond the bounds of their original usage'.[38] While, on the one hand Yugoslav thinkers saw the liberating potential of this new technology, others, such as Herbert Marcuse, saw in it the threat of 'a bureaucratic and technocratic culture that subordinated freedom of thought and action to the interests of the corporation'.[39] In the Soviet Union, as Slava Gerovitch has written, the understanding of cybernetics oscillated with wider political change, seen at different times as both antithetical and integral to the Soviet path towards communism. In the Soviet Union, cybernetics, with its emphasis on logic and objectivity, came to represent a counterpoint to the 'vague and manipulative language of Stalinist ideological discourse'.[40]

In the context of architecture and design, cybernetics offered a framework to reimagine the environment as a set of constantly changing relationships between people, their visual and material landscapes, through a dynamic process of feedback and control.[41] As Larry Busbea has argued, 'design can never simply respond to existing environmental circumstances, for it creates new relations – new environments – with every object or interface it produces'.[42] In the UK, borrowing from the cybernetic language of interrelated systems, feedback and control, William Holford offered a 'reconceptualisation of architecture and planning as "the continually changing end-result of all the smaller designs and their co-ordination – or lack of it".'[43] Soviet designers, on the other hand, outlined a critical approach to the environment that entailed 'the construction of milieux that enable new forms of information exchange and assembly to liberate the individual from a mind-set that engenders a passive relationship to objects, environments and ideas'.[44] Cybernetics, therefore, offered a fluid conceptual framework that architects and designers mobilised equally under capitalism as under state socialism.

As part of this international debate, the work of Tomás Maldonado and Gui Bonsiepe at the Hochschule für Gestaltung in Ulm, was particularly instrumental in the Yugoslav context and widely cited in local architectural and design press. The fourth issue of New Tendencies' *BIT International* magazine, published in 1969, was intended as a homage to the Ulm School, which had closed the previous year. At Ulm, Maldonado had adopted an approach to design described as 'scientific operationalism'.[45] In his view, designers needed to move away from aesthetics as the sphere of social and moral reformation, dominant in the early post-war years, to 'a more scientifically based sociological operation of product management and systems analysis' so as to 'help demystify and coordinate "our objective and communicative world".'[46] The same issue of *BIT* also featured an article, first delivered as a lecture at Princeton in 1966 which would later form the basis of his key text *Design, Nature and Revolution: Toward a Critical Ecology*. Here, Maldonado put forth his understanding of environmental design as the integration of the physical environment and the behavioural environment, invoking cybernetics as a way of addressing the 'urgent task' of 'conceiving here and now a new type of mediocosmos where not only the system of objects, but also the system of man can be optimised'.[47]

These principles were adopted in the Yugoslav understanding of environmental design, as laid out by Fedor Kritovac in 1969: on the one hand, the reference to design as a multidisciplinary science, on the other the cybernetic processes of feedback and control as a means of enabling individual creative agency.[48] Just like the system of self-management, the environment, as distinct from nature or space, was reimagined as one large cybernetic system, shaped by flows of information through mechanisms of feedback and control. The environment became a kind of technology.

Environment through planning and control

While environmental design provided a possible theoretical model for architecture and design, its application in practice remained less clear. How could such complex systems be designed? What objects or spaces could such systemic thinking be applied to? And what kind of political and social action would be necessary to put it in practice? In 1970s Yugoslavia, planning became the ideal form of intervention. Starting from the 1960s, urban planning was developed on an increasingly large scale through Republic-level plans, serving as a tool to address a wide range of concerns: industrial development and sustainable growth, social cohesion and environmental protection. In this context, environmental design offered a possible model for rethinking urban planning and addressing some of the critiques of urbanism framed in Marxian terms.

During the 1970s, alienation became a pressing concern in debates around architecture and urban planning. The art historian Žarko Domljan, writing in the magazine *15 Dana*, restated his previous argument that a functionalist view of urbanism had resulted in 'psychosocial urban destruction' and 'atrophy of social relations'.[49] The sociologist Melita Richter, on the other hand, argued in 1976 that 'one of the most negative outcomes of an urban lifestyle is the disintegration of the whole of a human being, the alienation and separation of its functions'.[50] She highlighted the lack of cohesive urban planning, writing that 'the spatial organisation of the urban tissue in large part enhances the disintegration of these functions. By treating each function as a separate whole and defining a dedicated place for its fulfilment, we are physically precluding the wholesome and simultaneous development of human life within a city space seen as a form of social unity'.[51] This critique of architecture and urban planning was, in essence, a critique of self-management.

Concerns about urban planning as an agent of alienation dovetailed with increasing awareness of environmental degradation and the impact of unregulated, unconstrained urban development on the quality of life. The UN's role was central in this regard, as Yugoslavia joined the 'Man and Biosphere' programme in 1969, with a dedicated event held in Zagreb in early 1972. As a result, a federal Yugoslav 'Man and Biosphere' council was set up with the aim of bringing together representatives from different institutions, from the army to the academy of sciences, to address environmental issues across all aspects of society.[52] That same year, the UN's Conference on the Human Environment in Stockholm further crystallised environmental concerns. Widely reported in the Yugoslav popular as well as architectural press, the conference became a catalyst for a series of initiatives: the foundation of the federal Yugoslav Council for the protection and enhancement of human environment in February 1973, the development of republican spatial plans that foregrounded environmental protection as their core aim, as well as a high-profile planning project for the Yugoslav Adriatic region whose first phase had already started in 1963. Further, environmental protections were formalised in a new act from 1973, with regional and republican Institutes for Urban Planning tasked with regulating '[m]any environmental aspects, such as the protection of natural resources, and the use and maintenance of public spaces and private gardens'.[53]

When the new constitution was introduced in 1974, environmental conservation was addressed through institutions of self-management at a local level. Drafted after a period of political dissent shaped by calls for the greater political and economic independence of Yugoslavia's constituent republics, the constitution set out a further extension of self-management to organs of local government via interest groups and local communes. Here, Yugoslav citizens were to 'organise themselves [...] for the fulfilment of certain joint interests and needs', among which were housing construction, social and children's welfare, education, culture, consumer protection, the protection and improvement of the environment.[54] Indeed, the 1974 constitution formally instituted the human right to a healthy environment, which would be enacted by local communes and supported through the work of self-managed interest groups (SIZs).[55] This extension of self-management was seen by some Praxis figures as one of the key aims of the Yugoslav system. 'Beyond the goal of control by the producers over their immediate productive activity', the sociologist Rudi Supek considered 'the primary function of self-management' to be the 'integration of the productive community into the civil community'.[56] Participation in decision-making in all aspects of life, from material production to educational, social and cultural activities, was to serve as the basis for the 'complete development and humanisation of the individual personality'.[57] Could self-management of natural as much as man-made environments constitute a form of praxis, an antidote to alienation?

In a pamphlet titled *Ecological Crisis, Marxism and Self-Management* the biologist and philosopher Ljubomir Berberović argued as much. He quoted Edvard Kardelj, the highest-ranking Yugoslav politician after Tito, writing that the environment could only be protected by,

> strengthening the knowledge of our working man, as a self-manager, that his relationship with nature is an integral part of his self-management function, which consists in 'managing things' in the broadest sense of the word. Namely, not only in managing those things created with his own hands, but the entire 'environment' in which he lives – both the one created by himself, as well as the one provided by nature.[58]

In this context, environmental design, formalised through the medium of the spatial plan, offered a tool through which to manage aspects of the social, physical and natural environment. As the Yugoslav council of urbanists claimed on the conclusion of their fourth congress, in 1975, 'The whole of the human being is established in space, which means that spatial-ecological problems need to be resolved in the holistic system of social planning'.[59] This emphasis on a more holistic approach to planning in relation to self-management offered the opportunity for Yugoslav architects and designers to reclaim the legitimacy of their profession. As Goroslav Keller argued in 1973, 'self-management and communal social organisations emerge as important preconditions for a successful establishment of the environmental system in the totality of its functions'.[60]

Branko Petrović's 1971 study, *The Systematisation of the Phenomenon of Human Environment*, was an early precursor of such thinking, built on the wider techno-utopian discourse of the period. A self-initiated project, the study sought to set out a blueprint for future spatial planning rooted in a cybernetic understanding of the relationships between individuals, social structures and the natural environment. Developed by Petrović while he was working at the Ministry for Urbanism, Construction, Housing and Local Communes, the intent was to offer an alternative method of design for addressing the environmental and social crisis. Petrović identified different subsystems of this cybernetic environment as socio-medium, techno-medium, space-medium, psycho-medium and bio-medium. Their interaction – the whole system – was presented through complex, yet visually appealing diagrams that offered a meticulously organised, structural vision of the complexity of interactions between human and natural environments.

And yet, this visual and structural complexity translated lived experience into abstract forms: the environment was dematerialised. By turning the relationship between humans and their environment into networks of relationships, managed through cybernetic processes of feedback and control, Petrović offered a technocratic solution to the 'problem' of the environment. This understanding was part of a wider epistemological shift, seen across both sides of the Iron Curtain, as architectural historian Simon Sadler has argued in his reflection on Maldonado's work. In this, he identified the central contradiction of environmental design: the problem of the environment, as it emerged in the late 1960s, was a 'political problem, not simply a technical one, in which nature [...] becomes replaced by technology.'[61] While such technocratic visions of the environment may have been aligned with Yugoslavia's political project, they were also questioned from within. Environmental debates provided a space for that questioning.

The criticism of techno-utopianism grounded in a reading of Marx extended to environmental design in the work of Matko Meštrović, one of the main figures involved in New Tendencies. His seminal text, *Design Theory and Problems of the Environment* (1980), can be seen as a culmination of two decades of debates around environmental design, cybernetics and self-management. In the text, Meštrović puts forward a Marxist critique of western science and, with it, a scientifically based design theory derived from the Ulm school. Meštrović argues that predominant scientific models – such as for example Jay Forrester's predictive mathematical model used for the Club of Rome report, one of the key texts informing environmental discourse – lacked insight

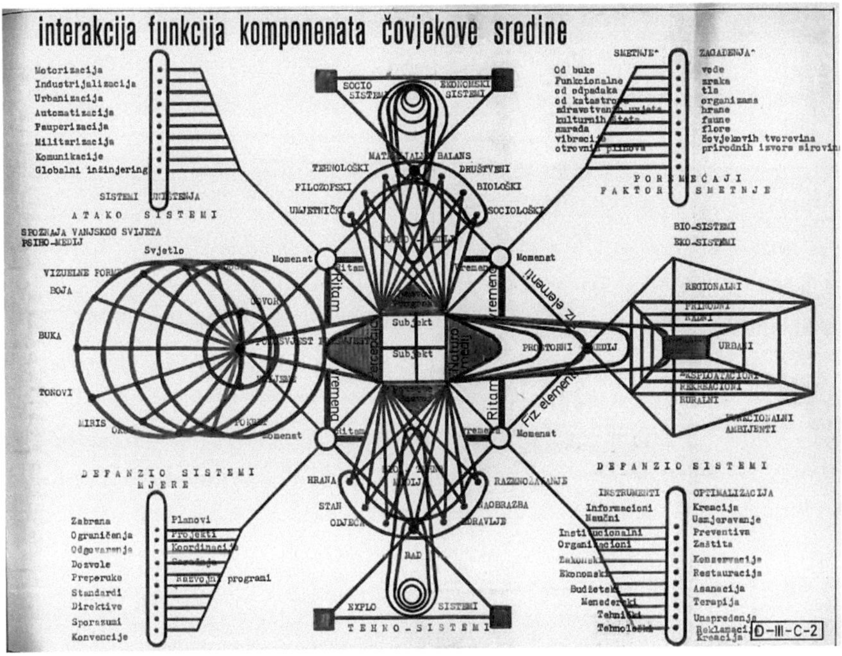

Diagram titled 'Interactions of the Function of Elements of Human Environment', from Branko Petrović, *The Systematisation of the Phenomenon of Human Environment*, 1971.

into social class relations and inequality, and thus failed to see social groups as key agents of historical change.[62] Meštrović followed Hans Magnus Enzensberger's ideas on the 'naturalism of men and humanism of nature' as endangered by mass-scale production, claiming that any design action seeking to restore the lost equilibrium has to see the environment not only as natural but, fundamentally, as social. In this context, Meštrović seemed to suggest that any change enacted by design may only be possible through a return to self-management.

Published in 1980, Meštrović's text needs to be seen in the wider context of late socialism, a period of economic and, increasingly, political crisis. As it became increasingly clear that self-management had largely failed to bring about wider social change, environmentalism turned into a critique of self-managed socialism. Zoran Oštrić, for example, has highlighted the ossified, performative institutions of self-management, arguing that the formalisation of the environmental movement through the foundation of the Yugoslav Council for the protection and improvement of the human environment, sounded the death knell for environmentalism as a social movement. By formally endorsing it, the Yugoslav government turned it into 'a bureaucratised institution lost in the labyrinths of delegation' under the system of self-management.[63] Vukašin Pavlović was much more explicit in his critique, writing: 'It is clear that socialism and ecology have a misunderstanding. Socialism, as we've known it until today, shapes its relationship towards nature with the logic inherited from the destructive and wasteful development of capitalist industrial societies. Many still measure the successes of socialism in tonnes of steel, wagons of mined coal, megawatts of consumed electricity. [...] Of Marx's Renaissance project aimed at reconciling people with nature, we can only dream'.[64]

It is in this context that the Yugoslav experiment with environmental design needs to be understood. Built upon the political, social and economic structures of Yugoslavia's 'third way' socialism, with workers' self-management at its core, environmental design failed to reimagine the relationship between humans and nature. Instead, it simply reproduced the contradictions of self-managed socialism: by breaking down the environment, or the totality of social, economic and political structures, into ever smaller, more individualised subsystems, an emancipatory project that sought to increase individual human agency through participatory action turned into a highly technocratic, systematised and, ultimately, formulaic instrument of control.

Notes

1 Goroslav Keller, "Socijalizam i ekologija", *Čovjek i prostor*, no. 241(April 1973), 24.

2 Juliana Yat Shun Kei, ' "What are People For?" Ecologists and the Articulation of the Built Environment', *Footprint* number 28 (2021), 151.

3 Tom Cubbin, *Soviet Critical Design: Senezh Studio and the Communist Surround* (London: Bloomsbury, 2019), 105.

4 Ibid., 106, 114.

5 Goroslav Keller, 'Futurologija', *Čovjek i prostor,* no. 245 (August 1973), 21.

6 Branko Petrović, *Sistematizacija fenomena čovjekove okoline* (Zagreb: Republički sekretarijat za urbanizam, građevinarstvo, stambene i komunalne poslove, 1971), 141.

7 Predrag Vranicki, *Historija Marksizma*, vol. II (Zagreb: Naprijed, 1961), 374, cited in Gerson S. Sher, *Praxis: Marxist Criticism and Dissent in Socialist Yugoslavia* (Bloomington and London: Indiana University Press, 1977), 9.

8 Sher, *Praxis*, 19.

9 Darko Suvin, "Diskurs o birokraciji i državnoj vlasti u post-revolucionarnoj Jugoslaviji 1945–1974. (II)." *Politička misao*, vol. 49, no. 4 (2012), 228–247.

10 Dušan Bilandžić, *Borba za samoupravni socijalizam u Jugoslaviji, 1945–1969* (Zagreb: Institut za historiju radničkog pokreta Hrvatske, 1969), 45 cited in Dennison Rusinow, *The Yugoslav Experiment, 1948–1974* (London: C. Hurst, 1977), 48.

11 Rusinow, *The Yugoslav Experiment,* 50–51.

12 Ibid., 58.

13 Sharon Zukin, *Beyond Marx and Tito: Theory and Practice in Yugoslav Socialism* (Cambridge: Cambridge University Press, 1975), 77.

14 See, for example, Igor Duda, *U potrazi za blagostanjem, O povijesti dokolice i potrošačkog društva u Hrvatskoj 1950-ihil 1960-ih godina* (Zagreb: Srednja Europa, 2005); Rory Archer, Igor Duda, and Paul Stubbs, (eds.) *Social Inequalities and Discontent in Yugoslav Socialism* (Abingdon: Routledge, 2016). On the discrepancy between the theory and practice of self-management see Igor Stanić, 'Što pokazuje praksa? Presjek samoupravljanja u brodogradilštu Uljanik 1961–1968. Godine', *Časopis za suvremenu povijest,* vol. 46, no. 3 (2014), 453–474.

15 Zukin, *Beyond Marx*, 78.

16 Ibid., 78.

17 Fedor Kritovac and Slavko Dakić, 'Okolina je proces: Teoretske mogućnosti jedne nove prakse', *Arhitektura* nos. 146–147 (1973), 35–38.

18 Bernardo Bernardi, 'Definicija i značaj industrijskog oblikovanja', *Arhitektura,* nos. 1–6 (1959), 18; for more on synthesis in Yugoslav postwar design see Jasna Galjer, *Dizajn pedesetih u Hrvatskoj: Od utopije do stvarnosti* (Zagreb: Horetzky, 2004).

19 Eve Blau and Ivan Rupnik, *Project Zagreb: Transition as Condition, Strategy, Practice* (Barcelona: Aktar, 2007), 250–281.

20 On *Naše teme* in relation to *Praxis* see: Sher, *Praxis* 31.

21 Žarko Domljan, 'Perspektive urbanizma', *Naše teme,* 11 (1964), 1771.

22 Ibid., 1767–1968.

23 Ibid., 1768.

24 This emphasis on conceptual unity between Marx's early and later writing distinguished Marxist humanists like the Praxis school from Soviet philosophers or European thinkers such as Louis Althusser. See Sher, *Praxis*, 70.

25 Mihailo Marković, *Humanizam i dijalektika* (Belgrade: Prosveta, 1967), 130–133; Mihailo Marković, *From Affluence to Praxis: Philosophy and Social Criticism*, (Ann Arbor, MI: University of Michigan Press, 1974), 64.

26 Rudi Supek, 'Le sort de la communauté productive,' *Praxis International*, nos. 2–3 (1965), 285–295, in Sher, *Praxis*, 129.

27 Fedor Kritovac, "Što je environmental dizajn?", *Čovjek i prostor,* no. 197 (August 1969) 8–9.

28 Armin Medosch, *New Tendencies: Art at the Threshold of the Information Revolution* (Cambridge, Mass: MIT Press, 2016), 4.

29 Eco cited in Ibid., 7.

30 Ibid., 8.

31 In total, seven issues of BIT International were published between 1968 and 1971, with each issue dedicated to a particular theme: the theory of information and the new aesthetics, computers and visual research, concrete poetry, dialogue with the machine, and so on.

32 Čalić in *15 Dana* (1962) 'Tribina 15 Dana: Suvremeni čovjek i tehnizacija', number 18 (15 June 1962), 6.

33 Karl Marx, "Third Manuscript", *Economic & Philosophical Manuscripts of 1844*, available online: https://www.marxists.org/archive/marx/works/1844/epm/3rd.htm

34 For an overview of the role of cybernetics in reforming self-management see Rujana Rebernjak, 'From Paperwork to "Mechanized Administration": Designing the Bureaucracy of Self-Management in Postwar Yugoslavia', *Grey Room,* no. 86 (Winter 2022), 50–77.

35 Borislav Bakić, *Kibernetika i samoupravljanje* (Belgrade: Zavod za ekonomske ekspertize, 1975), 23

36 Bakić, *Kibernetika*, 21

37 Fedor Kritovac, 'Arhitektura i kompjuter,' *Arhitektura*, nos. 02–103 (1969), 16.

38 David Crowley and Jane Pavitt, "The Hi-Tech Cold War" in V&A Museum, *Cold War Modern: Design 1945–1970,* (London: V&A Publishing, 2008), 165.

39 Crowley and Pavitt, 'Hi-Tech Cold War', 165.

40 Slava Gerovitch, *From Newspeak to Cyberspeak: A History of Soviet Cybernetics* (Cambridge, Mass and London: MIT Press, 2002), 8.

41 See, for example, Felicity Scott, *Outlaw Territories: Environments of Insecurity/Architecture of Counterinsurgency* (Cambridge, Mass: Zone Books, 2016); Reinhold Martin, 'Environment c.1973', *Grey Room,* no. 14 (Winter 2004), 78–101; Fred Turner, *From Counterculture to Cyberculture: Stewart Brand, the Whole Earth Network, and the Rise of Digital Utopianism* (Chicago: The University of Chicago Press, 2006).

42 Larry Busbea, *The Responsive Environment: Design, Aesthetics, and the Human in the 1970s* (Minneapolis: University of Minnesota Press, 2020), xvii-xviii.

43 Kei, 'What are People For?', 147.

44 Cubbin, *Soviet Critical Design,* 7.

45 Paul Betts, 'Science, Semiotics and Society: The Ulm Hochschule für Gestaltung in Retrospect', *Design Issues,* vol. 14, no. 2 (1988), 75.

46 Ibid., 75.

47 Tomás Maldonado, 'How to Fight Complacency in Design Education', *BIT International,* no. 4 (1969), 24.

48 Kritovac, 'Što je environmental dizajn?', 8–9.

49 Žarko Domljan, 'Prava smrt grada uvijek je samoubojstvo', *15 dana, nos.* 3–4 (May–June 1970), 13.

50 Melita Richter, 'Promjene u načinu života čovjeka u velikim gradskim naseljima i problem aktivnog angažiranja u slobodnom vremenu', *Arhitektura,* numbers 158–159 (1976), 142.

51 Ibid., 142.

52 Melita Richter, 'Čovjek I biosfera', *Čovjek i prostor,* no. 230 (May 1972), 18.

53 Tandarić, N., Watkins, C., Ives, C.D., 'Urban Planning in Socialist Croatia', *Hrvatski Geografski Glasnik* vol. 81, no. 2 (2019), 31.

54 Bojana Komadina and Vesna Popović, 'Perspektiva razvoja dizajna u mjesnoj zajednici', *Industrijsko oblikovanje,* nos. 37–38 (May–August 1974), 45.

55 Josip Čiček, 'Samoupravne interesne zajednice za zaštitu čovjekove okoline', *Čovjek i prostor*, no. 269 (August 1975), 21.

56 Supek in Sher, *Praxis*, 161.

57 Ibid., 161.

58 Ljubomir Berberović, *Ekološka kriza, Marksizam i samoupravljanje* (Sarajevo: Marksistički studijski centar Gradske konferencije SKBIH Sarajevo, 1980), 40–41.

59 'Zaključci IV kongresa Urbanističkog saveza Jugoslavije', *Čovjek i proctor*, no. 264 (March 1975), 25.

60 Keller, 'Futurologija', 21.

61 Simon Sadler, 'A Container and Its Contents - Re-Reading Tomás Maldonado's Design, Nature, and Revolution: Toward a Critical Ecology (1970, trans. 1972)', *Room One Thousand,* no. 1 2013, 42.

62 Matko Meštrović, *Teorija dizajna i problemi okoline* (Zagreb: Naprijed, 1980), 242–243.

63 Zoran Oštrić, 'Ekološki pokreti u Jugoslaviji: Građa za proučavanje razdoblja, 1971–1991', *Socijalna Ekologija,* vol. 1, no. 1 (1992), 85.

64 Vukašin Pavlović, 'Ekologija i politički sistem', in *Društvo i ekološka kriza,* ed. by Ivan Cifrić (Zagreb: Sociološko društvo Hrvatske, 1988), 78.

Chapter 5
'Brutalism as Class Architecture: The Case of Robin Hood Gardens'

Nicholas Thoburn, in conversation with Mark Crinson

Nicholas Thoburn's book Brutalism as Found: Housing, Form and Crisis at Robin Hood Gardens *(Goldsmiths Press) was published in 2022. The book focuses on the London social-housing estate (1968–72) designed by Alison and Peter Smithson which in its time was one of the most discussed examples of brutalism and, more recently with its demolition, became a salient casualty of the housing crisis in Britain. This conversation probes into and develops some of the book's implications for a Marxist critique of architectural form and social housing.*

MC: I think we should go straight to the main issue and ask what you mean by 'class architecture', which isn't as far as I know a term used in Marxist writing. What does the juxtaposition of these two words do to each? How far does the term come out of your previous work on Deleuze?

NT: Yes, 'class architecture' isn't a concept that appears elsewhere in Marxism, to my knowledge, although in forming it I draw on the Marxist architectural theories of Manfredo Tafuri and Fredric Jameson. It's a concept for grappling with how the working-class condition, as it is understood in Marxism, can be expressed in architectural form, working-class housing in particular.

To start with the first of the two words, the working class for Marx is a confounding and paradoxical concept and condition, poorly understood as such. In social analysis and architectural theory, the working class is too often understood to be a collective *identity*, typically an identity on the wane. But for Marx, the working class is not an identity but a *social condition of crisis*, a condition of dispossession, exploitation and insecurity, pulled out of shape by the tangle of social relations of which it is comprised. This was always true of capitalist societies, since the working class is a structural condition – workers' separation from their means of life and hence their subjection to work, whether they find work or not, and their tendential ejection from work as the ratio of machinery to labour increases over time. But since the 1970s, the working class has become ever more crisis-ridden, with manufacturing overcapacity creating deindustrialisation and rising un- and under-employment – first in the global north and then most everywhere else – and the corresponding collapse of the welfare-state settlement between capital, state and labour, in the regions where that settlement obtained. Turning conventional wisdom on its head, then, the recent demise of the relatively coherent working-class identities and cultures of the welfare-state period, as experienced by sections of the working class in the capitalist core, is characteristic not of the end of class society but of its intensification.

In being pulled apart in this way, by the social relations that cleave through and condition it, the working class is an impossible or paradoxical condition, a *non-identity*. It is a desperate condition, but also the radical force of class, as politics and theory. Without a place of its own, without an achieved and satisfied identity accommodated to society, or a positive ground upon which such an identity could be established, working-class politics must of necessity grapple with the social realm as a whole – a wrenching engagement with the gamut of social relations that cleave through and determine each particular working-class experience, what Marx calls the proletariat's 'restlessness within its very self'.[1] While liberal politics contents itself with fashioning and bolstering the 'liberty', in Marx's cutting phrase, of the 'confined individual, confined to himself', working-class politics recovers the flux of the social – indeed, the flux of the natural, the planetary, the cosmic – as the terrain of its practice, thought and vision, even as, or because, the social is lived as crisis.[2]

Turning to the second word in the conjunction, if there can be such a thing as working-class architecture, it must bear this impossible condition, the non-identity of class, in its built forms, or that's my contention. It's a big ask! Architecture is so interwoven with the social relations of land, construction and speculation that it's the most capitalist of arts. As Jameson puts it, 'Of all the arts, architecture is the closest constitutively to the economic, with which, in the form of commissions and land values, it has a virtually unmediated relationship'.[3] Tafuri draws the logical conclusion from this that there can be no such thing as a working-class architecture, making reference to Marx's method of critique: 'just as there cannot exist a class political economy, but only a class criticism of political economy, so too there cannot be founded a class aesthetic, art, or architecture, but only a class criticism of the aesthetic, of art, of architecture, of the city itself'.[4] He's certainly correct that any attempt at a liberated, autonomous, self-coherent working-class architecture – what Tafuri disparages as 'islands of realized utopia' – is mystifying, an ersatz solution that fails to reckon with, and leaves unchanged, the underlying structures of class society.[5] I find Tafuri's exacting standard powerful, but I twist it, taking his stringent disavowal of architectural autonomy to be less a refusal of the material existence of class architecture, than a wrenching and propulsive insistence that it can achieve *no self-coherent identity*. Just as the working class, as social condition and politics, exists not as an identity but as a grappling with the tangle of conflictual social and material relations of which it is comprised, so does class architecture.

From these premises, the concept can be schematised as follows. Class architecture is wrought out of fraught and hostile social relations, relations that course through and condition it from within. Just as the working class has no identity to realise, so class architecture does not declaim its autonomy from capitalist society, succumbing to 'the "resolve" illusion', wherein it would be lost to an accommodation with its social surround.[6] Rather, class architecture faces up to these social relations, modulating them in built form, exposing their limitations and contradictions, and therein forging new socio-architectural forms for living in, pulling against and visioning beyond capitalist society. These new forms are necessarily fragmentary. Just as the working class is a fraught and fractured non-identity, class architecture avers unifying wholes, revealing itself instead in parts, fragments and voids – which is not its limitation but its experimental force, its untimely opening to worlds in and against this society.

That's the conceptual framework. As a *method*, class architecture is flush with the conflictual social and material relations that course through its site and society – it's an immanent rather than transcendent architecture. And this is achieved through the methodological form of the 'problem'. You asked about the influence of Deleuze in my thinking about class architecture. The problem is one of these influences. It's also one of a number of instances where Deleuze comes into proximity with Alison and Peter Smithson, surprising though that may sound. Architectural forms, the Smithsons insist, are not dreamt up out of an architect's mind or available as a pre-given stock. Rather, 'form evolves out of circumstance', out of encounters in the social and material world (what the Smithsons call the world 'as found', their figure for an immersive, non-transcendent, self-decentring architecture).[7] There is an 'involuntarism' to architectural form here, in Deleuze's terms. 'Something in the world *forces us* to think', he writes, where this something is 'an object not of recognition but of a fundamental encounter'.[8] And it is these encounters that produce or solicit problems. The 'strangeness' of an encounter 'perplexes' thought, 'awaken[s] thought from its natural stupor' and forces it 'to pose a problem'.[9]

Architectural form emerges, then, through sensing, teasing out, grappling with, and materially fashioning problems. Provoked by encounters, problems and their forms can emerge in 'a range of affective tones: wonder, love, hatred, suffering'.[10] And as a process, form is experimental and faltering, cleaving to the fault lines, tensions, complexities and limits of social problems. In no way, then, are problems *resolved* in form. In grappling with problems, form is necessarily groping, incomplete and open.

MC: That's a fascinating answer and it takes us a long way. I want to ask you about several parts of it. Particularly interesting is how your conjunction of class and architecture seems to compel the second term to become as unfixed or non-determining, in your understanding, as the first – just as class is not an identity but a condition, so you seem to be suggesting that architecture is not only fixed form but spatial potentiality, to be claimed by experience and practice. This presents a problem for Tafurians, I think, because they remain committed to the architect and the studio as the creative centre of form-making,[11] and little interested in the claiming or appropriating of architecture by use. Even when Tafuri and Dal Co wrote about the Karl-Marx-Hof – the 1920s housing estate in 'Red Vienna', famous not only for the way it seemed to heroise working-class presence in the city but also for being bombarded by fascist artillery in 1934 – as establishing a difference 'pridefully counterposed' to the city around it, an 'epic tonality', they understood this as entirely the product of the estate's form-makers, its architects and clients.[12] And Tafuri's criticism of the estate was also along these lines – that it wasn't typologically innovative, which again is deemed a role for the architect who needs to respond to emerging socio-political formations by breaking out of conventions. Am I right in thinking, then, that class architecture attempts to go beyond this kind of formulation in which class is a representable thing, and the architect and client devise a programme and a design that brings this to realisation or not depending on their ability to fathom those emerging formations?

NT: Yes, I think of class architecture as spatial and social potentiality and process, so I use the modifiers 'deforming' form and 'processual' form, borrowing from topological thinking, where form is understood to bear at once continuity and transformation. Use is central to this, as you say. Built form is reproduced and transformed through the various ways it is lived in or used and adapted, where the user, we could say, becomes an architect: 'Everything is architecture. Everyone an architect', as a 1990s flyposter put it, which I once saw gracing the wall of a squatted social centre, Brixton's 121 Centre, a building very much transformed through use and adaptation.

But with the concept of class architecture, I wanted also to conceptualise and explore dynamic form-making prior to use. The concept of class architecture attunes to how built form can bear processes of deformation, as it channels, confronts and reshapes, as far as it can, the class qualities of the social, material and environmental forces which course through it. Here I'm closer to Tafuri, in according significance to the form-making work of architects (now more narrowly defined), but with this different understanding of how the dynamics of class play out in class architecture, which includes insisting that the working class is not here *represented* by architecture but is, in part, *produced* by it, as social, material and environmental form and experience.

MC: You say that it is class architecture that does the shaping. So, if class architecture is 'wrought out of fraught and hostile social relations' – to which you attach a strikingly fluid metaphor of 'coursing through' – then isn't that a situation in which the act of design is only one stage in a sequence of acts that extend before and well beyond what happens on the drawing board?

NT: That's an appealing formulation. The sequence of acts extending before and after the moment of design, as you describe it, is key to the method of the 'problem' I mentioned earlier, where intuiting, formulating, grappling with and responding to the problems of a project precedes and exceeds a building's emergence. Or we could say that this *is* design, in an expanded sense, which reaches backwards and forwards in time through the problems that shape it. Time here is multiple, layered and divergent, due to the many different temporalities and materialities of the components with which the different problems of a project grapple – landscapes, environmental factors such as light and sound, building materials, economic conditions, histories and patterns of local inhabitation, as much as the functions for which a project is built.

MC: You talked earlier about immanence and autonomy – that class architecture neither transcends its society nor is autonomous from it; instead, it is entangled with its site and its society. I like the way you bring in the Smithsons' notion of 'as found' here and suggest that it's not a strategy of absorbing or appropriating but instead one that sets up an encounter or a problem, in Deleuze's terms. To think of the Karl-Marx-Hof in this way is difficult, isn't it? There was an architecture that wanted to establish a certain image and space for the working class as part of the social-democratic city, but that didn't really set this up in an open or negotiable way. Can you contrast this with Robin Hood Gardens, which on the face of it also had heroic intentions or an 'epic tonality', if now counterposed to the deindustrialising city and its 'as found' elements? But how in the case of Robin Hood Gardens is this not just a Tafurian architect-led solution, and instead something else, something that you call class architecture?

NT: Picking up an earlier theme, I would say that Robin Hood Gardens *is*, in part, an architect-led solution, but differently so to what, in Tafuri's estimation, the Karl-Marx-Hof reaches for. The solution that is Robin Hood Gardens remains entangled with its site and society, its problems and forms remain open-ended, never resolved (it's a solution without resolution!). This is because, first, entangled with class society as it is, its forms can only engage, modulate and make liveable conflictual social relations, not resolve them, where this is the source of their wrenching, experimental quality, the non-identity of architecture bearing the fraught non-identity of class. Second, it's because these forms are enlivened, designed to be so, by the uses and experiences that they facilitate and that take hold of, actualise and deform them. And third, these deforming forms are not integrated with each other but are disaggregated, which has its own effect of open-endedness. We've discussed points one and two, but to say more about this third point, although Robin Hood Gardens had heroic qualities – the Smithsons at one point call it a 'Roman' endeavour – what is more original and exciting about the estate, and I would suggest more brutalist, is that these class problems and their forms are loosened from determination by formal unity. The scheme is what the Smithsons call an 'assemblage' structure, it holds its problem-forms together, but loosely, allowing each to have its own qualities, complexities and effects on the whole, where each is at once distinct, overlapping and folding into and out of the others, and experienced as such through use.

It might help clarify if I briefly sketch the problem-mediating forms of Robin Hood Gardens' class architecture, how its forms served to bear, confront and reshape class social relations. The central argument of my book is that Robin Hood Gardens comprised four deforming forms, forms which are at once material and social, and hence also spatial, environmental, sensory, affective, atmospheric, temporal, and so on. Each form can be named using (or rephrasing) a concept that the Smithsons coined amid their grappling of problems into form, at this site or elsewhere. First is the famous one, the 'streets in the sky', a form of deck access, conviviality and sensory intensity, elevated up in the expanse of open sky. The particular class problem that this form identifies and responds to is the crisis of the working-class street, damaged and diminished by the rise to dominance of automotive transport and high-rise towers.

Second, 'ordinariness and light' names the estate's problem-form of working-class 'home'. In contrast to the integrated autonomy of the bourgeois subject and its home – fashioned and consolidated by society to such an extent that society appears as a mere background, shut outside when the front door is closed – at Robin Hood Gardens, home renders liveable and expressive the working-class condition of being *riven* by the social. Home here is at once a pocket of 'homely' protection from the social outside ('ordinariness') and an unhomely opening to that outside, in all its social, environmental and sensory complexity ('light'). This co-determination of ordinariness and light was achieved at Robin Hood Gardens by a multiplication of thresholds across the estate – banks of windows on both sides of all apartments, 'eddy space' doorways, with their reciprocal exchange between street deck and home, visual thresholds between parents in the kitchens and children in the green.

The third of the estate's class forms I call 'repetition and difference', drawing from Peter Smithson's short essay 'Simple Thoughts on Repetition' and Deleuze's contemporaneous book *Difference and Repetition*.[13] This form concerns the estate's aesthetic handling of the class problem of 'mass', as in 'mass housing', through a class aesthetic of difference that is internal to the mass phenomena of industrial repetition – the rhythmic, nonorganic patterning and sun-enfolding quality of the estate's surface mullions, and the open-ended relay of repetition and difference between its paired structures. This class aesthetic of difference is in opposition to the 'individual' difference that is the affirmed aesthetic value of bourgeois culture, in its distinction from the denigrated class- and racially coded 'mass', and from the aesthetic that is usually imputed to the working class, in the global north, of mass 'standardisation'. Brutalism is known for its interest in the expressive texture of wood-shuttered and sand-blasted concrete, it has become a bit of a cliché. But the Smithsons' brutalist aesthetics, along with fellow brutalists Eduardo Paolozzi and Nigel

Robin Hood Gardens, London, in 2015, architects Alison and Peter Smithson, photographer Kois Miah.

Henderson, are so much more than this – as in the above example of the surface mullions of Robin Hood Gardens, and as your work has shown on brutalist 'ornament' and Ben Highmore's writing about Paolozzi and Henderson's company Hammer Prints, manufacturer of brutalist wallpapers, textiles and ceramics.[14]

The fourth form, the 'charged void', emerged through the class problem of the absence and degradation of landscape and nature in the estate's deindustrialising locale, amid London's former docks, and on its inhospitable site, bordered on two sides by thunderous roads. Instead of building a tower or two in the centre of an expanse of nondescript space, the Smithsons extended two long, cranked, mid-rise buildings pushed to either edge of the site, to create what they called a 'stress-free zone' at the centre. This green took over the architecture as the primary spatialising force, radiating outwards to incorporate the homes in its tranquil atmosphere. Devoid of instrumentalised use and economic functionality, the green was intensively charged by its relation to the sheer concrete walls of the bordering, nurturing buildings, while their monumental presence repelled nativist myths of nature and landscape. This was a nature threaded through with the fraught social relations of industry, damaged and yet made liveable, a quality that was confirmed by the anomalous mound placed at the green's centre, two storeys high, fashioned from the spoil of the estate's construction.

MC: That's fascinating, especially in the way it helps us to think differently, and architecturally, about the relation of the Smithsons to the politics of all this – that the Smithsons' exemplarity of approach is not dependent on whether they themselves held quite the same views on class and architecture as expressed in your analysis. Your idea of class architecture facing up to social relations reminded me of something the Smithsons said about architecture needing to 'face up to a mass-production society', and I guess their use of the 'as found' is the key here.

NT: The concept of the 'as found' captivates me. It's one of the many concepts and phrases the Smithsons' coined as means of provoking, problematising and channelling their practice. Figurative rather than instrumental, their concepts are open, subject to deformation, developed differently in relation to different problems and forms, and hence have been read differently by critics, rightly so. My feeling, though, is that the critical literature has tended to limit the scope of the 'as found' to the expressive qualities of materials and found objects. I don't want to diminish the importance of this dimension, where materials are to be valued in themselves for their expressive qualities, particular forces, morphological capacities and contingent effects, not covered over or modelled through geometric form – as against the International Style modernism of the 1920s and 1930s. But I understand the 'as found' to be no less a mode of relation to social forces than it is to materials, and hence it's an overarching concept of their architectural method as a whole, as we've been discussing it. Against the imposition of predetermined built form, the 'as found' names an immersive or immanent relation to materials, sites and social conditions, their flux and crises brought to light as integral to architectural form, which is all the more awkward, experimental and critical for it.

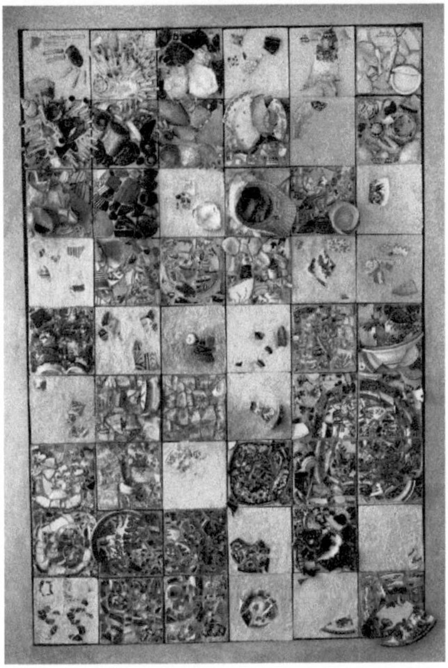

***Art of the 'As Found'*, tile mural, Alison and Peter Smithson, 1968–1970.**

It is instructive to reflect on what this immersive approach gives us in terms of the material practices of design we spoke about. In figuring form, concepts are key, but they don't work alone. The Smithsons deployed an array of textual, graphic, exhibitionary and aesthetic means, each intersecting and pulling apart, to discern, tease out, grapple with and be propelled by problems. The method was 'nonsystematic, synesthetic, collagistic', in Christine Boyer's characterisation.[15] At Robin Hood Gardens, it included such unusual practices as the collecting of fragments of found objects from the site prior to the build – shards of china tableware from ships' ballast or cargo fallout, pieces of clay pipe, shells, broken glass and clay bottles – which Alison arranged and set in 54 tiles of shutter-formed concrete to fashion a tile mural. Titled *Art of the 'As Found'*, the mural was embedded in the wall of the estate's Old People's Club Room, in this small way knitting the building with fragments of the site's material history – its connection to the Thames, to the docks, to its maritime routes and colonial connections. Or, representing the estate after its

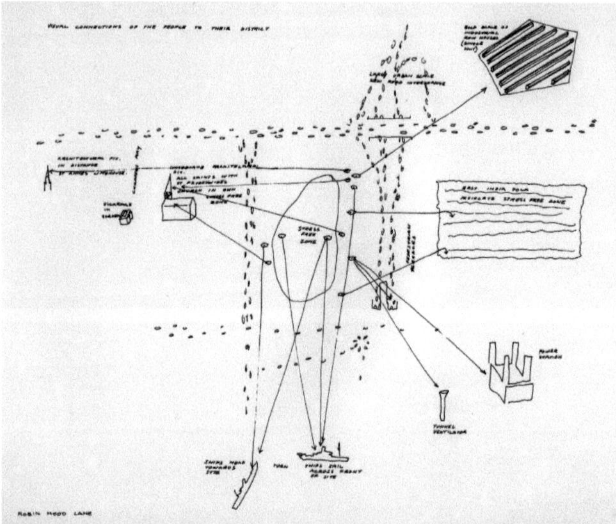

***Visual Connections of the People to their District*, Alison Smithson, c. 1970.**

completion, there is the Smithsons' appealing practice of photographing it in close-up, fragmented, from unusual angles, rather than as a whole, immersed in and expressing its particular qualities and forms.

A crucial role in this design practice was played by diagrams, schematic orderings of graphic and textual material – lines, images, words, arranged in space. I'm referring not to architectural plans, but to visual works that would grapple with particular problems and forms, using diverse techniques, often collage. One of these that I'm especially taken with is titled *Visual Connections of the People to their District*. It's a simple pen-line sketch of the sight lines of Robin Hood Gardens, centred around the green, seeking to figure the estate's qualities of openness and its visual connections to the locale. Stylistically influenced by Louis Kahn's 1952 diagram of Philadelphia traffic movement, the site is here demarcated by its pedestrian and automotive connectivity. Icons for eyes are distributed across the estate, with their sight lines connecting to built features of the neighbourhood, near and far, including ships routing around the Isle of Dogs, Brunswick Power Station, East India Dock, and Poplar's All Saints Church. But what's so striking and evocative is that the estate's buildings themselves, the means by which the views are achieved, are entirely absent from the diagram. It's a diagram of the sensory qualities of openness and visual connectivity that are so significant to the scheme that the architecture by which they are enabled falls away.

MC: How is class architecture to be separated from a statist notion of what public housing should do?

NT: The relation of class architecture to the question of the state has at least two dimensions, which I can address in relation to Robin Hood Gardens, in terms of the state programme of council-house building, and the identity it sought in this way to construct. First, in terms of the building programme, the relation is close, yet also awkward. It's close because Robin Hood Gardens is indubitably a product of the welfare state, the mass-building of council homes to house a large proportion of the UK working class in affordable, reasonably well-built, concrete-construction housing estates. But the relation immediately becomes more awkward, fraught and complicated. For Robin Hood Gardens was completed, in 1972, just as state priorities, ideologies and financing veered away to the state-promoted home ownership, private rent and welfare retrenchment of the neoliberal era, such that it was disparaged from the very start as a *too late* expression of the welfare state. This disparaging appraisal was wholly ideological of course, part of the vicious discursive assault on council housing to manufacture consent for privatisation and demolition, the major cause of the desperate crisis of housing affordability, safety and security we suffer today.

But the estate's awkwardness, its lack of fit with its times, is more existential than this, more internal to its brutalism and to its class architecture. The passage from the Smithsons that you mentioned earlier is key here. 'Brutalism', they write, 'tries to face up to a mass-production society, and drag a rough poetry out of the confused and powerful forces which are at work'.[16] I like to think of it as a crystalline definition of their brutalism, which invites unpacking, testing and developing through our engagement with their work. And you're right, it's the basis of my reading of their architecture as a confrontation with, and refashioning of, conflictual social forces, the forces of class society – where my unfurling and development of the class dimension of these 'confused and powerful forces' takes brutalism a step further than the Smithsons go, lacking a Marxist understanding of society as they did. An architectural form or practice cannot bear, confront and refashion the conflictual forces of class society and at the same time maintain a neat, self-identical fit with society. On the contrary, such class architecture is necessarily conflictual, ill-fitting, awkward at its core. As I said earlier, this ill-fitting, out-of-kilter quality is a feature of the four built forms of Robin Hood Gardens. But it is also a feature of the estate's relation to the state, to council housing, and this leads to the second part of my answer to your question.

At the heart of the postwar council-housing programme was the production of a fit, a social unity, between state, capital and labour. This fit is lionised by social democrats; it's integral to one of the two dominant narratives with which brutalism is championed today. But in this fit, this 'national compact' as Robbie Shilliam characterises it, 'class' was 'subordinated to national-racial affiliation', a patriarchal and industrious 'white working class' that was 'firmly installed within imperial coordinates and their racist determinations' vis-à-vis Black and other racially-minoritised subjects at home and in the Commonwealth.[17] An architecture that comfortably bears this ethno-national model of class, this state model of council housing, is *not* class architecture, as I formulate it.

To understand how the class architecture of Robin Hood Gardens confronted and diverged from this (pseudo-)class identity and its racial determinations we can return to the estate's form of 'home', now considering its postcolonial dimensions. Integral to the estate's history was its provision and facilitation of home to racially minoritised populations, those who were structurally excluded from council housing and the national compact through assorted racist social policies right up until the mid-1970s, and who, since then, have been disproportionately allocated to 'hard to let' estates and estates subject to disrepair and local-authority neglect. It gives us another example of how 'use', in its many variations, can at once be facilitated by built form and deform it in turn. The Smithsons did not design for Bengali, Somali and racially minoritised families and individuals, they didn't foresee them becoming typical of the estate's residents, but these social groups did become so, where they co-produced their social lives with the living architecture of the estate. It is not to exoticise the residents to say that, for example, the streets in the sky facilitated an open-air sociality which one resident, a second-generation British Bengali, described as reminiscent of Bangladesh: 'We always talked about the walkways being like Bangladesh. … [Robin Hood Gardens] gave you the opportunity to live an outdoor life'.[18]

Or take the estate's governing theme of 'protection', as the Smithsons described it. Protection was designed into the estate by the central stress-free zone against the noise and pollution of the bordering roads, but for racially minoritised residents in the 1980s and 1990s, it expanded to encompass protection from racism, through the pocket of home and collective space that the estate fashioned out of racialised society. As another Bengali resident explained, 'our recollection of the estate as we were growing up is as a safety net, a home. For my father it was the same. … When [the National Front] were marching in Brick Lane and he was in his home here, that was a safety net. So, yes, the estate in itself became a protection, a home'.[19]

My point is not that Robin Hood Gardens fully escaped from the structures and constraints of statist council housing, or that racism never impinged on the lives of its residents. In class architecture, the forces of class society are confronted and reshaped, but only insofar as they are always coursing through it. Protection from racism, then, was a chequered experience, where racialised relations and racist encounters at once intruded upon Robin Hood Gardens and were variously held back, dissipated, fought off and ejected by the estate-as-protection.

MC: That takes us nicely to the issue of the role of the residents in your book. They are certainly represented there – most obviously in the photographs by Kois Miah and through your own interviews with many of them. What were the formal means and purpose of these representations, and what role did the residents have in shaping them? What is their place in what you call 'a collective assemblage of enunciation'? How did your own interviews with estate residents work to restore a sense of agency, and how do you think your interviews and Miah's photographs deal with the issue of belonging, of how people create home out of their residential and domestic circumstances? On another level, can we use terms like 'community' or 'collectivity' about them even if they were denied agency in the decision to demolish the estate?

NT: Our project was very much a collective endeavour, in terms of the research process, the place therein of residents, and, in the book, its expressive voice. Runa Khalique, Aklima Begum, and I interviewed thirty-eight residents and two caretakers, in Bengali and English, and Kois photographed approximately thirty families or individuals, which have been shown in four exhibitions.[20] We sought to centre residents' experiences and understandings of the estate, in opposition to how they had featured in the prominent public debate about the estate's merits, failings and impending demolition, where they were either absent or their voices ventriloquised to support its destruction. The latter is a particularly underhand and pernicious practice which was endemic in government and press and is symptomatic of the discursive violence of class society, where the working class is variously spoken for, spoken against, stigmatised, or wrapped in clichés by those who claim to be acting in solidarity while effecting exactly the opposite. Certainly, the ventriloquised voices bore little or no relation to residents' actual views and experiences. The estate had suffered decades of local-authority neglect, which mired residents' experiences, sometimes desperately so, but they had so much insight, enthusiasm and deep emotional attachment to the social life and architectural forms of Robin Hood Gardens, and critical understanding of the social-cleansing forces of demolition. This shines through in the interviews and photographs.
Formally, we chose to visually represent residents through portrait photography, sometimes posed in or around their homes, other times in more naturalistic ways as they moved around the estate and its green. The images convey fulsome presence, a clear sense of agency, and express the richness of domestic and social life on the estate – even as, you rightly noted, this agency was blocked or marginalised with regard to the decision to demolish their homes. In terms of the architecture, in placing residents front and centre in

the images, often with only parts of the architecture visible, the images are rather different, and deliberately so, to the way brutalist buildings are usually photographed, devoid of people and in high-contrast monochrome. The point wasn't to diminish the architecture but to present the estate as lived-in socio-architectural form, as 'living architecture', to borrow a phrase from the artist and communist Asger Jorn. We also consciously sought to repel the pitfalls in photographing working-class and racially minoritised populations – paternalistically 'giving voice' to them, incorporating them in a class-obscuring 'civic exchange', or rendering their images a depoliticised 'consumer sensation'. To this end, the co-determining relation between photographs, interviews and analysis has been especially important to the project's exhibitions and book.

As for the enunciative voice of the book, my aim was for it to be an expression of the estate itself, 'as found' in the present, in all its various, overlapping and divergent constitutive parts – a 'collective assemblage of enunciation', in Deleuze and Guattari's terms. Not a unitary or integrated collective voice, and not the voice of the residents or of myself, albeit that these are integral to it; rather, it is the expressivity of lived experience, social relations, architectural and critical ideas, and also built structures, materials, objects, atmospheres, landscapes – the deforming forms of Robin Hood Gardens coming into expression. At different points in the book, different contributing parts come forward more and others recede. It's in the four central chapters, each focused on one of the estate's forms, where this mode of expression is most evident. But I don't labour the point; I wanted this mode of expressive voice to feel intuitive to the study, and I see it as in keeping with the brutalist method of the 'as found', where the architect – or writer – is decentred as the leading agent to become a part of a more complex, immanent and distributed expressivity. I also think of this approach as an articulation of Alison Smithson's wonderful notion that, 'For us, a book is a small building'.[21]

Notes

1 Karl Marx and Friedrich Engels, 'The Holy Family; or Critique of Critical Criticism', in *Collected Works*, vol. 4 (London: Lawrence and Wishart, 1975), 36.
2 Karl Marx, 'On the Jewish Question', in *Early Writings*, trans. Rodney Livingstone and Gregor Benton (Harmondsworth: Penguin, 1975), 230, translation modified.
3 Fredric Jameson, *Postmodernism: Or, the Cultural Logic of Late Capitalism* (London: Verso, 1991), 5.
4 Manfredo Tafuri, *Architecture and Utopia: Design and Capitalist Development*, trans. Barbara Luigia La Penta (Cambridge, Mass and London: MIT Press, 1976), 179.
5 Manfredo Tafuri, cited in Gail Day, 'Manfredo Tafuri, Fredric Jameson and the Contestations of Political Memory', *Historical Materialism* 20, no. 1 (2012): 31–77, 56.
6 Day, 'Manfredo Tafuri', 62.
7 Peter Smithson, 'Think of it as a Farm! Exhibitions, Books, Buildings. An Interview with Peter Smithson', in *This Is Not Architecture*, ed. Kester Rattenbury (London: Routledge, 2002), 94.
8 Gilles Deleuze, *Difference and Repetition*, trans. Paul Patton (New York: Columbia University Press, 1994), 139, emphasis added.
9 Ibid., 139, 140.
10 Ibid., 139.
11 Tafuri recognised this as a 'residue' that he had tried to leave behind: Manfredo Tafuri, 'Note to the Second (Italian) Edition', in *Theories and History of Architecture* (London: Granada, 1980), unpaginated (iv).
12 Quoted in Eve Blau, *The Architecture of Red Vienna 1919–1934* (Cambridge Mass and London: MIT Press, 1999), 328.
13 Peter Smithson, 'Simple Thoughts on Repetition', *Architectural Design* 41 (1971): 479–481.
14 Mark Crinson, 'Eye Wandering the Ceiling: Ornament and New Brutalism', *Art History* vol. 41, no. 2 (April 2018): 318–343. Ben Highmore, *The Art of Brutalism: Rescuing Hope from Catastrophe in 1950s Britain* (New Haven, CT and London: Yale University Press, 2017).
15 M. Christine Boyer, *Not Quite Architecture: Writing around Alison and Peter Smithson* (Cambridge, Mass and London: MIT Press, 2017), 393.
16 Alison and Peter Smithson, 'The New Brutalism', *Architectural Design*, vol. 25, April (1957), 113.
17 Robbie Shilliam, *Race and the Undeserving Poor* (Newcastle: Agenda Publishing, 2018), 75, 80
18 Motiur Rahman, author interview 4 December 2015.
19 Musa, author interview 28 October 2020.
20 See www.brutalismasfound.co.uk
21 Alison Smithson, in Alison Smithson and Peter Smithson, *The Charged Void: Urbanism* (New York: The Monacelli Press, 2005), 15.

Chapter 6
Groundwork: Viollet-le-Duc, Marx and the Metabolic Rift

Alistair Cartwright

This chapter proposes a Marxist reading of the French architect and theorist Eugène Emmanuel Viollet-le-Duc (1814–1879). Notwithstanding Viollet-le-Duc's contradictions – ardent republican and favoured restoration architect of the Second Empire, builder of barricades in 1830 and troubled spirit of post-1871 revindication (for whom the Communards of Paris were 'bands of drunkards' desecrating an already humiliated nation) – the link with Marx is bound to seem odd.[1] And yet two themes in Viollet-le-Duc's work suggest a potential affinity: his intense focus on construction as a form of labour, and, related to this, the question of nature. In examining these two themes together it is the 'ecological' Marx of recent readings that proves particularly amenable to a radical re-interpretation of Viollet-le-Duc. It is also this ecological Marx that offers the possibility of a materialist counter-critique to revisionist accounts of the latter's work.

The analysis that follows centres on two texts from Viollet's later written work: his millennia-spanning 'world history' of architecture, *Histoire de L'Habitation Humaine depuis les Temps Préhistoriques jusqu'à Nos Jours* (1875), written ostensibly for young readers, and the slightly earlier pedagogical fable of the same series, *Histoire d'une Maison* (1873). The allegorical reading demanded by these books makes them particularly suggestive in terms of the underlying concepts that came to obsess its author following the great political and personal defeats of the last decade of the Second Empire: the war with Prussia, the Commune, and his failed curriculum reform at the Ecole des Beaux Arts.[2] The underlying theme of catastrophic collapse, of disaster both social and material, invites a Marxist reading centred on notions of contradiction and crisis, and, more specifically, the concept – developed by Marx but assembled into a more systematic framework by later scholars – of the so-called 'metabolic rift' in social-natural relations. Reading these works through a Marxist lens, I will draw on interpretations by John Bellamy Foster, Paul Burkett and Kohei Saito, as well as selected original texts by Marx and Engels themselves: principally, Marx's account of the labour process in Volume 1 of *Capital,* and Engels' writings on labour and human evolution in *Dialectics of Nature.*[3]

A materialist counter-critique

Regarded by an earlier generation of critics including John Summerson and Nikolaus Pevsner as the 'prophet of the modern movement',[4] a very different Viollet-le-Duc has emerged in recent reinterpretations. This postmodern or contemporary Viollet-le-Duc is a thinker haunted by the symbolic and physical acts of violence of his own era, expressing in elaborate theoretical form tropes that continue to mark the discipline to this day: rival nationalisms, colonial conquest, ruination of the past and the relentless drive to modernisation and 'reconstruction'.[5] This chapter is indebted to that revisionist historiography. And yet in overturning the image of Viollet the 'structural rationalist', something, I want to insist, has been lost.

Two things stand out from interpretations since the 1990s: 1) the restitution of a romantic, anti-rational, anxious-melancholic tendency in Viollet-le-Duc; and 2) the centring of 'race' as a guiding concept.[6] Whether it is the pillaging of Rome by invading 'Gothic' tribes, or the conquest of a hostile nature by 'noble primitive races', authentic innovation always emerges, in this interpretation, from 'a prior act of destruction'.[7] Approaching the climax of his career in an atmosphere of national humiliation and revindication, Viollet's theoretical quest for origins resulted in what Martin Bressani calls a 'racial-constructive typology' of the most deterministic kind[8] – whereby architectural culture evolves according to an embryonic genius (or retardation) in combination with the influence of the natural environment.[9]

The racism coursing through Viollet-le-Duc's work and his affinity with the romantic movement are one aspect emphasised in this revisionism, and they are undeniable. And yet there is a substratum of thought that resists this interpretation. Take the following passage from *Histoire de L'Habitation Humaine,* set in ancient Egypt:

> The workers, however, being used to building with unbaked bricks, rammed earth and reed, were not yet very skilled in stone cutting; [...] To split the stones in the quarry, having observed that limestone naturally presents itself in beds, they laid bare the exterior horizontal surface; then, at regular intervals along a continuous line [...] they sunk, by means of copper punches, a series of narrow oblong holes [...]. This done, they drove into these holes wooden wedges that had been thoroughly dried; they then whetted these wedges consistently, which, in swelling, split the stone along the line traced by the sinkings [...].
>
> Being a patient and laborious people, they ultimately succeeded in sizing these blocks evenly, [...] and gouging in them characters and figures; since, in the same way that everything in the way of life upon the banks of the Nile was subject to rules, so each construction, every object, had to state the reasons in view of which these constructions or objects were established.[10]

What is striking about this passage is not only the sustained attention to material details, but the very ordinariness of the narration; its groundedness, its patience, its *laboriousness* even. There are countless passages like this, which taken together argue for the centrality of the concept of labour in Viollet-le-Duc's work: passages, for example, describing the complex assembly of trusses in a roof, and the carpenter's knowledge of how a log split lengthwise will bow outwards following the greater shrinking of the sapwood layers; or the method of inserting an arch within an arch to let in a basement light in a barrel vaulted cellar, a tricky piece of geometry that has the young protagonist of *Histoire d'une Maison* scratching his head but poses no great difficulty for the builder in charge; or, returning to the ancient world, the quarry of Cava di Cusa in Sicily described in the *Entretiens sur L'Architecture* (1872) as a series of labour steps frozen in time as if only 'yesterday', where the extraction of enormous cylindrical blocks, cut with square holes for lifting and rolling them to their site of assembly as columns, displays the 'still fresh traces of human labour'.[11]

There is indeed something strangely moving about the modesty of Viollet-le-Duc's prose, which insists on the most intimate attention to the labour process. In the extended passage above, the reader is made to feel the resistance of stone to metal, the nervous precision in the siting of the pilot holes, the ingenuity of leveraging the living qualities of wood against the inertness of rock, and the final triumph when the stone is freed from the ground. Yet the insight here goes beyond a romantic identification with the workers of antiquity and feudalism (the two modes of production that most taxed his historical thinking).[12] The 'constructive gestures' of the past are rather grasped precisely in their transition from an ephemeral, mobile force to an artefact of relative permanence, from 'unrest [*Unruhe*]', to use Marx's phrasing in his account of the labour process, to 'being [*Sein*], as a fixed, immobile characteristic', in a manner that alters both nature and human nature alike;[13] or, as Bellamy Foster has highlighted in his reading of the ecological dimensions of Volume 1 of *Capital*, embodied labour that 'mediates, regulates and controls the metabolism between himself [humanity] and nature'.[14]

It is this laser-like focus on the transition from living labour to immobile product of labour – and, eventually, the erection of a social-material edifice that comes to rule over labour – that ultimately distinguishes Viollet-le-Duc from his architect-contemporaries. Pevsner was surely right to single out Viollet-le-Duc and John Ruskin as the two towering figures of nineteenth-century architectural theory who gave labour a sacrosanct place in their systems of thought. But he is wrong to say that what distinguishes them is simply the degree of romantic sentiment: Ruskin the 'conjurer with feeling' versus Viollet-le-Duc the 'dry reporter of facts'; Ruskin for whom the essential question remained 'was the carver happy?', versus his French counterpart who admired above all 'the designer for his grip on the logic of rational construction'; the one who forbade 'the use of cast or machine-made ornaments of any kind', versus the other who embraced cast iron and the ornamental possibilities of prefabrication.[15] Though carefully controlled, there is as much 'feeling' in passages like the one above as anything in Ruskin. What fundamentally enables the second two distinctions by Pevsner is rather the *striving* by Viollet-le-Duc to positively integrate the alienation of labour into his system, rather than decrying it. His ultimate failure to do so conditions the symbolic violence of his work, including, most importantly, the logic of 'race'.

This critique can be carried through to more recent authors, who in some ways have simply re-aligned Viollet-le-Duc with Ruskin's romanticism, and indeed nationalism. To argue, as Charles L Davis II does, that Viollet's method amounts to the expression of an 'organic' principle in architecture, analogous to or derived from an essential 'race type', fails to accurately account for what is going on in passages like the one above. Viollet's descriptions of the labour process in fact display no sense of natural unfolding but rather a series of conscious technical steps. To the extent that there is a fusion, or rather a closely woven dialectic, of labour and nature, it is rather an 'inorganic' relationship in the double sense implied by Marx when he spoke of the tool (and indeed all natural elements that labour appropriates to its own ends) as an extension of the body,[16] and of the labourer, in ancient slave economies and feudalism, as being 'inorganic' to the reproduction of the non-producing part of the society, which posits the labourer as an 'accessory of the earth', a natural being or 'speaking animal'[17] – a condition of unity with nature enforced and appropriated from without that is indicated quite explicitly earlier on in the narrative.[18]

Race, of course, is present; the builders are drawn from the stock of a 'patient and laborious people'. Rule-bound and traditional, their architecture nevertheless supplies the other side of the creative dialectic that Bressani speaks of: the stone blunts the tool, resists the will of the builders, confronts them from the beginning with failure, and finally forces the innovation of a certain geometry. And yet if there is a dialectic at work here, it can be reduced neither to an organic principle, nor, as Bressani claims, a metaphysical battle between 'order' and 'chaos', the interior clockwork of a personal 'cosmology'.[19] Such an explanation, where it isn't reduced to a psychological diagnosis, is simply too withdrawn from the matter at hand; too lofty, too idealistic, and ultimately not sufficiently distanced from the ideological schematism that Viollet-le-Duc himself falls prey to. Viollet's internal *method* in these passages evidences a *materialist* dialectic. This materialism is only cut short from its fitful approach to what can properly be called a *historical materialist* perspective by the final impossibility of its author reckoning with the concrete development of labour power in his own day.[20] The racial schemas that he resorts to must then be understood as violent and distorted philosophical resolutions to a problem that cannot be resolved other than through practical, revolutionary means.

To substantiate this argument, I want to examine the multifaceted treatment of labour in Viollet-le-Duc's work, tracing its development from a 'force of nature' to a true social force; to an 'inorganic' component of ancient slave-based and feudal societies; to, finally, an abstract quantity of labour power that finds its direct equivalent in the reduction of natural materials to commodities and the widening 'metabolic rift' that results from this.

Becoming human

L'Habitation Humaine begins with prehistory; begins in fact with the emergence of human beings as a species, that is with natural history. This placing of the beginnings of architectural history in deep historical time distinguishes it from a host of earlier examples of the genre of 'world histories of architecture', in particular Thomas Hope's widely read *Historical Essay on Architecture* which directly influenced Viollet-le-Duc.[21] The book's prologue opens on a primeval scene with two 'beings' contemplating a 'vast' and untamed landscape. One says 'All is as it should be', and the other replies 'Nothing is complete' – pointing to the signs of an emerging humanity below.[22] These two, Epergos and Doxi, are the book's time-travelling narrators, one embodying the spirit of progress, the other the counsel of tradition. Coming across a group of 'creatures [*d'êtres*]' sheltering pitifully beneath a tree, Epergos is 'seized with compassion' and sets about showing them how to fashion a structure to better protect them from the elements: a simple tent-like arrangement of bent saplings, packed with rushes and mud.

These opening pages show Viollet-le-Duc grappling with the concept of labour from first principles. The 'creatures' or 'beings' are not yet human; it is through labour that they become human, 'set[ting] in motion', as Marx writes, 'the natural forces which belong to [their] own bod[ies], [their] arms, legs, head and hands' in order to 'act upon external nature and change it, and in this way [...] simultaneously chang[e] [their] own nature'.[23] This dialectical motion, which operates between labour as a force of nature betokening emergent social qualities and the rest of nature, embodies the principle that Marx – drawing on the biological theories of his own day – called 'metabolism', meaning the constant physical exchange of nutrients, waste products, heat, light and other sources of energy needed to maintain life. As Kohei Saito points out, this metabolism is common to all living organisms but with human beings becomes a veritable *social* (and, we might add, *technical*) metabolism, embracing much more than the physiological functions of the body and the immediate environment. Humanity in this way 'mediates, regulates and controls the *metabolism* – [...] between himself [*sic*] and nature'.[24] Viollet-le-Duc also begins with the labouring body that attempts to consciously regulate its energetic and material exchanges with nature. Epergos, 'hoisting himself up' on one of two young trees, makes the trunk 'bend under the weight of his body'. The creatures/beings, 'with their hands and some sticks', 'uproot' other nearby young trees and 'drag' them towards Epergos, who by the end of this effort is 'covered in sweat and mud'.[25] The process set in motion by Epergos embraces both his own body and the collective body of the group. The Hegelian *spirit* here is dragged back down to earth in the very act of catalysing the essential sociality of human beings.

There is, of course, something wilfully idealist about imputing a human capacity for conscious labour to a mythical, external spirit. Read allegorically, however, as the text clearly asks of its young audience, an unmistakably materialist dialectic reveals itself. The real 'spirit', i.e. conscious labour, emerges from the material, from the body, from the natural world; from sweat, mud, trees and rocks. Equally, these acts of an emerging human consciousness return, as it were, to the material world. They are effective insofar as they leave in that world relatively permanent artefacts that can mediate the constant flux of metabolic exchange, slow down and modify those processes of decay and disassembly (as well as the circulation of air, absorption of sunlight, etc.) that, as Engels wrote, are just as much a part of natural systems as forces of growth and reproduction.[26] Architecture, as a historical-material artefact characterised by its *duration*, as well as its primal identification with shelter and habitat, becomes the sign under which are inscribed all the objects of human labour that mediate human beings' environmental milieu.

The first chapter of *L'Habitation Humaine* thus closes with an exchange between the two narrators that can be read as an allegory of the idea that the Marxist political ecologist John Bellamy Foster, drawing on contemporary biology as well as Marx's own reading of Darwin's theories, has called social-natural 'coevolution':[27] 'Would you then want to teach the birds how to make their nests, beavers to build their dams other than those they know how to fabricate?' asks Doxi. Epergos replies: '[L]et us come back here in one hundred thousand days and we will see if these beings have forgotten my instructions to live as they did yesterday. If it is so, then I have been wrong to meddle in their affairs [...] but if they have benefited from my opinions, if the huts that we will see then are in fact better than these ones, then there you have it, for these beings are not animals.'[28] Epergos's wager voices the crucial factor of temporality. What sets human beings on a differential pathway to other species is the fact that we have the capacity to alter our environment at a greater rate, more permanently and with more far-reaching effects than the environment, in its unchanged state, changes us. Architecture is thus conceived as a crucial mediatory factor interposed between human nature and non-human nature with the capacity to both outlast (in duration) and outpace (in changes of form) natural constructions – constructions which Viollet-le-Duc, not unlike Engels, nevertheless has the greatest admiration for.[29]

Race and the metabolic rift

The opening sequences of *L'Habitation Humaine* designate an individual parcel of natural-historical time, limned on all sides by an environmental milieu (a 'habitat', in contemporary parlance). If Viollet-le-Duc the materialist is at his strongest in the analysis of these spatialised parcels of time, then it is in the movement from one natural-historical situation to another, in the grasping of history 'as such', i.e. social, cultural, political and economic history – which has played an increasingly essential role in the transition between different natural historical situations or even epochs (*plantationocene*, *capitalocene* etc) – that another, distinctly anti-materialist logic, the logic of race, rears its head. In *L'Habitation Humaine* these historical transitions are marked by the individual chapters. The abjection of the creatures or beings encountered in the Prologue and first chapter – with skin, so we are told, a 'livid yellow' – thus contrasts with the physical beauty of the 'aryan' tribes-people who are the subject of the next chapter.[30] This racial comparative mode violently denies humanity's common evolutionary ancestry. A racial sequencing of the different 'stages' of history thus composes the overall structure of the book, taking the reader through ancient Egypt, Assyria, central Asian nomadic society, the marshlands of southeast Asia and so on, and finally Europe from the Middle Ages to the Renaissance. As an overarching schema it both ties together the different epochs and regions, *and* effectively constricts the materialist dialectic.

And yet to the extent that this dialectic operates within the bounds of the individual chapters, each one understood as a different environmental milieu, it itself generates the possibility of a decisive historical shift. It does so through one of the most remarkable features of Viollet-le-Duc's materialism: via the mechanism of disaster, understood as both social and natural, or, as Marx conceptualised it, as a 'rift' in the 'social metabolism' with nature.[31] The second chapter of *L'Habitation Humaine* (like the first) thus begins with a storm. The book's spiritual meta-characters, Epergos and Doxi, are once again mortalised, re-earthed, their transhistorical vision blinded by storm water. Rescued by a shepherd, the pair take shelter in his family's 'dwelling', before the house itself – a wooden structure built up against the side of a cliff with projecting roof supported on forked trunks and walls of stacked tree trunks – finally succumbs to the storm. A discussion ensues in which Doxi argues that the family should rebuild the house just as it was, while Epergos proposes to reconstruct it in stone and divert the water away from the cliff-edge. It is this option, the side of technical innovation, that wins out. What follows is a

Reconstructed house of the 'Aryas' after the storm, from Eugène Emmanuel Viollet-le-Duc, *L'Habitation Humaine*, 1875.

careful description of the whole construction process, from the base of large stones, to the fitting together of smaller ones by means of a bevel, to the kind of mortar (made from moss and clay), and the creation of a channel up above to carry water away from the house.[32]

What is remarkable about this sequence is the way a 'natural' disaster is depicted as enmeshed with built modifications to the environment (the house's vulnerable position against a cliff side). The disaster, a 'rift' in the existing social metabolism, as well as being partly human-made, further catalyses an all-sided expansion of modifications to the environment – not just rebuilding the house in more durable materials but diverting the natural course of the mountain run-off. Viollet-le-Duc's prescience in intuiting this complex dialectic between nature and the built environment goes far beyond ascriptions of a hostile or beatific nature, the one associated with romanticism's destructive-creative impulses, the other with an enlightenment teleology (as in Laugier's primitive hut).[33] It is precisely this understanding of environmental disasters that, as Kohei Saito has shown, Marx came to grasp through his reading of natural sciences and analysis of ancient as well as contemporary environmental breakdown, and that today has become a foundational insight of disaster studies.[34]

This understanding of disaster is taken further in a later chapter on the 'Delta of the Nile' in the era of the 'kings of the first three dynasties' (i.e. from about 3000 to 2500 BC). The extended quotation above is taken from this same chapter and we are now in a position to understand its full significance. The quoted passage follows a 'violent earthquake', which 'threw down many of [the] houses' particularly those newly built along the fertile river shore.[35] One of the reasons for the quarry workers' exertions, the work of the 'common people', who exist in a condition 'bordering on serfdom', is the demand to produce earthquake-proof constructions – for 'those who had enriched themselves and who occupied the functions of the state' and 'no longer contented themselves with such simple lodgings of limited durability'.[36] Following Epergos's intervention at a council of elders, it is realised that buildings with inclined walls (like the pyramids) show greater stability and that further modifying the line of stone or brick courses to give a concave form prevents slippage. The work of the stone cutter – replacing buildings of rammed earth and cane, and following precise geometric prescriptions 'promulgated' by 'royal decree' – answers the challenge of the foregoing disaster.[37]

The disaster here takes on an elaborated social form in line with the move from a type of pastoral clan society structured around the family as an economic unit (as in the 'aryan' shepherd and his hut), to a fully fledged agrarian slave economy.[38] Environmental vulnerability is a direct consequence of economic development, expanded settlement intertwining with the strategic geography that Viollet-le-Duc posits as the hallmark of despotic rule within the riverine society of ancient Egypt. A specific 'configuration' of the landscape thus surrounds the legendary fertility of the Nile, such that the broad, low-lying delta and its agrarian inhabitants are subject to the 'surveillance' of the mountain dwelling rulers, who control the narrow upper reaches of the water course.[39]

The result of this geographical distribution of wealth and power is a form of architectural hybridisation reiterated elsewhere in *L'Habitation Humaine*.[40] It is the villages that proliferate along the lower shores that sustain the most damage from the earthquake, particularly the more poorly built houses constructed out of a maladapted hybrid of 'stone and mud', fusing materials from the rocky hillside origins of the conquering elite with the rammed earth techniques of the subjugated peoples of the delta.[41] Drawing on his knowledge of the archaeological literature of the time and the writings of predecessors such as Thomas Hope, Viollet-le-Duc thus constructs a speculative, political-ecological account of the development of both architecture and class society. While the vector of development, the link in the chain between different natural-historical epochs, may well be the act of conquest – predicated on a racial schema of supreme and subordinate peoples – the powerful internal drive exercised by the materialist method ultimately leads Viollet-le-Duc to the same conclusion that Marx and Engels drew in *The German Ideology* regarding pre-capitalist societies: 'Nothing is more common than the notion that in history up till now it has only been a question of "taking"' – so, for example, 'The barbarians "take" the Roman Empire' – but this act of taking, of conquest, ultimately involves 'submitting to the conditions of production and intercourse of the country taken'.[42] The result, manifested with unusual clarity in the architectural object, is a form of difference in fusion, a hybridisation that differentiates (on the basis of wealth and power) rather than homogenising or equalising its human material.

The reconstruction in carefully calibrated cut stone that Viollet-le-Duc hypothesises as the outcome of earthquakes in ancient Egypt thus retrenches this stratified pattern, further deepening the metabolic rift, and with it, the development of class society. Viollet-le-Duc reserves a final word of (uncharacteristic) doubt for Epergos, who wonders what gratification the new architecture promises for 'the poor wretches who will have passed their lives in laboriously raising these dwellings exactly like the former ones' except in more recalcitrant materials.[43]

If race provides the overarching schema that guarantees the sequence of historical epochs, it is rather the interaction of class (as the concrete historical development of labour) and nature (in the form of natural phenomena which only become disasters through their technical-social interaction), that generates the internal motivation of *L'Habitation Humaine*. Architectural form, moreover, is read as a palimpsest of this process. The house in cut stone preserves (for example, in the form of the projecting cornice, a relic of the fillet of

Building with reeds and rammed earth in ancient Egypt, from Eugène Emmanuel Viollet-le-Duc, *L'Habitation Humaine*, 1875.

bundled reeds designed to retain the mass of earth composing the roof) a trace of the more 'natural', metabolically attuned structure that it extinguishes. Offered here in allegorical form, this insight is made absolutely explicit in the *Entretiens*, in a section about ancient Assyria rather than Egypt.
The reckless 'spoliations' of the Assyrian empire, which denuded its territories of majestic cedar forests as well as 'men' [in the form of slaves], can then be read in inverted fashion in a 'refine[d]' and now ruinous architecture.[44] The highly regulated water courses displayed the astonishing feats of command over labour that characterised everything else in the kingdom; 'for while those fierce Assyrian monarchs created a desert around their empire, it was their pleasure to live amid pleasant gardens and verdant fields' [*des campagnes les mieux arrosées et les plus riantes*]. With the 'argillaceous earth' taken from the excavation of the canals, huge numbers of fired or sun-dried bricks were fabricated, 'and with these materials were raised veritable hills or plateaux' surmounted by 'vast and lofty palaces [...] more like towns than residences'. The ornamentation of these palatial artificial landscapes, consisting of vertically grouped cylinders resembling 'the pipes of an organ', can be seen as 'a last reminiscence' of timber stockading, i.e. of a natural material now extinguished. Thus when this empire 'crumbled', toppled finally by

invasions from the neighbours it oppressed, 'there no longer remained anything of its glory but the piles of bricks that are still to be seen on the banks of the Euphrates and Tigris.'[45]

Just as Kohei Saito has noted with regards to Marx, Viollet-le-Duc studied the environmental disasters of ancient society for clues as to the ruinations of his own era.[46] Architecture takes on a special significance in this context. As one of the crucial artefacts of human labour it helps mediate our social metabolism with nature. But with increasing submission to the only semi-conscious and often irrational behaviour of class society, this same architecture contributes to a potentially calamitous 'rift' in those social-natural relations.

The commodity and the clerk of works

Although published two years earlier than *L'Habitation Humaine*, Viollet-le-Duc's *Histoire d'une Maison* (1873) picks up the historical narrative just where the later work leaves off, with the contemporary era and the transition from the feudal past. The latter theme is figured in the book's main subject – the rebuilding of the principal house of a great estate ['*une belle terre*']. The owner of the *terre*, Monsieur de Gandelau, is preparing, so we are told, 'a transition between ways of life which are weakening even in the countryside, but which are nonetheless still alive, and those which must replace them'.[47] The bearer of the transition will be his son Paul, acting under the tutelage of his architect cousin, who assumes the role previously filled by Epergos as conduit for Viollet's opinions. Set against the background of the 1870 war with Prussia (in which its author had direct experience leading a company of sappers armed with picks and shovels), and a restive peasantry foreshadowing the revolutionary upheavals of the Paris Commune, the role of disaster as social catalyst, the 'metabolic rift', returns in *Histoire d'une Maison* – but, as we will see, in a form where blockages in the political-economic system predominate over natural hazards.[48]

The challenge of effecting the desired 'transition' from the old, semi-feudal way of life is indeed one of those potential blockages. The 'weakening' but surviving ways of life extend to the forms of labour on the estate and the surrounding countryside, including the nature of building labour. This is figured principally in the character of le père Branchu, 'a good country mason' like his father before him, who is now regularly employed on odd jobs around the estate but was once known to have undertaken the building of the mayor's mansion.[49] Both Branchu and his fellow builder, Jean Godard the carpenter, belong to the past: 'old fellows [...] who cannot go soldiering', they drink to the health of de Gandelau for providing them with opportunities to earn a living.[50] Neither, we are told, has the capital to undertake the works on the new house by themselves. They are not general contractors but small masters or workmen who employ only 'un garçon', and as such have themselves to be employed directly by the estate, with materials purchased by de Gandelau or supplied 'on account' from the estate grounds: from its forests and natural beds of stone.[51]

Viollet-le-Duc thus draws out the nature of building labour and materials that are still partially rooted in the feudal past. The builder is attached to the estate practically and psychologically, an extension of its agricultural life, just as the old house appears as an extension of its owner and his family, a matter without which his authority would disappear. The house is an active hub of the rural economy, as well as a psycho-social symbol of the collective body; the master's upstairs 'bureau' its thinking head, the large kitchen – where 'the harvest men [...] come to supper' and the shepherds 'settle their accounts' – its ruminating belly.[52] As Saito notes with regards to Marx's analysis of feudal landed property: 'The estate is individualised with its lord: it has his rank, is baronial or ducal with him, has his privileges, his jurisdiction, his political position, etc [...] It appears [along with its workers] as the inorganic body of its lord.'[53] Corresponding to this, the materials for the new house come directly from the lands of the estate and bear the names of its significant places: the oak from a stand of trees near a particular farm, for instance, that testifies to the '*provenance des charpentes*'.[54]

This is the poetics of an architecture of traditional rural relations. Rather than an artefact of labour as a force of nature, as seen in *L'Habitation Humaine*, architecture here is an expression of that primary form of alienation that predates and pre-conditions the all-sided alienation found within capitalism: namely, private property in the land. This is the historical background intimated by *Histoire d'une Maison*. The book establishes all this only to show how, in the rationalised, capitalistic construction process enacted by its author's avatars (Paul and his architect cousin), these semi-feudal relations must be subtly yet thoroughly transformed.

This transformation takes place first of all through the familiar trope of the division between drawing board and building site, design and construction, architect and builder, the latter increasingly 'discipline[d]' by the former's synoptic knowledge of the 'site'.[55] This division is figured in the narrative structure of *Histoire d'une Maison*, which proceeds, like the method of the rational, modern architect, from the ground upwards, from plan to elevation, as well as in the alternation between chapters centred on the site and chapters dedicated to 'theoretical studies'.[56] Secondly, it is actively enforced and put into practice via the introduction of an intermediary, the '*Inspecteur des Travaux*', or 'clerk of works'.[57] Sérgio Ferro has argued that the emergence in certain European cities towards the end of the twelfth century of individual masters who took charge of the 'project-contract' and removed themselves from the building site coincided with the development of a layer of intermediaries needed to transmit to the workers the resulting plans.[58] It is the tradition of these intermediaries – known in medieval France as *parleurs* – that Viollet seems to gesture to with the appointment of Paul to the role of '*Inspecteur des Travaux*'.

For the young boy this role can only ever be make-believe, a peculiar rite of passage enforced by his unconventional elder. For Paul's cousin, however, it is deadly serious. The '*Inspecteur des Travaux*' is the architect's eyes and ears on the building site. He ensures that work is carried out to a predetermined standard, that corners are not cut, that materials are checked for quality, that tools are kept under lock and key, that an accurate account is made of those materials extracted directly from the estate grounds, and that nothing surreptitiously leaves the site once it has been brought there.[59]

It becomes clear that the role of the *Inspecteur* is necessary not only because, as Ferro has argued, construction remains a kind of 'manufacture' in which

From the ground up, from Eugène Emmanuel Viollet-le-Duc, *Histoire d'une Maison*, 1873.

the worker – despite his subordinate and increasingly atomised status under capitalism – retains something of his unique craft knowledge,[60] but equally because the (at this stage) *natural* materials forming the physical fabric of the building have become commodified. If commodities, i.e. objects alienated in exchange, certainly existed in the ancient societies that Viollet-le-Duc preoccupied himself with in *L'Habitation Humaine*, here they become virtually universal. They become the only generally possible means of subsistence, and of much else besides; the only way to satisfy the needs of labour, which, separated from the means of production, must also sell itself as a commodity, as labour power, to impart its transformative capacities to yet more commodities in the form of surplus value, realisable as exchange value. As Paul Burkett argues, under this near universal rule of exchange value over use value, even objects and materials taken as 'free gifts' from nature must now be treated as commodities – as bearers of surplus value – 'as if' they were recipients of so many hours of abstract labour power, and be carefully counted as such.[61] Working from the ground up, the modern architectural procedures of rational design and scrupulous site management decompose, in this way, not only the traditional forms of building labour, but also the status of natural materials and resources. One of the fundamental ecological contradictions of modern capitalism emerges from this nexus of social-environmental relations brilliantly illustrated by Viollet-le-Duc. Every object about to enter the building site has a double value. As use value it is oak, cedar, limestone, granite and so on, with their particular qualities and vestiges of traditional meanings (their '*provenance*'). Viollet is intensely interested in these qualities and in *Histoire d'une Maison* he draws on his wide reading of natural history – particularly geology but also the history of France's 'noble' and now much depleted forests ('*belles futaies*')[62] – to convey this dual nature of value. This is indeed the first lesson conveyed to the young Paul, aspiring architect and soon-to-be clerk of works: 'a knowledge of the ground is the first among all those things that the architect must possess'.[63] Walking the grounds of the estate his cousin acquaints him with the basic elements of geology, the difference between 'crystalliform rocks' such as granite, and those deposited in layers like sandstone, gravels and marls which make for ideal foundations;[64] likewise the influence of different qualities of soil on timber production and those where disease has weakened the wood.[65] But no sooner does Viollet-le-Duc establish a certain allegiance between the exactitude of modern science and the earthbound, immemorial qualities of earlier modes of production, than another logic brutally interrupts this pairing. The ground, in its materiality and its spatiality, comes to embody a steadily augmenting set of exchange values, values that the 'clerk of works' is charged with keeping track of.

Nature itself thus reproduces the dual status of the commodity as use value and exchange value. However, the potential contradiction between these two characteristics now grows even more profound. If the use value of an 'ordinary' commodity, whether a shirt or a sack of unspun wool, is determined by its place in the capitalist production process (as raw material, subsistence good, etc), the social 'usefulness' of a 'natural' commodity, be it water, air, trees, or rocks – materials and resources which persist in nature despite their industrialised extraction – can never be delimited in quite the same way. While the 'ordinary' commodity, just like the means of production, sustains its liveliness for capitalist society through mobilisation in the production process (wool left unspun is devoured by moths; idling machinery rusts and depreciates relative to more scrupulous rivals), the same cannot be said for commodities which remain deeply embedded in natural ecological processes. Rather, it is precisely through the increasingly rapid through-put of resources, that nature is ravaged, laid waste to, and ruined.

In the thought of Viollet-le-Duc, two contrary notions of disaster thus exist in painful combination. For Viollet the scientific-romantic, the scholar of antiquity and decipherer of Gothic structural genius, the contemporary sense of ecological devastation as a form of creative destruction litters the soil as well as the pages of history. Production devours the natural world. For Viollet-le-Duc the bourgeois organiser of works, however, an even more acute disaster hangs overhead. For it is, in his own day and age, precisely when the productive apparatus threatens to return to nature – when the site falls silent, deserted of workers and abandoned to the elements – that he feels most keenly the nightmare of capitalism: work stopped. As architecture gives way to unmediated metabolic processes of decay and growth – the incomplete timbers of the house in *Histoire d'Une Maison*, showing 'black with damp' in contrast with the 'veil' of snow that mimics the surrounding social misery – precisely then does his boyish avatar, Paul, the architect apprentice, experience his first true grief, 'the first deep disappointment' of impending adulthood (*'la première douleur, le premier dur mécompte'*).[66] This is not simply pathetic fallacy, a romantic overidentification with natural effects, but rather represents a fusion of political-economic and ecological crises. The abrupt halt to the works cannot be separated from the dislocation of the rural economy: at that time when groups of peasants might be found 'speaking in excited tones' on the road to town, when lights were seen burning in the cottages late into the night and the cattle were driven afield beyond the normal hour, a 'painful shudder' (*'un frémissement douloureux'*) seemed to pass through the country.[67]

That this lamentation issues from the extreme crisis of 1870–1, with the French army's rout by Prussian forces and calls for the popular defence of Paris spurring on the rising of the Commune, should not obscure the fact that Viollet-le-Duc zones in with uncanny acuity on the general mechanism of capitalism's 'metabolic rift'. These two aspects of his thought, the one bearing on social relations with nature, the other on the unresolved destiny of labour (saviour of the nation or gravedigger of the entire capitalist system?) should be read as two sides of the same coin, forever spinning in an incompossible unity. Architecture's capitulation to natural forces represents, for Viollet, a crisis of labour, nature's resurgence being tied to labour's own reassertion of its independent power. The subjection of labour meanwhile – as in the resolution to an earlier crisis that Viollet-le-Duc placed great store in, namely the Carpenter's strike of 1840, 'solved' through the accelerated production of structural iron, that apparently 'inexhaustible' material which neutralises and even encourages the destruction of forests – goes hand in hand with the obliteration of natural limits.[68] Fear, and out of that fear, brutality, are thus intermingled in Viollet-le-Duc's thought with a profound respect for both labour and nature, contradictory attitudes which the logic of race ultimately fails to contain.

Notes

1 John Summerson, 'Viollet-le-Duc et le Point de Vue Rationnel', trans. Dirk Depreeuw, in Geert Bekaert ed., *A La Recherche de Viollet-le-Duc* (Brussels: Pierre Mardaga, 1980) (originally 1947), 99–114; Martin Bressani, *Architecture and the Historical Imagination: Eugène-Emmanuel Viollet-le-Duc, 1814–1879* (London: Routledge, 2016); Eugène-Emmanuel Viollet-le-Duc, trans. Benjamin Bucknall, *Discourses on Architecture*, vol. 2 (London: Sampson Low, 1881), 247.

2 Jean-Michel Leniaud, *Viollet-Le-Duc ou Les Délires du Système* (Paris: Éditions Mengès, 1994), 110.

3 John Bellamy Foster, *Marx's Ecology: Materialism and Nature* (New York: Monthly Review Press, 2000); Paul Burkett, *Marx and Nature: A Red and Green Perspective* (Chicago: Haymarket Books, 2014); Kohei Saito, *Karl Marx's Ecosocialism: Capital, Nature and the Unfinished Critique of Political Economy* (New York: Monthly Review Press, 2017); Karl Marx, trans. Ben Fowkes, *Capital*, vol. 1 (London: Penguin, 1990); Friedrich Engels, trans. Clemens Dutt, *Dialectics of Nature* (Moscow: Foreign Languages Publishing House, 1954).

4 Robin Middleton, 'Viollet-Le-Duc's Influence in Nineteenth Century England', *Art History*, vol. 4, no. 2 (June 1981), 203; Summerson, 'Viollet-le-Duc', 103 and 109. See also Nikolaus Pevsner, *Ruskin and Viollet-le-Duc: Englishness and Frenchness in the Appreciation of Gothic Architecture* (London: Thames and Hudson, 1969), 16–17.

5 For an early example see Martin Bressani's 'Notes on Viollet-le-Duc's Philosophy of History: Dialectics and Technology', *Journal of the Society of Architectural Historians*, vol. 48, no. 4 (December 1989), 327–350.

6 Jean-Michel Leniaud, *Viollet-Le-Duc ou Les Délires du Système* (Paris: Éditions Mengès, 1994), 109, 127–8; Richard A Etlin, 'Le Corbusier, Choisy, and French Hellenism: The Search for a New Architecture', *Art Bulletin*, vol. 69, no. 2 (June 1987), 265 and 272.

7 Bressani, *Architecture and the Historical Imagination*, 87.2 and 1245.4.

8 Ibid., 1111.5. See similarly Charles L Davis II, 'Viollet-le-Duc and the Body: the Metaphorical Integrations of Race and Style in Structural Rationalism', *Architectural Research Quarterly*, vol. 14, no. 4 (2010),. 341–2.

9 Davis, 'Viollet-le-Duc', 345.

10 Eugène-Emmanuel Viollet-le-Duc, *Histoire de L'Habitation Humaine depuis les Temps Préhistoriques jusqu'à Nos Jours* (Paris: J Hetzel, 1875), pp. 87–8. This translation, as for all subsequent citations from the original French texts, is my own.

11 Eugène-Emmanuel Viollet-le-Duc, trans. Benjamin Bucknall, *How to Build a House: An Architectural Novelette* (London: Sampson Low et al., 1874), 66–7, 98; Eugène-Emmanuel Viollet-le-Duc, *Entretiens sur L'Architecture* (Paris: A Morel, 1863), vol. 1, 45.

12 Martin Bressani, 'Eugène-Emmanuel Viollet-le-Duc (1814–1879): Gothic as Constructive Will', in Kenneth Powell ed., *The Great Builders* (London: Thames and Hudson, 2011), 115.

13 Marx, *Capital*, 287.

14 Marx, *Capital*, quoted in John Bellamy Foster, *Marx's Ecology: Materialism and Nature* (New York: Monthly Review Press, 2000), 157.

15 Nikolaus Pevsner, *Ruskin and Viollet-le-Duc: Englishness and Frenchness in the Appreciation of Gothic Architecture* (London: Thames and Hudson, 1969), 16, 18 and 22.

16 Bellamy Foster, *Marx's Ecology*, 201. Bellamy Foster refers to Marx's *Paris Notebooks* of 1844 (often known today as the *Economic and Philosophic Manuscripts*). See also Saito, *Marx's Ecosocialism*, 30.

17 Karl Marx, *Grundrisse: Foundations of the Critique of Political Economy (Rough Draft)*, trans. Martin Nicolaus (London: Penguin, 1993), 489; Perry Anderson, *Passages from Antiquity to Feudalism* (London: Verso, 2013), Ebook, 117, n. 38.

18 Viollet-le-Duc, *L'Habitation Humaine*, 68.

19 Bressani, *Architecture and the Historical Imagination*, 79.3 and 86.0. See also Martin Bressani, 'Viollet-le-Duc's Rationalism', in Martin Bressani and Christina Contandriopoulos eds., *The Companions to the History of Architecture, Volume III: Nineteenth Century Architecture* (Hoboken NJ: Wiley Blackwell, 2017), 228.

20 In fact Summerson, somewhat inconsistently, used precisely this word 'materialist' to characterise Viollet-le-Duc's thinking. Summerson, 'Viollet-le-Duc', 109.

21 Thomas Hope, *An Historical Essay on Architecture* (London: John Murray, 1840), especially 11–16; Martin Bressani and Aniel Guxholli, 'Circumstances, Habit, and Adaptation: Thomas Hope's An Historical Essay on Architecture (1835)', in Petra Brouwer, Martin Bressani and Christopher Drew Armstrong eds., *Narrating the Globe: The Emergence of World Histories of Architecture* (Cambridge Mass: MIT Press, 2023), 198.

22 Viollet-le-Duc, *Habitations of Man,* 1, 4–5.

23 Marx, *Capital,* 283. Emphasis added.

24 Saito, *Marx's Ecosocialism*, 101.

25 Viollet-le-Duc, *L'Habitation Humaine*, 6 and 7.

26 Engels, *Dialectics of Nature*, 387.

27 Meaning evolution determined by both natural factors and social-cultural ones. Bellamy Foster, *Marx's Ecology*, 201.

28 Viollet-le-Duc, *L'Habitation Humaine*, 7.

29 Viollet-le-Duc, *Habitations of Man*, 15; Eugène-Emmanuel Viollet-le-Duc, trans. Virginia Champlin, *Learning to Draw, or, The Story of a Young Designer* (New York: GP Putnam's Sons, 1881), 114–7; Engels, *Dialectics of Nature*, 240–1.

30 Viollet-le-Duc, *Habitations*, 4 and 27–8.

31 Marx, *Capital*, vol. 3 (London: Penguin, 1981), 949.

32 Viollet-le-Duc, *Habitations*, 17 and 20–3.

33 *Contra* Martin Bressani's assertion on this point. See his 'Notes on Viollet-le-Duc's Philosophy of History', 328–9.

34 Saito, *Karl Marx's Ecosocialism*, especially 158, 198 and 203–5; and for example Ian Davis, *Shelter After Disaster* (Oxford: Oxford Polytechnic Press, 1978).

35 Viollet-le-Duc, *Habitations*, 88.

36 Viollet-le-Duc, *L'Habitation Humaine*, 89, and see also n. 26.

37 Viollet-le-Duc, *L'Habitation Humaine*, 90–2.

38 See n. 26 above.

39 Viollet-le-Duc, *L'Habitation Humaine*, 82–3.

40 Viollet-le-Duc, *Habitations*, 45–7.

41 Ibid., 88.

42 Karl Marx and Friedrich Engels, ed. and trans. R Pascal, *The German Ideology*, Parts I and III (London: Lawrence and Wishart: 1938), 62.

43 Viollet-le-Duc, *Habitations*, 85.

44 Viollet-le-Duc, *Discourses,* 179.

45 Ibid., 179

46 Saito, *Marx's Ecosocialism*, 240–245.

47 Eugène-Emmanuel Viollet-le-Duc, *Histoire d'une Maison* (Brussels: Pierre Mardaga, 1978), 29.

48 Viollet-le-Duc, *Architecture and the Historical Imagination*, 1404.3.

49 Viollet-le-Duc, *Histoire d'une Maison,* 37.

50 Ibid.,72.

51 Viollet-le-Duc, *Histoire d'une Maison*, 75 and 77–8; Linda Clarke, *Building Capitalism: Historical Change and the Labour Process in the Production of the Built Environment* (London: Routledge, 1992), 73–8.

52 Viollet-le-Duc, *Histoire d'une Maison*, 26–7.

53 Karl Marx, *Paris Notebooks*, quoted in Saito, *Marx's Ecosocialism*, 37.

54 Viollet-le-Duc, *Histoire d'une Maison*, 77.

55 Viollet-le-Duc, *Histoire d'une Maison*, 38.

56 Ibid., Ch. 18 'Etudes Theoriques', 154, or similarly Ch. 16, 'Le Critique', 135.

57 Viollet-le-Duc, *How to Build a House*, 74.

58 Sergio Ferro, trans. Ellen Heywood, 'From Strasbourg to Paris' in Sérgio Ferro, eds. Silke Kapp and Mariana Moura, *Architecture from Below: An Anthology* (London: Mack, 2024), 53.

59 Viollet-le-Duc, *How to Build a House*, 74.

60 Ferro, 'Dessin/Chantier: An Introduction for Newcastle', in Ferro *Architecture from Below*, 26–28.

61 Burkett, *Marx and Nature*, 58–9 and 82; see also Georg Lukács, trans. Rodney Livingstone, 'Reification and the Consciousness of the Proletariat', in *History and Class Consciousness* (Pontypool: Merlin, 1971), 91.

62 Viollet-le-Duc, *Histoire d'une Maison*, 65; and Viollet-le-Duc, *Discourses*, vol. 2, 332–3 for a brief but impassioned account of the depletion of French forests. On the interest in geology see Pierre A. Frey and Lise Grenier, *Viollet-le-Duc et La Montagne* (Grenoble: Glénat, 1993).

63 Viollet-le-Duc, *Histoire d'une Maison*, 43.

64 Ibid., 43.

65 Ibid., 78.

66 Ibid., 177.

67 Ibid., 39–40.

68 Eugène Viollet-le-Duc, *Entretiens sur L'Architecture*, vol. 2 (Gollion: Infolio éditions, 2010), 443-6.

Section 3
Ideological Formations

Chapter 7
Architecture's World History

Mark Crinson

World histories of architecture have never been as widely discussed and practised as they are today. Books on the subject proliferate, from large format popular versions to academic studies, each claiming ever more inclusion and coverage. Banister Fletcher's *A History of Architecture on the Comparative Method*, first published in 1896, is now into its 21st edition and re-titled *Sir Banister Fletcher's Global History of Architecture* (2019), a change just as interesting for the insertion of that apparently value-neutral word 'global' as for the continuation of the anachronistic Banister Fletcher brand. A global or world history of architecture (hereafter WHA) indicates a claim to master not just time but space: to deal with all the (significant) architecture on planet Earth, the boundary beyond all others. Architectural history thus seems to join the humanities' search for relevance as framed in terms of a 'global turn'.[1] The consensus: the global is not a perspective, not a horizon or a greater if variable scale of reference, but simply a given, something irrefutably and objectively *there*, boundary and terrain. This seems to move us (whoever we are) beyond Eurocentric approaches and condescension towards, or outright ignorance about, vast areas of the world. Such globalism is rhetorically democratisation, a universal suffrage of all places, but also a tonic, an exaltation of privilege, a goad to address absence.

There is something different here from previous attempts to address architecture across continents. Wide surveys of architecture were initiated in the Enlightenment and then proliferated in the Victorian period. That they didn't have 'global' or 'world' in their titles but instead terms like 'a history' or 'a general history', for which they might be a 'handbook' or 'manual', is not a pedantic point. Their work was not conceived as having some necessary duty to cover all of the Earth: 'history' meant a commanding view of the past but also ways of structuring it or organising it into hierarchy and narrative; and

Cover of Banister Fletcher, *A History of Architecture on the Comparative Method*, 1938 edition, design originally by Banister Fletcher senior, 1897.

where 'world' might creep into these texts it meant the world known to be of importance already, the world of global hegemons and their spheres of interest and trade networks, what had already undergone formal subsumption in the architectural domain. (Contrast this with what Marx and Engels called the 'cosmopolitan character' of production and consumption that would give rise among other effects to a world literature and a world history based, dialectically, on the everyday and a 'local being', something perhaps mirrored in recent decolonial ideas about 'worldness' and 'border thinking' in relation to globalisation.)[2] This was these histories' front story, populated and sometimes even structured by ideas like spirit or genius, trees of architecture, historical and non-historical, peoples or races, comparative method, the true and the imitative. Recent WHA – a revival of the Victorian genre – may acknowledge multiple contributions and 'specialist topics or micro-histories', but these are understood as tesserae (albeit often misshapen and ill-matched) fitting into the bigger mosaic to be surveyed.[3] Key terms – core and periphery, connectivity, mobility, exchanges and networks – spread architecture, or imply its spread, to all parts.

To criticise the global turn might easily seem reactionary. Contesting Eurocentrism and exposing racial assumptions behind architectural history have been vital moves in the discipline, but they neither produced the global turn nor are they necessarily inherent in it. To be clear, what is being questioned in this chapter is not globalism, world-making as an imaginary totality (or perhaps 'planetarity' as an ethics of global responsibility),[4] and certainly not serious studies of neglected areas of the world, but instead the assumptions and practices of WHA as a revived form of a discredited genre with new links and parallels to globalisation as a neoliberal discourse, indeed in many ways its 'vanity mirror'.[5] (Here I agree with certain decolonial critiques of the singularity of world history, as having a particular epistemological perspective, which is also an inherent problem in WHA.)[6] It is important to provincialise western ideas about architecture – to demonstrate their misrecognition of the world – and crucial to understand the place of architecture in a range of societies and periods well beyond the west as well as those imposed upon by it. It is much less clear, however, whether WHA with its idea of a globe-filling history offers any fundamental corrective to this when it is the imperialist idea of complete coverage that is itself part of the problem. It is not often asked, furthermore, how this approach itself relates to globalisation.

As will be argued later, the alternative to WHA is not a return to national categories or formerly canonic accounts, but instead a set of very different approaches to how architecture relates to the spaces of the Earth, and to signal these I coin the term 'vectorial totality'. 'Totality' is, of course, a concept deeply rooted in Marxist thinking (in which it has also often been contested). For Marx himself, totality was what would be aspired to or summoned up when the 'simple material production of life' was related to civil society, the state, and 'different theoretical products and forms of consciousness', as all of these developed over time, including the 'reciprocal action of these various sides on one another'.[7] Marx's 'concrete, mediated totality'[8] was thus a distinctly non-Hegelian concept, but his optimistic idea of history as a progressive movement has long been qualified with notions of particular temporalities or indeed, as will be developed later here, of coexisting temporalities. As well as uneven forms of development we might also think of deglobalisation and slow globalisation, in other words, ways of understanding global forces that undercut the notion of an inevitably ever-increasing globalisation and, arguably its accompaniment, an ever-increasing global architectural knowledge.

WHA are often justified as providing two services, which are sometimes separate and sometimes overlap. On the one hand, the global account creates 'maps' or 'outlines' for both lay reader and student. These are analogies, of course, and they are not neutral; they are determining constructs which guide and contain what is to be known, indeed they naturalise the phenomenon as if what it is and how it might be found are already self-apparent. The globe here is a kind of map; the survey is identical with 'the overall field of knowledge', the outlines it draws need to be populated.[9] On the other hand, reflective forms of the genre stake their credentials on a more representative coverage, more even-handed or symmetrical to offset past imbalances and asymmetries; and so, filling the gaps on those maps is essential work that might even re-centre or entirely re-orient them. However, this anti-Eurocentric argument is at best a prescription, neither a method nor a type of analysis, promising always an illusory form of completion; and it is premised on a moralising call simply for raising awareness of places previously ignored. As it turns out, moreover, anti-Eurocentrism is not really the effect at all. The map, the outline, the illusion of the global itself, all retain their normalising effects, behind which is still an essentialising and imperialising idea of the global.

Two approaches to writing global histories are coterminous with these homogenising normalisations. One is the product of teams of specialists whose work is located all round the world, while the other is produced by the figure of the omniscient scholar roving the world. The first organises scholarly labour by fitting the specialist to the area that needs filling; the whole is then the multi-faceted conspectus designed by the editors. The second depends on synthesis, much-travelled experience, the smoke-and-mirrors of detail and broad sketch. Inevitably, there are discursive tropes that follow from these practices and that are also elevated as principles: diversity models the former, while connectedness reigns over the latter. But, while they might agonise over narrative as much as over what to include, both approaches assume the inherent truth of the global as survey. This is both the ground they attempt to fill and, necessarily, their ever-receding horizon.

Neither approach substantially questions the nature of the history it purveys – the ways causation works, the relation between architecture and other spatial phenomena, the measure of temporality and its multiple forms, what is to count as context, and even whether context is a viable metaphor – indeed to do so would put at risk the very foundations of what they seek to portray and enlarge on. They accept the normative conditions, practices and expectations of architectural history, attempting to further them by scaling up to the global. And so they still depend on ideas of the canon, however re-geared, inclusive or expanded, and they still choose the exceptional, the pioneering, and the vanguard. They create a curious kind of history, the product of an architecture culture that depends on a particular conception of architecture as designed object projected from its context and superordinate to its environment, and what follows is a kind of soft humanist populating of the world with multiple (architectural) varieties of identity. And thus WHA manages to be, in Michel Foucault's terms, both a 'concerted carnival' (of which he approved) and a 'monumental history' (which he attacked).[10] Very few architectural historians, including those practising WHA, would today claim an absolute autonomy for architectural change, for histories of form alone. And so, WHA has written into its accounts 'contextual' matters like dynastic and regime changes, climate differences, technological innovation, and so on. But these are treated as a kind of background from which architecture is projected, rather than integral to its actualisation. The global in WHA is nothing other than a map to be filled; it is not the global as the universal or the generality, and not – more relevantly here – the global as totality, a compass both to show what social structures organise territories of architectural production and to enable critique of false categories of its containment.

This revived genre of WHA, whatever the good intentions of its authors, is entangled with neoliberal conceptions of the global. This is surely as little controversial an assertion to make as to say that Victorian world histories – by James Fergusson, Edward Freeman, or Banister Fletcher, say – were products of the colonial rivalries of their time, the 'expanded interstate system', Britain's control over world markets and its particular kind of imperialism, combining territorialism and capitalism.[11] Imperialism as world system superseding a world economy, in Immanuel Wallerstein's terms, was the frame and the enabling condition by which Victorian WHA understood the world and Free Trade was its ideology.[12] As Giovanni Arrighi writes, 'no territorialist ruler had ever before incorporated within its domains so many, so populous, and so far-flung territories as the United Kingdom did in the nineteenth century'.[13] As historians it is necessary then to understand the global – like the nation, like the region – not as having some geographical truth but as a concept with historical time already in it. It follows: that if the global has a history, then the WHA genre must be understood as having its own historical conditions of possibility, and these overdetermine its form beyond what may be claimed for it.

Before coming to recent WHA and the link with neoliberalism as claimed earlier, we need to recognise the often-forgotten proliferation of WHA in an earlier transitional period in neoliberalism. It is no coincidence that the expansion of capitalist world trade and production, and new forms of globalisation in the 1960s and 1970s – containerisation (globally standardised in the late 1960s), for instance, or OPEC (1960), or the emergence of new media relationships, the relocation of manufacturing to low-income regions, or a new kind of world economic crisis in the 1970s – were faintly echoed in the appearance of 'world' and 'global' in the titles of the first wave of WHA books after a suspension in their publication that had lasted some fifty years (except for new editions). While academic scholarship was working on lower scalar levels like the region and nation, these new popular WHA had a bigger scale but tended to be passively descriptive and to assume aesthetics as transhistorical – as in the surveys published by Hamlyn (1963), Prentice-Hall (1961), SI (1963), Studio Books (1964), Studio Vista (1968), Hamlyn (1971), Octopus (1973), Macmillan (1977) and Blandford (1980). These may not be of much inherent historical value now but at the time they responded to the new loosening and opening up of world relations beyond the Cold War, and they generated a market to which later academic accounts needed to respond.

The ascendancy of Thatcher and Reagan, their response to the economic crisis of the previous decade, and then the crises of 1989 and 2008, only pushed further the tendency of neoliberalism to expand to an extreme the search for new markets and new forms of extraction, working less by dominance or territorial conquest than by the kinds of front-of-house exploitation and back-of-house expropriation that Nancy Fraser has described.[14] Framing this were the transnational Bretton Woods bodies that took on a new activism in the 1980s becoming a worldwide apparatus ensuring the safe navigation of capital through the global system.[15] There was also a new sense of 'neoliberal rationality acknowledged as a historical construct and a general norm of existence', in which the valorisation of the self was made equivalent with the market and projected onto the world.[16] The parallels are striking with how recent WHA search for new parts of the map previously ignored, their striving for scope or reach in a further intensification of the imperial WHA idea – shared by modernist historians – that the west's own history had already been overmined. There is also often an uncritical acceptance of globalisation, hence a packaging of the world for its better consumption whether for the architectural studio, the view from the airliner, or indeed for its use in the competitive marketing campaigns of urban boosterism.[17] As a result, WHA always presents architecture as multi-coloured, glitzy, individualised; its tone is upbeat ('the epic story of humans ... shaping communities through the act of building');[18] and it works as a kind of real subsumption in the architectural domain, marginalising or appropriating counter-temporalities, sifting them so they accord with the always-reaching completion, the shape-adapting 'story' of the global.

One response to the expansion of US architecture schools in this same period, was the marginalising of history survey courses, partly out of intellectual enquiry, the need to address students from other parts of the world, and new research programmes, but also partly out of the economic logic of growth in the tertiary sector and the new hires that went along with it. What could architectural historians recommend to the students taking their survey courses in world or global architectural history? The WHA as course reader offered an instructional commodity, one that claimed to hold everything students needed to know between its covers, to be parcelled out over the length of the course. The ways in which universities were reshaped and expanded elsewhere should also be figured into this, especially of course in the architecture and environmental humanities. The often self-congratulatory tone in the response to these phenomena through expanded survey courses hides the problems that these global surveys produced. Recent WHA provide select examples of representative exceptionalism, a vertical model that is meant to complement a horizontal model of democratic inclusion by place. Not, then, or only marginally, architecture's embroilment with practices of expropriation and exploitation, of coercion, of slow violence and theft, but instead architecture's transcendence of or even autonomy from such matters in 'the stories these buildings have to tell'.[19]

Neoliberalism is characterised by a globalising dynamics exerted through the multinationalism and financialisation of capital, the evolution of transnational institutions of governance into guardians of economic behaviour, and the emergence of new media platforms and their neo-feudal owners, and all this is accompanied by a 'hollowing out [of] political capacities … at both the state and geopolitical levels'; in short, of cannibal or vulture capitalism.[20] At the same time these developments are both 'unitary and differentiated',[21] particularly accompanied by new differentiations on the level of temporality rendered as 'functional to capital' and by a 'surcharge of multiple or "parcellated" subject positions', both with distinct relevance to a critique of the avowedly pluralist WHA.[22] Compare, for example, what WHA writers call their 'celebration of the astonishing diversity of efforts … that different cultures around the world have taken … to shape their built environments', or their 'story of how environments are created that shape experience and communicate identity'.[23]

This play of variety within deeper homogenising structures is typical of recent WHA, indeed unavoidable in reading them; they have to pass the postmodern test of relativist heterogeneity. Local colour and global mobility, the relation between the two unproblematised and often unexplained; we can as it were experience all these different architectural worlds at once – a Babel of architectural tongues, an aggregate of localities and their architectures, a faceted pattern of national and regional tendencies. Clearly, if not admitted by WHA, as well as having a history and becoming a world system, the global is always a representation, inferred or mediated from statistics, images, dimensions. (Is it a set of geographies? Social forms? Trade routes? Weather systems? A topological relation of functions?) Within the framing and imagining condition of the global, there is a kind of thin celebration of diversity, of local colour as the faces of the multi-aspected or mosaic idea of the global, clustering around an essentially empty category, placed on an indifferent ground, as if they make up the global or form its justification. Fredric Jameson's words on this are useful – 'the opposition between global and local is an ideological dualism which generates not only false problems, but false solutions as well'; relatedly, the terms of resolution here are 'pluralism' or 'multiplicity' which act to synthesise an 'imaginary resolution' in the form of a fantasy; a collective identity of architecture across the globe.[24] The globalised social relations of production, practice and need, are replaced in another related model of the global by an ontology of association – of agency and actors and actants – that arise in the magical form of the network spread across the hemisphere and either indifferent to the human (and its history) or decentring it.[25]

In thinking about global approaches other than WHA, and in drawing on Marxist work on matters like the coming into being of global capital and its value-form, as well as multilinear histories within that, and even on world literature, we have to recognise the oddness of discussions about the global in architectural history. How little they engage with other disciplines and their global turns, how different they are from discussions of global history or world literature: on translatability and untranslatability as well as on translation as displacement and interpretation; on methods of 'distant reading', and on how national dynamics may be absorbed by relationships with global hegemons.[26]

One moment when architectural history engaged with debates about the global predated and largely bypassed postcolonial theory and came more from the social sciences. This was the work of Anthony D. King, whose acknowledgements in his earlier writing frequently thanked the subaltern studies historian Ranajit Guha, the sociologist Janet Abu-Lughod, the anthropologists Bernard Cohn and Amos Rapoport, and the planning consultant Otto Koenigsberger. He would later be sympathetic to what postcolonial theory brought to studies of culture but, as these names indicate, King's work of the 1970s and 1980s was much more a part of recent intellectual concerns in the social sciences.[27] Differently put, he was a Marx-influenced scholar whose work in London and Delhi in the 1960s, and then later, exposed him to development studies, urban studies, the sociology of race, systems theory, structural anthropology, the historical semantics of Raymond Williams, and early forms of subaltern studies.

When King applied Wallerstein's world systems theory to architecture, it was partially as an antidote to the phenomenon of globalised architecture in the 1970s and 1980s. Wallerstein's rigid core/periphery relation of unequal exchange and its premise that capitalism originated in a world economy may no longer be tenable,[28] but his work did ask what was immanent to capitalism in its global forms and, in the idea of one system with 'different sectors performing different functions',[29] it offered ways to spatialise and therefore as it were to architecturalise the global, and this is what inspired work such as King's *The Bungalow: The Production of a Global Culture* (1984).

As its subtitle implies, King's book is very different from those studies of building type which seek formal isomorphisms across the world, some of which are still being produced and typify what I earlier called the view from the studio. In such studies – King was reacting to Nikolaus Pevsner, but one might think of P.V. Aureli's recent work on grids and on longhouses – we seem to return to another nineteenth-century WHA approach, that of J.N.L. Durand, where redrawn schematic plans of buildings of a particular type are grouped across pages so they focus attention on repeated formal characteristics.[30] Typological or diagrammatic identity, extracted from but indifferent to global spaces, is a distilled, abstracted product of Aureli's methods as much as it was of Durand's. Rather than this assumption of an *inherent* identity, in King's interpretation it was the *situational* identity of bungalow cultures that was stressed, an anthropological angle that was drawn from Amos Rapoport, at the same time as King understood the bungalow – as Marx had understood

A European Gentleman Entering a Bungalow in India, watercolour by Samuel Davis, c. 1800.

working people's experience whether in India, Ireland or England – as creating a commonality of experience produced by globalised capitalism.[31] The bungalow exemplified how the global was cathected by colonialism, yet it was also a global vector of property increasingly built for the nuclear family and the single household dwelling.[32] If colonial rule was the means by which industrial capitalism moved from certain European areas to forge global relations of production, then the bungalow was effectively both a transmitter and a manifestation of capitalist relations around the world; it was, then, a vector whose totality, in Marx's sense of 'different theoretical products and forms of consciousness', was to be filled out by King's study.

This is architecture seen in movement: as King puts it, 'its global diffusion represents … the transfer of institutions, images, of ways and models of living,

Mr. Croft's bungalow, near Madras, watercolour by Samuel Davis, c. 1800.

of a particular kind of material and non-material culture which is produced by the modern, industrial free market economy'.[33] The 'global' is a noun that activates – it diffuses, it transfers, it expands, And, in the case of the bungalow this is a process of suburbanisation dependent also on car industries and oil production.[34] The word 'bungalow' itself attested to this – a word ubiquitous in many different languages, the form found in every continent.[35] It could not be explained only culturally, but also by 'questions of supply and demand, the ownership of land, the right to private property, and the principles behind the organisation of the state.'[36] If colonial rule was the means by which industrial capitalism moved from certain European centres to become 'global relations of production', then the bungalow was effectively a transmitter and a manifestation of capitalist relations around the world. Colonialism was the 'instrument' enabling 'the penetration of subsistence, peasant or semi-incorporated economies by the system of industrial capitalism in which peripheral economies were … linked to those at the core'.[37] Immanuel Wallerstein was behind some of this, with his idea of the capitalist world economy as 'a single division of labour within which are located multiple cultures'.[38] King was rightfully tentative about this – pointing for instance to the issue of local societies maintaining control over their own economy and thus also over their 'distinctive building and urban forms'[39] – but he followed its broad implications.[40] It was, for instance, particularly relevant to 'the managerial or organisational functions of the developing capitalist world economy and which are used by colonial or *Comprador indigenes*. Hence, the bungalow of the plantation manager and the cultural standards or traditional accommodation of plantation labour'.[41] Again King was not citing postcolonial theory at all, but writers such as John Rex, David Harvey and Wallerstein, and a little of what has come to be called the new imperial history (notably Chris Bayly).

Otherwise, debates in architectural history have not really resolved the issue of how to deal sufficiently with local specificity while also creating epistemological frameworks on the planetary level. Our discipline depends too much on understanding architecture as object related to other such objects, each necessarily extracted from the tessellated locality of landscape, property, infrastructure, and so on. The inadequacy of our current constructs of the global is most telling in their concealment behind a veil of the commonsensical, or their resort to intellectual history. The global in them – like a Freudian account of desire – is about the multiple giving the illusion of the whole but constantly deferring consummation. The global seems to offer completion through geographic spread, but doesn't offer historical process and structural intelligibility that might qualify as totality – in fact, it is an avoidance of the task of explaining deeper relationships through the reciprocity between culture and the world, forms of memory and utopia, material practices and structuring forces.[42] While the map in WHA is to be filled, the workings of complexity are not to be explained but, as neoliberalism does, to be obscured by spectacle or bypassed.[43]

The vector, rather than the globe or the network, or even the decolonial project of multiple local histories building macro-narratives,[44] is, then, one way to think of totality in terms of form and space – it extends across boundaries to expose the historical logic in disconnection as much as connection, understanding boundaries from both sides rather than accepting their spatial authority as inherent. The vector is a metaphor, of course, and no doubt it implies too much a sense of uni-directional movement and dynamism where movements might be two-way or multi-directional and where stasis, glacial change, or even regression might sometimes be better analogies. It might be otherwise metaphorised as a pattern or a stain or, deeper, a geological formation. It is an act or a movement, something that may peter out or may be intersected by other vectors. An approach of this kind asks, then, not what architecture there is across the world and how it is architecturally significant, but how it is organised across territorial arcs or segments of the globe, how it is the product and expression of concrete social and historical forces, how indeed those trajectories or vectors are meaningful and indeed how architecture and space are made meaningful even world historical by them. This relates to totality and to the cognitive mapping of totality, both of which oppose a concept of the global which resorts to a supposedly natural or neutrally geographic category but one with no necessary correlation to the production of space.

Fundamentally different from the perspectival and surveying acts of WHA and the limitations of accounts of the global based only on architectural cultures,[45] a vector might operate at different ranges and scales, tracing from the global to the hyper-local; how, say, the global is both representation and pressure in an Exchange building housing the abstracted dealings of a world-girdling trade, and how that dichotomously impacts upon its immediate urban surrounds as its globalising success demands more space for its trading floor from its locality; or how industry in one place is seen to produce cultural institutions in another when fossil fuels and pollution are cognitively mapped across space.[46] Indigenous agency might be one such vector, challenging neoliberal concepts of property rights, either reaching across space in forms of architectural resistance or deploying scale (small scale, or anti-scale) as itself a destabilising force, a 'strategic delinking' from dominant geographies.[47] A vectorial approach might understand architecture and landscape as bound up in the ramifying effects of global connectedness on locality, or in what Edouard Glissant distinguishes as *mondialité* (globality or worldness) as opposed to *mondialisation* (globalisation):[48] it might take an international airport interconnected across the globe and study not its high-tech structures and its airport typology, but how it first erases a particular history and landscape then reaches out into its immediate hinterland affecting it in numerous ways from aerial and noise pollution to business, warehouse and hotel accommodation, and so on. Or a vector might show how the global spread of an architecture of control, whether in scattered form like postwar US military bases or in a directional form like recent infrastructural corridors (such as the Chinese Belt and Road Initiative), manifest a set of globalised spatial norms whatever the local setting.

Already a number of architectural histories have explored such vectorial totalities, if not necessarily in Marxist ways. Sibel Zandi-Sayek's understanding of mid-nineteenth century Istanbul as a multidirectional meeting point for exchanges of expertise between the Ottoman Empire and Britain, enables her to see architecture as both embedded in locality and the result of certain intercontinental economic and geographical vectors.[49] The climate zones of colonialism have been recalibrated as 'colonial technoscientific networks and circulations' in Jiat-Hwee Chang's work.[50] In Lukasz Stanek's research, export architecture between Communist eastern Europe and west Africa is comprehended as a vector for world-making through architecture as gift as well as flows of technology and expertise.[51] There are indications in Daniel Barber's work of how a vectorial approach might be particularly useful in thinking about architecture's relation to environment, including pollution and climate change, all indifferent to national and global frames.[52] Relatedly, as in Peter Christensen's work, vectors of transport or vectors of materials and their production and use across regions and even continents bring together infrastructural, architectural and landscape issues in the 'vast gray zone between binary formations'.[53]

In these examples the vector is something with deep historical, economic and political substance, which enables us to grasp its relational integrity as a totality, as opposed to the dutiful space-filling of WHA with its imaginary world of architecture and its non-acknowledgement of its compliance with globalisation. Vectors also cut across differences for too-long hallowed in our discipline (between, say, vernacular buildings and architecture, or infrastructure and designed landscape, property relations and natural forms), and made into its police. (Complementary to this is the emphasis on 'flows' and constant border-crossings, which is as much a form of police injunction as its opposite.)[54] Furthermore, instead of a text/context model these vectorial studies work much more by models of imbrication, of overlap and adjacency, or models of architectural mobility and new shifting geographies of connection. Such vectoral totalities help us properly to think of the global not as pre-existing but as motivated, as practised, as historical construct. A vectorial approach asks, then, not what architecture there is across the world and how it is architecturally significant, but how it is organised, what needs it responds to or creates.

It is not far from here, as the concept of totality implies, to several related Marxist theories of divergent trajectories and temporalities on a global stage. Specifically posed against theories of globalisation and the singularised time of the nation-state, the revived interest in ideas of 'combined and uneven development' emphasise the dynamic interdependence between and within regions and the anti-linear collapsing or compression of stages in conjunction with capitalism's metabolic system. This goes beyond merely the production of unevenness as a structural feature of disproportionately advanced forms of capitalism across nation-states (whose architectural historical equivalent is theories of 'third world modernism' or 'alternative modernities'), instead delving into apparently contradictory levels of development – the molecular and the molar - in the same place.[55] In other words, various historical modes of production may be found in the same economy in 'synchronous nonsynchronisms'.[56] This explains the coexistence and mutual enabling of the 'torn halves' of vernacular (or indigenous culture) and mainstream (including avant-garde) architecture in the same place as well as their uneven articulation with extra-national entities. Any state is, in Trotsky's formulation, 'full of contradictions, gaps, lack of coordination, vague fermentation – in a word, of phenomena in which the inheritance of the past is interwoven with the shoots of the future'.[57] This bypasses the rigidity of world-system theory and its compartmentalising by core, periphery and semi-periphery, by developed and undeveloped. And it also eclipses the merely pluralistic, multi-aspected image of the world we get in postmodern global histories – the way they sanitise and ahistoricise opposition and resistance by the means of 'autonomy' or of 'difference' or the abstract metaphors of networks, and their often-assumed model of progress or development as the key criterion for inclusion. These produce a commodified form of architectural history in which comparative method or claims of originality and innovation are abstracted from the material conditions of labour and locality.

The concept of combined and uneven development recognises both integration on a scalar level and unevenness – local, cultural, technical – as constantly dynamic and contradictory, the 'contemporaneity of apparently anachronistic forms'.[58] A vectorial approach would show how these temporalities are articulated together under particular conditions and purposes. Combined and uneven development also addresses the soft ways in which WHA have absorbed the postcolonial critique of Eurocentrism by attempting a supposedly more balanced coverage of the world.[59] The gap between a western-centric architectural history and a provincialising of that history is simply filled in by a set of examples of the forms of modernity in a range of non-western locales. This leaves a myth of western modernity as sealed and completed, neither provincialising modernity within Europe nor acknowledging its temporal discrepancies. Combined and uneven accounts are also multi-lineal accounts, showing how socio-economic domination extends beyond direct political or military domination, plotting real connections between different parts of the world, real forms of spatial imposition and change, as well as those surplus to or remaindered by these changes.[60] Focusing on these real forms and connections gives us historical depth, from which planetary links or vectors are plotted, not global survey.

The issue of temporality is key to combined and uneven development and to other related Marxist work on the dynamic of formal and real subsumption. One such resource is Massimiliano Tomba's call for historical paradigms that can measure the 'combination of a plurality of temporal strata in the violently unifying historical dimension of modernity', and how these phenomena might be understood as synchronised by the world market, even as other phenomena are structured by a different, sometimes syncopated time of difference from, struggle with, or alterity to this synchronisation.[61] In other words, to recognise globalisation at the same time as rejecting its forms of instrumentation. Such an approach offers a way of accounting for the highly advanced, the emergent, the regressive, the residual and the somewhere between, all in the same terrain, a co-existence which WAH's mosaic approach, when it notices it, tends to treat as being in a 'state of reciprocal indifference' rather than as violently synchronised by the world market.[62] How else, after all, to understand the coexistence of slums, vernacular huts, neo-medieval villages, neoclassical government buildings and high-tech towers than as the contrapuntal outcomes of the provision of migrant labour, extractive rent and financial services across the same fractured landscape?

Notes

1 Jason W. Moore, '"The Modern World-System" as Environmental History? Ecology and the Rise of Capitalism', *Theory and Society*, vol. 32. no. 3, June 2003, 307–377.

2 Karl Marx and Frederick Engels, *Manifesto of the Communist Party* (1848) (Peking: Foreign Languages Press, 1975), 37. Harry Harootunian, *Marx After Marx: History and Time in the Expansion of Capitalism* (New York: Columbia University Press, 2017), 237–8; Walter Mignolo, *Local Histories/ Global Designs* (Princeton: Princeton University Press, 2000), 40, 49–88.

3 Murray Fraser, 'A Provisional Collectivised Global History of Architecture', in Petra Brouwer, Martin Bressani, and Christopher Drew Armstrong, eds., *Narrating the Globe: The Emergence of World Histories of Architecture* (Cambridge Mass and London: The MIT Press, 2023), 516.

4 Mary Louise Pratt, *Planetary Longings* (Durham, NC: Duke University Press, 2022), 10–11. On 'aesthetic worldedness' see Eric Hayot, *On Literary Worlds*, (Oxford: Oxford University Press, 2012), 45.

5 Ben Highmore, 'Art's Work' (review of Caroline A. Jones *The Global Work of Art*), in *New Formations*, no. 94, 2018, 161.

6 Mignolo, *Local Histories/Global Designs*, 21–22, 54.

7 Karl Marx, *The German Ideology*, ed. R. Pascal (New York, 1968), 28.

8 Martin Jay, *Marxism and Totality* (Berkeley and Los Angeles: University of California Press, 1984), 125.

9 Fraser, 'A Provisional Collectivised Global History', 517.

10 Michel Foucault, *Language, Counter-Memory, Practice* trans. Donald F. Bouchard (Ithaca: Cornell University Press, 1977), 161.

11 Giovanni Arrighi, *The Long Twentieth Century: Money, Power and the Origins of our Times* (London: Verso, 1994), 50, 54. Germany also saw the production of many WHA – by C. L. Stieglitz, Wilhelm Lübke, Franz Kugler, Albert Rosengarten and others – which require explanation in terms both of disciplinary developments and the country's emergence first as nation-state then as global power.

12 Immanuel Wallerstein, *The Modern World-System* (New York and London: Academic Press, 1974), 348.

13 Arrighi, *Long Twentieth Century*, 55.

14 Nancy Fraser, *Cannibal Capitalism* (London: Verso, 2023), 30–40.

15 Ellen Meiksins Wood, *Empire of Capital* (London: Verso, 2003), xi.

16 Pierre Dardot and Christian Laval, *The New Way of the World: On Neoliberal Society* trans. Gregory Elliott (London and New York: Verso, 2013), 4, 255, 264, 267.

17 Kathleen James-Chakraborty, 'Daring to Craft a Canon (Almost)', in Brouwer, Bressani, and Drew Armstrong eds., *Narrating the Globe,* 492; Fraser, 'A Provisional Collectivised Global History', 516.

18 Spiro Kostof, *A History of Architecture – Settings and Rituals* (New York and Oxford: Oxford University Press, 1985), Preface.

19 Michael Fazio, Marian Moffett, and Lawrence Wodehouse eds., *A World History of Architecture* (London: Lawrence King, 2003), x.

20 Nancy Fraser and Rahel Jaeggi, *Capitalism – A Conversation in Critical Theory* (Cambridge: Polity, 2018), 39.

21 Fraser, *Cannibal Capitalism*, xvi.

22 Massimiliano Tomba, *Marx's Temporalities* trans. Peter D. Thomas and Sara R. Farris (Chicago: Haymarket, 2013), xiv; Fredric Jameson, *Archaeologies of the Future* (London and New York: Verso, 2007), 214.

23 Murray Fraser ed., *Sir Banister Fletcher's Global History of Architecture* (London: Bloomsbury, 2020), vol 1, xi; Kathleen James-Chakraborty, *Architecture Since 1400* (Minneapolis: University of Minnesota Press, 2014), xvii.

24 Jameson, *Archaeologies*, 215–6.

25 Peter Osborne, 'The Planet as Political Subject?', *New Left Review*, vol. 145, Jan-Feb 2024, 110, 114.

26 Emily Apter, *Against World Literature: On the Politics of Untranslatability* (London and New York: Verso, 2013); Franco Moretti, *The Modern Epic: The World System from Goethe to García Márquez* (London and New York: Verso, 1996); Franco Moretti, *Distant Reading* (London and New York: Verso, 2013), 47–9; Roberto Schwarz, *To the Victor, the Potatoes* trans. Ronald W. Sousa (Leiden and Boston: Brill, 2020).

27 Anthony D. King, 'Preface to the Paperback Edition', *The Bungalow: The Production of a Global Culture* (New York and Oxford: Oxford University Press, 1995), xii.

28 See for instance Ellen Meiksins Wood, *The Origin of Capitalism* (London: Verso, 2017), 18-19..

29 Immanuel Wallerstein, *The Capitalist World-Economy* (London: Cambridge University Press, 1979), 68.

30 On urban grids see Pier Vittorio Aureli, *Architecture and Abstraction* (Cambridge, Mass and London: The MIT Press, 2023), 86–122. The work on the longhouse is an ongoing project of Aureli and his office Dogma: see https://www.youtube.com/watch?v=KXda5ANA33A (accessed 10/6/24).

31 Kevin B. Anderson, *Marx at the Margins* (Chicago: University of Chicago Press, 2010), 187.

32 King, *The Bungalow*, 3.

33 Ibid., 259.

34 Just as certain films, forms of popular music styles and television programmes manifested an 'interlinguistic standardisation of culture', so too this happened with certain styles of living: Erik Hobsbawm, quoted in King, *The Bungalow*, 8.

35 Ibid., 2.

36 Ibid., 247.

37 Anthony D. King, 'Culture and the Political Economy of Building Form', *Habitat International*, vol. 7 nos. 5/6 (1983), 244.

38 Immanuel Wallerstein, *The Capitalist World-Economy* (London: Cambridge University Press, 1997), 34; King, *The Bungalow*, 7.

39 King, 'Culture and the Political Economy', 248.

40 It was a 'framework in which to analyse built form': King, 'Culture and the Political Economy', 244. See also Anthony D. King, '"The World Economy is Everywhere": Urban History and the World System', *Urban History Yearbook 1983*, ed. David Reeder (Leicester: Leicester University Press, 1983), 7–18.

41 King, 'Culture and the Political Economy', 245. In another example, the forms of a Lancashire cotton town must be seen within 'a global political economy which has a physical and spatial dimension and which includes the cotton exchange in Manchester, the transport links to the cotton supply ... as well as the cotton plantation and the accommodation of those connected with it': Ibid., 245.

42 Jay, *Marxism and Totality*.

43 Douglas Spencer, *The Architecture of Neoliberalism* (London: Bloomsbury, 2016), 17.

44 Mignolo, *Local Histories/Global Designs*, 22.

45 Tom Avermaete and Cathelijne Nuijsink, 'Architectural Contact Zones: Another Way to Write Global Histories of the Post-War Period?', *Architectural Theory Review*, vol. 25, no. 3 (2021), 350–361.

46 Mark Crinson, *Shock City: Image and Architecture in Industrial Manchester* (New Haven and London: Mellon Centre for Studies in British Art, 2022), 137–188.

47 Swati Chattopadhyay, *Small Spaces: Recasting the Architecture of Empire* (London: Bloomsbury, 2023), 27.

48 Mignolo, *Local Histories/Global Designs*, 77.

49 Sibel Zandi-Sayek, 'The Unsung of the Canon: Does a Global Architectural History Need New Landmarks?', *ABE Journal*, 6 (2014), https://journals.openedition.org/abe/1271

50 Jiat-Hwee Chang, *A Genealogy of Tropical Architecture* (London and New York: Routledge, 2016).

51 Lukasz Stanek, *Architecture in Global Socialism: Eastern Europe, West Africa, and the Middle East in the Cold War* (Princeton: Princeton University Press, 2020).

52 Daniel Barber, *Modern Architecture and Climate – Design Before Air Conditioning* (Princeton: Princeton University Press, 2020).

53 Peter Christensen, *Germany and the Ottoman Railways: Art, Empire and Infrastructure* (New Haven: Yale University Press, 2017); Peter Christensen, *Precious Metal: German Steel, Modernity and Ecology* (University Park PA: Penn State University Press, 2022).

54 'The police order is always at once a system of circulation and a system of borders': Jacques Rancière, *Dissenting Words: Interviews with Jacques Rancière*, ed. and trans. by Emiliano Battista (London: Bloomsbury, 2017), 239.

55 Harootunian, *Marx After Marx*, 20–24.

56 Ernst Bloch as quoted in Harootunian, *Marx After Marx*, 72.

57 Leon Trotsky, *Problems of Everyday Life* (New York: Monad, 1973), 271.

58 Tomba, *Marx's Temporalities*, 148–9.

59 Alexander Anievas and Kerem Nisancioglu, 'Troubling Time and Space in World Politics: Reimagining Western Modernity in the Atlantic Mirror', in James Christie and Nesrin Degirmencioglu eds., *Cultures of Uneven and Combined Development* (Chicago: Haymarket, 2021), 86–7.

60 Anderson, *Marx at the Margins*, 177–8, 244–5.

61 Tomba, *Marx's Temporalities*, 47.

62 Ibid., xiv.

Chapter 8
The Myth of the Architect

Luisa Lorenza Corna

Parricides and filiations

In the early 1960s, the architect Marta Lonzi (1938–2008) receives several postcards from tourist destinations. The fronts of the cards depict images of pristine natural landscapes and picturesque villages, typical of tourist photography. However, the backs are strikingly different from what one might expect from a relative or friend on holiday. There are no 'greetings from', 'wish you were here', or 'see you soon' messages. Instead, they all bear only a succinct signature: Ludovico Quaroni, and a date.[1]

Quaroni (1911–1987) was an important figure in the Italian architectural milieu, playing a pivotal role in establishing a new discourse at the onset of the postwar reconstruction period.[2] Among his most notable achievements were the Tiburtino houses in Rome, one of the foremost examples of Italian architectural neorealism, and later, the urban and architectural housing project La Martella in the southern Italian town of Matera. In the early 1960s Quaroni held a position at the University of Florence, where Lonzi worked on a master's thesis under his supervision. There appears to be a relationship of mutual respect and esteem between the two, yet the power hierarchy is evident in their written exchanges. While Quaroni communicates through formal, concise postcards, Lonzi responds with lengthy, sincere letters, reflecting on her design upbringing.[3]

Lonzi will graduate in 1963 and will soon begin her career as a practitioner. The same year Quaroni will leave Florence and return to his *alma mater*, the University of Rome, where he will appoint a new graduate, Manfredo Tafuri, as a staff member. Notably, the appointment happened just a few months after Tafuri had published his first book, a monograph on Quaroni.[4] Secondary literature describes it as an attempt to read the urban and architectural

Postcard from Ludovico Quaroni to Marta Lonzi, 1962.

transformation in postwar Italy through the lens of his persona, but we could also regard it as tribute to a mentor.[5]

Tafuri's official entry into academia coincides with Lonzi's definitive departure. In the early 1970s, Lonzi was a practising architect but she still entertained the idea of engaging in design pedagogy. Prompted initially by architect Alberto Samonà and later by Quaroni, she decided to return to university as a voluntary assistant. However, the experience was short-lived. A 1973 letter to Quaroni states her decision to resign: 'Looking ahead, I can't but dissociate myself in a clear and definite manner from the course'.[6] Quaroni did not respond until 1979, with a phone call.

With and contra Marx

I have chosen here to take my cue from the (broken) relationship between Marta Lonzi and her teacher Ludovico Quaroni (triangulated by the figure of Tafuri for reasons we will see later) to introduce her singular and little-known attempt to reread postwar architectural theory and history through the lens of feminism, and her simultaneous endeavour to set up a *different* practice. I stress the term *different* here as Lonzi was involved, for a decade, in a type of feminism that went under the name of 'feminism of difference'. This latter approach diverged from the dominant egalitarian feminism due to its inability to recognise the assimilationist logic implicit in the claim of 'universality of rights'.[7] At first glance, Lonzi's work couldn't appear more remote from Marxism and Marxist-inflected analysis of architecture, the theme of this book. And a closer reading will confirm this hypothesis. She is distant from the feminist materialist analyses of space and the built environment that started surfacing in the 1970s–80s, in the aftermath of second-wave feminism and its struggles over reproductive labour.[8]

Yet, I want to approach her writings in partial defiance of her declared political position; forget for a moment that she would not call herself a Marxist nor make conscious reference to Marxian analytical categories. There is much to gain, I think, from an oblique reading of her work for anyone interested in critique of ideology. In the following text I will argue that Marta Lonzi's analysis of the figure of the (male) modernist architect opens a new critical perspective on the foundations of twentieth-century architectural discourse and history, unveiling their materialist shortcomings. As I will expound, her enquiry into the ways the protagonists of modernist architecture fashion themselves doesn't take labour as its central category, but this latter – or better, the absence of it – will be one of her main discoveries. The fabrication of the myth of the modernist architect – a process she analyses by mainly focusing on architects' first-person accounts – is thus revealed in its full complicity with the broader concealment of the material conditions of designing and making.

The image of the architect

The letter previously mentioned was reprinted by Lonzi in her first book *L'architetto fuori di sé* (*The Architect at Variance with Himself*) in 1982. Released by Prototipi, an independent publisher associated with her feminist separatist group *Rivolta femminile*,[9] the book is composed of two parts. The first part provides an autobiographical account of the author's initial steps in the design profession, while the second one offers an analysis of the figure of the (male) modernist architect. Here, Lonzi seems to shift from biography to essay, but the use of the first-person perspective and colloquial language remains consistent throughout the text. Building on 1970s feminism, the book places daily experience at its centre, treating it as both the generative space for speculative endeavours and their testing ground.

Dividing the two parts is a photographic report of Lonzi's project for her residence in Rome – a majestic refurbishment of a top-floor loft in a building designed by Giulio and Enrico Gra, two eclectic, little-known architect-engineers from the 1930s. This is not the most significant project Lonzi had completed by the time *The Architect at Variance with Himself* was released, but perhaps it best represented both the theme and the narrative style of the book. Images of the interior design for her home double the biographical incipit, while photographs of the exterior, designed by the Gra brothers, testify to Lonzi's study of the building's history and structure, in the attempt to stage a critical dialogue with the protagonists of the discipline.

The cover's illustrative style sharply contrasts with the clean, photographic language of the inside. Below the title, there's a drawing of a man with oval glasses and a bow tie, his hair rendered with broad brush strokes standing on end, seemingly reaching out to the world. Drips from the painting cover his face, disfiguring it. The man appears to be Le Corbusier. This representation is unusual compared with his most popular portraits. Like his buildings, Le Corbusier's appearance was a constructed set of elements evoking rigour and sturdiness. He was known for dressing meticulously, for both clients and the camera, aware of the significant role photographic images played in promoting architects' work and shaping their public personas.[10] If the official images testify to his precision and the ability to comply with professional codes and social rules, Lonzi's drawing is exactly the reverse. All the rigour and restraint are quashed, or perhaps parodied. His head appears to be both exploding and liquefying, with the drips of paint obscuring his iconic glasses and his view.

To make sense of this iconoclastic gesture, one must delve into the first chapter of the book and then reconsider the image alongside the title. *The Architect at Variance with Himself* is an expression Lonzi coins to indicate a specific positionality of the twentieth-century male architect. Positionality here

Cover of Marta Lonzi, *L'architetto fuori di sé*, 1982.

is perhaps not quite the right term, as the title doesn't allude to the architect's location in relation to his various social identities, but bears an introspective, psychoanalytic inflection. For Lonzi, male architects are 'outside their selves', detached from their inner worlds, and hesitant to engage in self-reflective approaches that could reveal a personal connection to their project. From this perspective, Le Corbusier's usual image of steadfast rigour appears less as a mark of strength to be admired and more as a defensive mechanism. As his authority begins to crumble, so too can his iconic image be détourned.

Architecture, architects and myths

The built environment is certainly not the primary concern of Lonzi's analysis. Unlike most of her contemporaneous feminist counterparts in architectural scholarship, her work shows little interest in how gendered power relations are produced and reproduced through specific designs and urban forms. Instead, she directs her research toward written texts. Architects' treatises, methodological precepts, declarations and biographical accounts are the main sources for her investigation into a topic she believes has been largely overlooked by feminist scrutiny: the figure of the (male) architect.[11] Up until now, she laments: 'Architecture has always been discussed as an expression of the ruling classes, as if this were a given, while the idea of architecture as an expression of the power of the architects themselves has been largely ignored.'[12]

Here, Lonzi seems to challenge some well-rooted Marxist convictions. If we assume that the primary cause of architecture's failure in its social mission lies exclusively at the structural level, what space remains for architects' agency, either to uphold or challenge the system? Lonzi's interest lies less in singling out exceptional cases that defy the status quo, and more in scrutinising architects' overall complicity with power. Power here is not explored as a sphere of production, but more in its superstructural reverberations. How do architects, asks Lonzi, implicitly conspire to create an image of themselves *au-dessus de la mêlée?* In their writing, what concepts, definitions and visions recur that affirm their privileged class and social position? And how does this self-picturing contribute to obfuscating the capitalist and gendered nature of their labour? Lonzi doesn't ask these questions openly, but in setting for herself the goal of unveiling the 'myth' of the twentieth-century architect, as she herself calls it, she answers them all, and ventures into the terrain of ideology critique.

Her endeavour begins with a meticulous reading of some of the classic texts of the 'fathers' of twentieth-century western architecture. Quotations from Le Corbusier, Otto Wagner, Marcel Breuer, Mies Van der Rohe, Frank Lloyd Wright, among others, punctuate the book's first chapter, where the tenets of her critique are expounded. In selecting the excerpts, Lonzi is guided by specific questions: how do modernist architects define themselves and their discipline? How do they relate to their social role and profession? What commonalities can be identified in architects' positions, language and posture? It must be admitted that her research is neither extensive nor methodologically rigorous – the works from which the texts are excerpted are only referred to in footnotes, and contextual information on the architects and dates is missing. However, the quotations selected have a stark similarity, and all point to an exaltation of architecture's power and scope. From the architects' words transpires a desire to endow the discipline with a demiurgical role, a quasi-divine force, we can say. Take, for example, Wagner in *Moderne Architektur*: 'It should come as no surprise to hear that architecture can reach the highest peaks of human expression, occasionally touching upon the divine.'[13] Or, again, Wright: 'I know that architecture is the supreme spirit.'[14] And finally Breuer: 'In its best conditions, the architect serves two deities: the client and architecture itself.'[15]

Commenting on these declarations, Lonzi argues that modernist designers have turned the architectural object into a myth, a term she uses with only loose reference to Barthes's definition.[16] In her reframing of the concept, a myth is what an object becomes when disconnected from its maker (for Lonzi, the architect) and the true reasons for its creation are obscured. Architecture as a myth lands on the Earth 'delivered by a stork' rather than being the result of a painful 'birth giving',[17] she laments. Here lies its miraculous origin, its divine substance.

At first glance, we may glimpse theories of alienation and commodity fetishism in these words, but a closer look reveals no trace of reference to the capitalist mode of production as a possible cause of this separation. Lonzi replaces 'capitalism' with 'dominant culture', as if domination were not entwined with class disparity. Her focus is often too narrowly centred on gender, failing to grasp its imbrications with capitalism. Still, as I will argue, if reassessed with a critical eye and a broader conceptual framework, there is something that Marxists can learn from her analysis of the architect's mythology.

We started, through Lonzi, by exploring how modernist architects constructed their own mythical personas, but we soon veered into a different direction, and ended up discussing the mythical status of architecture itself as portrayed in the treatises of modernist architects. I want to place emphasis on this drifting, since as I will explain shortly, it represents the most innovative aspect of Lonzi's understanding of the mechanics undergirding the fabrication of the architect-mythology. Before proceeding, however, I want to briefly explore a different yet closely related area of inquiry that inspires Lonzi's analysis: the history of the (male) artist genius and its feminist critique.

The artist and the architect

Art history and aesthetics have long championed the concept of the artist's genius, as testified by their seminal texts. The sixteenth-century *The Lives of the Artists*, among the oldest art historical treatises, presents a biographical narrative of those Giorgio Vasari deemed the most exceptional painters, sculptors and architects of his time. Centuries later, Kant's philosophical work solidified this narrative, establishing the connection between genius and the work of art: 'Genius', he writes in *The Third Critique*, 'is the talent (natural endowment) that gives the rule to art'.[18] Or, to put it otherwise, the individual will of the creator is the *sole* determinant of the form and content of an artefact. Building upon these foundations, modern art history perpetuated the myth of the autonomous creator, insulating itself from efforts to situate artistic practice within broader contexts of production and social relations.
There is a crucial oversight in this brief overview: the revered figure of the artist was unquestionably *male*, like all other heroes, until feminism offered a new historical perspective. If it is true that Marx and Engels tried to ground the labour of artists within a fabric of social relations constraining their creative autonomy, it wasn't until the 1970s and 1980s that critiques of the mystique surrounding artistic labour began considering gender and broadened their scope to encompass diverse cultural discourses and practices. This critical effort was advanced by a generation of scholars and activists, with Griselda Pollock making particularly insightful contributions to the field.[19] Her work on Vincent Van Gogh remains essential for a more detailed understanding of the discursive structures through which the discipline of art history constructs 'an artistic subject for works of art'.[20] This specific dynamic, where the artist becomes the ultimate signifier, is well encapsulated in the following sentence: 'Art and the artist become reflexive, mystically bound into

an unbreakable circuit which produces the artist as the subject of the art work and the art work as the means of contemplative access to that subject's "transcendent" and creative subjectivity.'[21]

There is, however, another feminist theorist much closer to Marta Lonzi whose work arrives at similar conclusions. This is her older sister Carla, an established critic in the 1960s Italian art scene, known for her resolute decision to leave her profession and embrace a new feminist life.[22] Carla Lonzi's theoretical contributions result from a tortuous professional and intellectual journey, rendering her written interventions particularly vivid but perhaps less coherent than Pollock's. For this reason, in exploring how Marta Lonzi addresses the myth of the modernist architect in relation to her sister's analysis of the artist, I wish to bear in mind Pollock's lesson about the concealment of the material conditions of artistic practice on which the ideology of the genius rests.

Carla Lonzi looms large in Marta's book. In the first part of *The Architect at Variance with Himself*, Marta briefly retraces her sister's decision to leave the artworld for feminism, and recalls the moment she joined her collective as 'the event that changed [her] life'.[23] Besides Carla, another woman is evoked in association to that experience: artist Carla Accardi. I emphasise her exclusive references to two women involved in the arts, as this suggests a centrality of the figure of artist, and the extant debates about his social role, in her attempt at reconsidering the image of the modernist architect. This assumption seems further confirmed by her mention of Carla's experimental book *Self-Portrait* (1969), an investigation into artists' modes of living and working. *Autoritratto* marks Carla Lonzi's first attempt to disengage from her role as a critic by allying with what she regarded at the time as the much more 'authentic' figure of the artist.

There is indeed more to say about this milestone book, but in the context of this chapter, I will limit the focus to Marta's reference. Her emphasis lies not so much on her sister's initial idealisation of the artist's exceptional subjectivity, but rather on her later disappointment.[24] Only a few years after its release, Carla Lonzi would reassess *Autoritratto* with a new feminist consciousness, shedding light on the exploitative logics which defines the figure of the artist.

Although more implicit in its approach, the text addresses the same ideological concealment discussed by Pollock, while emphasizing the role played by the female spectator in this dynamic. Whereas Pollock examines how the figure of the 'artist-genius' reframes the work of art as a manifestation of his unique individuality, Lonzi argues that the establishment of this very figure implicitly assumes the presence of a non-exceptional, less creative counterpart: the woman-spectator. The existence of the modern artist rests on a clear division between creative and uncreative labour, mirrored by a separation in the realm of artistic consumption and vision between the observer and the subject being observed. From two slightly different yet complementary perspectives, both Pollock's and Lonzi's studies shed light on the artist's ideological function in detaching artistic practices from their broader context of production and gendered social relations.

Marta finds her sister's later critique of the artist 'comforting',[25] as it helps her understand the disappointment stemming from her architectural collaborations with the 'masters' of the discipline. She shares with Carla a sense of estrangement from her professional milieu and its key figures, but she perceives subtle differences in the ways the myths of the artist and the architect are manifested. To better grasp this distinction, we need to revisit the statements of modernist architects that Marta Lonzi quotes in her book. As previously mentioned, these excerpts reveal the architects' attempt to elevate their profession to a divine status. Their words endow architecture with a quasi-autonomous agency, likening it to a holy spirit serving the universal needs of humankind. In examining these statements, Lonzi seems to allude to the way artists define their personal work and profession, as reported in her sister Carla's *Self-Portrait.*

It is precisely this comparative approach – gained partly through her proximity to her sister's work as an art critic and partly through her shared feminist experience with artist Carla Accardi – that allows Lonzi to grasp a distinction in the triangulation between the creative subject, the artefact, and the divine attribute. While the artist seems to openly embrace the socially constructed role of the unique creative subject, the architect appears more inclined to project this exceptional status onto the object itself. For Lonzi this is not an act of modesty but rather the result of a different position within the division of labour. While modernity has granted art and the artist an autonomous status, it has left the architect deeply entangled in the harsh realities of capitalist relations, and curbed his space of manoeuvre. 'Unlike the artist …', says Lonzi, 'Architecture has a specific recipient: the client, to whom he can't say "I'm divine", but "my architecture is divine".' 'In the first instance' she adds 'he would lose him, while in the second one he captures him, turning him into the accomplice of an omnipotent idea.'[26]

As the above sentences clarify, the shift in focus from subject to object is not a materialist turn. Instead, the object becomes an abstraction, or, as Lonzi puts it, a 'substitution'. The 'reflexive, mystic and unbreakable' circuit connecting creator and artefact exposed by Pollock, remains largely intact, but is now more insidious, less easy to detect. Albeit architects may not enjoy the same privileges as artists, they still seek a comparable autonomous status, using various subterfuges to enhance their position while preserving their commercial appeal.

'An idea born out of an idea'

Lonzi's critique of the 'architect' develops through two distinct experiences and contexts: her professional practice, particularly her early collaborations with Quaroni, and her work as a voluntary assistant at the University of Rome. It is to the latter that she primarily refers in her book, as it provides her with a privileged vantage point into the architect's upbringing and the specific mentoring role played by the 'fathers' of the discipline in Italian academia. Unlike Tafuri, Lonzi's return to university in 1973 is detached from any aspirations for an academic career – at that time, she is actively working as an architect and raising her three children. Her interest lies instead in observing the students' design process, specifically the very early phase that precedes ideation, and in the various ways this phase could be expressed and discussed in class. Recalling this experience, she writes: 'Discussions with students, with their blank sheets of paper to transform into projects, were exactly what interested me and what I wanted to clarify.'[27]

Lonzi's fascination with the 'degree zero' of the project seems aligned to her interest in consciousness-raising, a practice that involved reaching a 'degree zero' of the self, a new unexpected subjectivity that had remained buried under layers of societal expectations. But this same fascination with the origin was also a reaction to universities' canonisation of design methods that prioritise project development over the analysis of foundational premises. This complex relationship is articulated in the following sentence: 'It was not easy to pinpoint this, nor to subject it to the investigation I was interested in, as the transition from nothing to the idea was not recognised as a fundamental step in design. Instead, it was seen as a leap into the void, suddenly [the project] would appear.'[28]

After presenting a general critique, Lonzi delves into a detailed description of the design process as taught in 1960s Italian architectural faculties, highlighting its blind spots and their consequences for the designer's creative development. In her account, the project develops through two phases. The first phase, named preliminary research, involves the collection of data and gathering of samples to frame the brief, both methodologically and formally. For Lonzi, however, this research is not guided by specific criteria, but by pure data hoarding, turning the whole process into an 'exhausting endeavour' whose 'termination happens almost by chance and likely for quantitative reasons'.[29] Following the research phase is the ideation part, which Lonzi critiques just as starkly, reframing it as 'looting' existing models and styles. The term 'looting' (*saccheggio*) is crucial here, as it implies an uncritical appropriation of samples from the past and present, replacing critical engagement with obedient adherence to the discipline and its lineage. This 'learning by following' approach, she concludes, is reinforced by the entire professorial class, whose role is limited to 'steering the students' preferences towards a [Louis] Kahn rather than a [Saverio] Muratori'.[30]

Lonzi takes a resolute distance from the kind of pedagogy that occludes the possibility of examining how research morphs into projects and instead imposes an idea of design as a self-generating, circular activity where 'an idea is always already born, no one knows how, from another idea'.[31] Having suffered under this approach as a student, she is dismayed to witness it being imposed once again on a new generation of architects. In response, she decides to peruse 'the interval of thought that occurs before the project'; 'an 'interval', she adds, that 'the architect conceives but fails to recognise'.[32] Her gaze turns to the blind spot of the architect's *consciousness.*

Her interest lies not in the architect per se, despite his persona being the target of her critical analysis in the book's inaugural part, nor in the architectural artefact in its finished form. Instead, she focuses on what ties the former to the latter: 'the relationship', as she terms it, using the lexicon of consciousness-raising. Lonzi's endeavour goes beyond reinterpreting architects' writings through a feminist lens. Her stakes are higher. She wants to transpose her feminist experience into both architectural pedagogy and practice. Midway through her book, we read her posing a series of rhetorical questions to the architect – 'Why design?' 'Niemeyer, where are you? What do you experience? What do you understand?'[33] – in an effort to uncover a subjectivity often hidden behind a reassuring social role and ultimately *at variance* with his inner self. Architects are imaginatively drawn into a consciousness-raising session and questioned about the more recondite aspects of their creative journey.

At first glance, some of Marta Lonzi's propositions may seem aligned with processes of subjectification within neoliberal societies, a phenomenon paralleled by an affective turn in architectural practices and theories. These trends have received insightful criticism from various Marxist quarters, which highlight how the emphasis on the emotive and affective effaces the possibility of a 'passionate form of reasoning', reinstating a Cartesian dualism between mind and body.[34] Such a critique holds some validity and, to some extent, applies to Lonzi's texts, especially when they place too much faith in a true creative self as opposed to a public and institutional persona. Nonetheless, her criticism was not aimed at affirming the presumed authenticity of the creative individual but at illuminating the relationship between the designing subject and the architectural object, a relationship that has become, in her view, increasingly opaque.

Indeed, the origin and meaning of the term 'relationship' here diverge significantly from the Marxian 'relations of production'. There is little of the coercive aspect Marx had in mind when he coined this definition. For Lonzi, a relationship is the result of a choice, not a necessary condition under which people must operate to survive within capitalist societies. Despite this, Lonzi's attempt to transpose consciousness-raising to the field of architecture – by interrogating the design process and its transmission or codification – succeeds in unveiling the discipline's materialist shortfall. A shortfall aptly encapsulated in her quip about buildings being 'delivered by a stork' rather than resulting from the painful process of 'birth giving'. The stork stands here for a mythical origin that obscures the real reasons, processes and beneficiaries of architectural design.

We can also relate her endeavour to a critique of late modernist design. By the 1970s, the decade in which Lonzi began drafting the thoughts that would culminate in her book, the utopian spirit of modernist architecture had run out of steam, and its early precepts appeared increasingly dogmatic. Lonzi's call for a return to the incipient moment of the design project sounds like a wake-up call for her colleagues, who cling to the carcass of modernist design, retaining its rules while discarding its ideals. No longer shared and lived scripts, methods have become, for Lonzi, artifices to justify, a posteriori, the necessity of one's own project, leaving no room for critique. This is why, while she devotes her attention to the 'origin' of the project, she announces that she will bracket its afterlife, or, better, 'what the architect says after [the project's completion]'.[35]

This is, however, a *faux* promise, since Lonzi's 1982 work is largely a close reading of what architects have to say about their own and their colleagues' designs once these projects enter the world. The book can also be regarded as a literary analysis of the architects' texts: a mapping of recurring terms, expressions and figures of speech. This endeavour leaves Lonzi at a loss in front of the plethora of what she calls 'castrating periphrasis'[36] – circumlocutory speeches that expose architects' tendency to evade the core of the matter and avoid naming things for what they truly are. Her scrutiny contains the germ of a critique of specialised languages and their gendered nature, a field addressed in the same years by other practitioners like Matrix. Yet, while Matrix focused on the gendered and middle-class nature of professional codes,

Lonzi examines the values informing the texts produced *ex-post* and explores how these texts helped maintain the discipline's borders intact.

Tafuri, again

We began by recounting Lonzi's fallout with her mentor Quaroni and juxtaposing it with the successful academic trajectory of her peer Manfredo Tafuri. There is no mention of this contrasting story in Lonzi's 1982 book, yet Tafuri's name does appear at the very end – and not for favourable reasons. Tafuri is widely regarded in architectural history as the epitome of critique, as the best representative of non-dogmatic Marxism and the starkest opponent of 'operative history'. However, in the final chapter of *The Architect at Variance with Himself*, Lonzi challenges this image, presenting him in a markedly different light. Here she stages an imaginary polemic, quoting and commenting on lengthy excerpts from his well-known works *Theories and History* and *The Sphere and the Labyrinth*. She focuses on passages that best reveal Tafuri's vigorous judgements – both positive and negative – towards notable figures in postwar architecture. On the positive side, she highlights Aldo Rossi, a well-known Tafurian favourite; on the negative side are Kahn, Venturi, Samonà, Copcutt, and Stirling. Lonzi first critiques Tafuri's analysis of Venturi's ambiguity and historical subjectivism, then challenges his unconditional endorsement of Rossi's retreat to pure forms.

There are evident limitations to Lonzi's position. Her critique of Tafuri's view of Venturi overlooks the broader context: the critique of postmodernist architecture and its alignment with the existing economic-political models. Tafuri skilfully identified the opportunism often disguised as radicalism in many postmodernist proponents, and he challenged Venturi's ambiguity as a viable alternative to the constraints of modernist principles. However, Lonzi's aim was not merely to defend Venturi's position against Tafuri's critique. This becomes evident a few pages later in the chapter, when her initial enthusiasm for the postmodern icon is tempered by several critical remarks. More than the content of the dispute – namely, the viability of ambiguity and contradiction as design principles – Lonzi is interested in the different modes of address employed by the two architects. The narrative voice in Venturi's *Complexity and Contradiction in Architecture* (1966) contrasts with what she calls the 'obscuration of the I' in Tafuri's response. This difference can be attributed to the distinct purposes the two texts serve: while *Complexity and Contradiction* supports Venturi's architectural practice, Tafuri's *The Sphere and the Labyrinth* is purely a work of criticism. Yet, Lonzi seems to argue, this is rational distinction as much as it is a smokescreen. 'Does Tafuri really believe that his historicisation is free from this limitation (of subjective bias) and that the Theory of Art or History are not also the versions of those who produce them?', she asks.[37]

It's tempting to interpret Lonzi's rhetorical question as a full capitulation to modern grand narratives and a defence of subjectivism as a repository of truth, but once again, we must be careful not to throw the baby out with the bathwater. Her polemic exposes the fragility of any Marxist criticism and history that refuses to acknowledge its epistemic limits, thereby turning into a self-validating discourse. Of course, these limits are not intentionally set by the subject; rather, the subject is a complex space where numerous biases converge, making it into a cog in the machine of 'perfect vision'. While Lonzi may not fully share this perspective, she does help reveal that what may have been perceived as Tafuri's uncompromising stance is also a universalising one.

Coda

Marta Lonzi published another book, *Authenticity and Project*, in 2006, a couple of years before she died.[38] By then, Lonzi had established herself as a professional working on projects of various scales, from urban planning to product design. Consequently, the cover of the book reflects less of a polemical stance – there are no attacks on modernist icons – and more of a desire to showcase Lonzi's own contributions to the field. Beneath the title, the cover features plans and a maquette of a museum project designed by Lonzi for the municipality of Rome. The inside of the book aligns with its exterior in its chosen feminist perspective on the architectural project, as testified by the core chapter, titled 'What is creating for a woman?' Here, Lonzi maintains her focus on architects' texts, but this time the selection includes female representatives of the modernist movement: Eileen Gray and Margarete Schütte-Lihotzky, in particular. We read Lihotzky wishing her kitchen to be a place for living, besides working, and Gray speaking of her project for a domestic interior as a space of imperfection, where problems are never fully solved. In another excerpt, Gray engages in a polemical discussion against the common interpretation of 'type' in architectural discourse. While for many, 'type' is seen as a simplified version of an object to be endlessly replicated, Gray argues that a type is optimal only within the specific context in which it is realised and must be adapted to concrete conditions. Lonzi's research into the writings of female designers associated with the modernist movement reveals their hesitations and struggles to fully adhere to its abstract precepts. The myth of the *machine-à-habiter* finally cracks, like the cover image of her first book had foretold.

Notes

1 Marta Lonzi's Archive, Fondazione Elvira Badaracco, Milan. Visited in April 2024.

2 Among the secondary literature on Quaroni in English language see *Ludovico Quaroni 1911–1987*, P. Ciorra (ed.) (Milan: Electa, 1987).

3 Marta Lonzi's Archive, Fondazione Elvira Badaracco. Visited in April 2024.

4 Manfredo Tafuri, *Ludovico Quaroni e lo sviluppo dell'architettura moderna in Italia* (Milan: Edizioni di Comunità, 1964).

5 Andrew Leach, *Manfredo Tafuri. Choosing History* (Ghent: A&S Books: 2007), 22.

6 Marta Lonzi, *L'architetto fuori di sé* (Milan: Prototipi, 1982).

7 For a historiographical account of 'feminism of difference' in the Italian context, see F. Restaino, *Il pensiero femminista. Una storia possibile*. In A. Cavarero, F. Restaino (eds.), *Le filosofie femministe* (Milan, Bruno Mondadori, 2002), 3–77.

8 I implicitly refer, here, to the work of the British collective Matrix and of the American historian Dolores Hayden.

9 Rivolta Femminile was the name of a separatist collective founded by Marta Lonzi's sister, Carla in 1970. For an analysis of the political work and feminist philosophy of the collective, consider Jamila Mascat, Leaving and Living: Mascat, J. (2023). Carla Lonzi. Leaving and Living: Mascat, J. M. H. (2023). Leaving and Living. In L. L. Corna, & J. M. H. Mascat (Eds.), *Carla Lonzi, Feminism in Revolt: An Anthology* (pp. 101–132). Seagull Books.

10 For an analysis of Le Corbusier's relation to his photographic portraiture consider: Klaus Spechtenhauser, 'Snapshots and Poses: Le Corbusier in Photographs' in Nathalie Herschdorfer, Lada Umstätter (eds.) *Le Corbusier and the Power of Photography* (Ashgate: Farnham, 2013).

11 There is indeed literature addressing the profession of the architect, but it primarily focuses on its position between the humanities and sciences rather than through a feminist lens. Among the most recent publications on the theme, albeit not translated into English, consider: Marco Biraghi, *L'architetto come intellettuale* (Turin: Einaudi, 2019).

12 Lonzi, *L'architetto fuori di sé*, 124.

13 Wagner in Lonzi, *L'architetto fuori di sé*, 68.

14 Wright in Ibid., 73.

15 Breuer in Ibid., 73.

16 I say this as Lonzi's sister Lidia is the translator of the first Italian edition of Barthes' *Mythologies*, and her other sister, the art critic Carla Lonzi, makes extensive use of the term in her critique of the artist and the notion of artistic creativity. Therefore, although the choice of the term "myth" is not accidental and bears resonance to Barthes's usage, there is no evidence of a proper engagement with his complex semiotic theory

17 M. Lonzi, *L'architetto fuori di sé*, 20.

18 Immanuel Kant, *The Critique of Judgment* (1790) (Indianapolis: Hackett Publishing Company, 1987, 1790), 307.

19 Linda Nochlin's academic contribution to the theme should be mentioned here, though her analysis focuses more on how the figure of the male artist blocks women's access to art, rather than on the discourses and institutions that contribute to establishing the ideology of the artist genius. Linda Nochlin, 'Why Have There Been no Great Women Artists? *ARTnews*, vol. 69, no. 9, (1971), 22–39 and 67–71.

20 Griselda Pollock, 'Artists, Mythologies and Media – Genius, Madness and Art History', *Screen*, vol. 21, no. 3, Autumn 1980 59.

21 Ibid., 59.

22 On Lonzi see L. L. Corna, J. Mascat, *Feminism in Revolt*.

23 M. Lonzi, *L'architetto fuori di sé*, 26.

24 In this regard, it may be worth referring to a passage from Lonzi's diary where the disappointment towards the artist is associated with his mythological status. There we read: 'The artist is burdened with too much myth', Carla Lonzi, *Taci. Anzi Parla* (Milan: Prototipi, 1978), 378. For a more extended critique of the artist's complicity with the status quo and his myth, consider instead Carla Lonzi, *Assenza della donna dai momenti* celebrativi *della* manifestazione creativa maschile (Milan: Prototipi, 1972).

25 M. Lonzi, *L'architetto fuori di sé*, 30.

26 Ibid., 73.

27 Ibid., 31.

28 Ibid., 31.

29 Ibid., 31.

30 Ibid., 38. Saverio Muratori (1910–1973) was an Italian architect and educator. He is considered the founder of the Italian morphology school.

31 Ibid., 38.

32 Ibid., 16.

33 Ibid., 66.

34 See in particular Douglas Spencer, *The Architecture of Neoliberalism: How Contemporary Architecture Became an Instrument of Control and Compliance* (London: Bloomsbury, 2016). Also by Spencer and Peg Rawes 'Material and Rational Feminisms: A Contribution to Humane Architectures', Hélène Frichot, Catharina Gabrielsson, Helen Runting (eds), *Architecture* and *Feminisms, Ecologies, Economies, Technologies (London: Routledge, 2017).*

35 M. Lonzi, *L'architetto fuori di sé*, 16.

36 Ibid., 21.

37 Ibid., 148.

38 Marta Lonzi, *Autenticità e Progetto* (Milan: Jaca Book, 2006).

Section 4
Building the Racial Regime of Modernity

Chapter 9
Policing the Crisis: Locating the Urban in British Cultural Studies

Nick Beech

In this chapter I argue that *Policing the Crisis: Mugging, the State and Law and Order*, written by Stuart Hall and his students – Chas Critcher, Tony Jefferson, John Clarke and Brian Roberts – at the Centre for Contemporary Cultural Studies (CCCS) in the 1970s, provides a form of urban study that can make a significant contribution to the architectural history of mid-twentieth century Britain.[1] *Policing the Crisis* provides us with a means to respond to a series of questions that continue to trouble historians of architecture and urbanism.[2] These pertain to the *ideological* determinants of urban change in post-Second World War welfare states: what 'notion[s] of the city', were operative in the period from the mid-1940s through to the late-1970s; what '*picture[s] of the collective*' were produced, which urban planners and architects were responsive to? And what were the consequences of 'decolonisation' and 'notions of emancipation reliant upon the existence of a non-emancipated class ... the members of western European states' former colonies' for these ideologies?[3]

A twin danger exists in the formulation of responses to these two questions. One is that the first question of the ideological is reduced to a superstructural and epiphenomenal 'reaction' or 'expression' of the deeper socio-economic social relations (of colonialism and decolonisation, and of the struggle between social classes constituted in that process). A second danger (more typical in architectural discourse) is to respond to these questions descriptively or functionally: either presenting design and planning ideology as a discrete, differentiated practice/discourse with its own logic, range of action and history; or trying to explicate a practice/discourse 'reacting' to external forces or pressures. What *Policing the Crisis* offers is a form of analysis ('conjunctural analysis'), that can situate the specific ideologies of design and planning in broader ideologies and practices of social reproduction (in particular mass media, policing, the justice system and political ideology) showing how design and planning were already implicated in programmes of colonisation and class struggle, without reducing them to the same.

For many architectural and planning historians, answering the above questions has meant demonstrating the continuities of modernism with earlier planning and design paradigms; showing how the 'mixed economy' of the 1950s and 1960s was in fact dominated by private developer/consumer market imperatives; arguing for the dynamism and continuing relevance of modernist planning and architecture beyond the mid-1960s; and identifying the contradictions within the urban and architectural projects of the period, resulting from a failure to recognise the reconstitution of Britain following deindustrialisation and decolonisation.

In his history of modernist urban planning in Bradford, Simon Gunn, for example, has highlighted the consequences of immigration policy, and the emergence of 'planning from below' produced by the new Asian communities of the 1960s – the informal, but sophisticated re-organisation of urban life:

> In the corner shops, cafes, mosques, temples, and cinemas, which gave Pakistani and Indian populations a permanent presence in the urban landscape [of Bradford] for the first time during the 1960s.[4]

It was, Gunn argues, developments like these that resulted in the 'emergence of the "inner city",' as a term 'introduced into circulation by the Local Government Act of 1966' that reconstituted 'such populations as a significant social problem'.[5] It was this phenomenon, and a parallel process of deindustrialisation, which damaged confidence in a prior modernist project for Bradford, dominated by technological and functionalist ideological motives. A great deal is gained as a result of this account, foregrounding the role of decolonisation and post-imperial migration, the dominance of commercial interests and the role of 'declinism' as an ideology, resetting the terms on which the architecture and planning of the period are given – critically, expanding the category of architecture itself, to include non-designed elements of urban life.

Nevertheless, the ideology of planning and design, and indeed the material discourse of the same, remains 'sealed off' from the wider set of social practices identified as operative; the highly suggestive 'planning from below' remains a negative 'outside' to the official planning practices of the state; 'inner city' policy – initially a policy of population dispersal followed by 'ghettoisation'[6] – is treated as strictly parallel to urban design and planning; planning ideology and discourse is assessed as inadequate to, rather than implicated in or conditioned by, either colonial or decolonial practices in the metropole. Though rarely, if ever, directly engaging with urban design and planning, the work of the CCCS in the 1970s offers a model of Marxist analysis that might enable an integrative, non-reductive, explanatory framework for this period, in the process, fleshing out some answers to the questions posed at the beginning – what 'image' of the city, and the people, were urban and architectural designers responding to? What were the consequences of 'notions of emancipation reliant upon the existence of a non-emancipated class' drawn from former colonies, on such images?

Origins of *Policing the Crisis*

Policing the Crisis was a product of the CCCS at the University of Birmingham. Founded by Richard Hoggart in 1964, the Centre was small – the faculty amounted to Hoggart as Director, and Stuart Hall as Research Fellow – and marginal. Though attached to the English Department, and encouraged to engage in a dialogue with the Department of Sociology, the methods, working practices and objects of study at the CCCS were strongly resisted by established disciplines in both the humanities and social sciences.[7] Hoggart understood the project of the Centre to be a continuation of his work published as *The Uses of Literacy* in 1958 – a project of left-Leavisite criticism, scrutinising popular arts and mass media and discriminating between material that subordinated working-class cultures and practices and material that enabled reproduction and extension of the same.[8] *The Uses of Literacy* comes to very similar conclusions as the contemporaneous study, *Family and Kinship in the East End*, by Michael Young and Peter Willmott.[9] While Young and Willmott deployed a method of survey and interview through research assistants,

Hoggart developed a form of auto-ethnography, drawing on his own experience growing up in a working-class community in Leeds. Both works identify extended kinship networks that operated in and through social lives that were sustained in urban forms – markets, streets, clubs, pubs, music halls – threatened by modernisation. Both argued that British working-class culture was vulnerable to fragmentation through slum clearance and council housing schemes and the reorganisation of landscapes with the introduction of major infrastructural works and decanting to new towns. Hoggart additionally read mass culture as dominated by – increasingly America – commercial values that were strictly contrary to the values and motives of working-class cultures in Britain. Unlike the Leavisites, Hoggart understood that cultural artefacts (whether poems of the canon or copy for newspaper columns) were transformed by readers or audiences in their reception. The purpose of cultural studies was to interpret the processes of cultural change that resulted from this complex process.[10]

Though a great deal is shared between them, the basic assumptions from which Hall's work develops can be contrasted to Hoggart's. Hall's own formation was manifestly different from Hoggart's, a colonial formation in Kingston, Jamaica, of the 'brown middle-class', saturated with the culture of English imperialism, but whose texture of life (landscape, inhabitation, rhythms of life and speech) could not be more different to industrial urban England.[11] As with many other members of the Caribbean diaspora in the period – that generation of West Indian writers which includes George Lamming, Andrew Salkey, and Sam Selvon, as well as earlier figures such as C.L.R. James – Hall was sensitive to the landscape he encountered in England. The contradictory condition of recognising so many of the landmarks and make-up of metropolitan life – the result of a colonial education – while confronting the profound alienation produced by the distinct form of racialisation, class and gender relations in the metropole, all further conditioned by an ambivalent relationship to migration, meant that Hall and these other writers consistently registered and explicated the dynamism and transformations of modern urban life in their works.[12] These experiences conditioned Hall's engagement with Marxist concepts and categories, as well as political praxis – not least, the problems of class formation and class-consciousness, the formation and reproduction of the capitalist (and imperialist) state, ideology and race.

As an active, leading intellectual figure in the New Left of the 1950s and 1960s, Hall had paid particular attention to the housing conditions of working-class migrants in London, as he did later in Birmingham.[13] He was responsive to the Notting Hill race riots of 1958, alerted to them by his pupils (Hall was then working as a supply teacher in a secondary modern in south London) travelling by bus to participate in the violence.[14] Working with George Clark (a fellow New Left and CND campaigner), Hall recognised the deeper problems of housing, welfare and cultural provision that were racialised by the radical right, and exacerbated by 'the short-sighted and temporising policies of local council planners and builders'.[15]

Later, Hall would contribute to discussions with Gus John, responding to his report for the Runnymede Trust published as *Race in the Inner City* (1970), and the subsequent formation of the Harambee Project, established to provide facilities for African Caribbean families in the Handsworth area of Birmingham.[16] Throughout these and related engagements, Hall identified how the experience of urban life was undergoing radical transformation under twin pressures from 'above' (through developer- and state-led modernisation) and 'below' (through the transformation of community life resulting from mass migration), both of which were heavily mediated through newspapers, radio, television, cinema and popular music.[17]

As such, Hall's experience of urban Britain radically diverged from Hoggart's. Where the latter began analysis from a conception of an organic community of working-class life, beleaguered by commercial culture, but able to fashion coherent responses through communitarian institutions and moral codes, Hall was alert to the already mediated, contradictory and unstable conditions of working-class consciousness, undergoing radical transformation. This resulted in a challenge by Hall to Hoggart, but also to fellow leading intellectuals of the New Left and emergent cultural studies – E.P. Thompson and Raymond Williams – on the grounds that, despite their wide political and intellectual divergences, they all shared a specific humanist problematic that could not resolve itself.

There was both a theoretical problem – of the limits of what Hall would later refer to as a 'culturalist' project – and practical, political problems generated by a succession of new social movements, including the student movement, Women's Liberation, national liberation movements, Black Power and Gay Liberation. As a result of these problems, Hall initiated and embraced a programme of theoretical innovation at the CCCS – engaging the works of continental theory, including Frankfurt School critique (particularly Theodor Adorno, Walter Benjamin, Herbert Marcuse and Wilhelm Reich), and French structuralist anthropologists and semioticians.[18] Hall's paper 'Encoding and Decoding in the Television Discourse', developed from 1968 and eventually published in 1973, has become the classic reference of this period of work.[19]

However, this moment, from 1968, is also marked by a deep engagement with the work of Marx (particularly *The Eighteenth Brumaire*, and the recently translated *Grundrisse*) and in quick succession, the works of Louis Althusser and Antonio Gramsci.[20] It was Hall's wager, that a set of theoretical tools could be fashioned from Marxism, that could successfully challenge the organicist, humanist and historicist approaches to culture that cultural studies had inherited. The location of culture within a social totality, its relationship to the economic, the relation of consciousness to social relations and material practices, the identification of determining and dominant forces and structuration, the necessity of theory and abstraction in order to interpret and intervene politically, these and concomitant questions were elucidated through exegetical work on Marx, Althusser and Gramsci, published over the course of the 1970s.[21] These readings were conducted in relation to practical research of cultural phenomena and following confrontation with the major disciplinary paradigms that produced theories of 'culture' in the period – English literature, anthropology, and sociology. The result – 'conjunctural analysis' – retains the central features of classical Marxist concern (class struggle, mode of production, forces and social relations of production, 'economic base and institutional and ideological superstructures') complicated by Marx and Engels's own commentaries and historico-political analyses, as well as later neo-Marxist developments.

In particular, conjunctural analysis drew on Althusser's psychoanalytically informed concept of 'overdetermination' and its subsidiaries 'condensation' and 'displacement' to replace both reductive causal determination (the 'economic base' determining the 'superstructures') or humanist or historicist notions of organic holism/expressive totality. The key term in conjunctural analysis – 'articulation' – again an adaptation from Althusser, identifies the moments at which configurations of internally differentiated social formations (both within and between 'base' and 'superstructural' levels) are determined by one or other element of that complex structure. The advantage of 'articulation' is that, as a term, it signals the contingent, forceful and transformative 'bringing together' of elements that might otherwise remain autonomous.

The adaptation and elaboration of Althusserian concepts and categories conducted at the CCCS was conditioned by the simultaneous reading of the Italian communist Antonio Gramsci. Gramsci provided Hall with a means to counter the hardening of Althusser's structuralism (evident, Hall argued, in *Reading Capital*, and the essay 'Ideology and Ideological State Apparatuses' in particular) and enriching of analytical vocabulary. In particular, Hall recognised Gramsci as operating at a 'lower level of abstraction' – closer to the political analyses of class fractions, cultural and political institutional specificity and historical contingency, of *The Eighteenth Brumaire* than the epochal analysis of modes of production (ancient, feudal, capitalist) of *Capital*. Hall's conceptions of ideology, the State, political praxis and 'conjuncture' itself, owe more to Gramsci than any other Marxist. Larry Grossberg has referred to this approach as a 'radical contextualism',[22] as Hall himself put it in the second edition preface of *Policing the Crisis*:

> In the *Grundrisse* Marx argues that the only way to produce 'the concrete by way of thought' is to add more determinations: 'the concrete is concrete because it is the concentration of many determinations'. Contextualising is thus not the invocation of an inert 'background' but involves treating these articulated processes as a real movement through time and identifying, in their historical specificity, the links between the different levels of abstraction.[23]

Beyond the obvious problems of compression and a failure to fully elaborate a complex theoretical practice, the above summary fails to do justice to conjunctural analysis for the singular reason that it was not elaborated theoretically: work at the CCCS was produced out of empirical research. While Hall's extensive writing on Marxism is, then, useful, it is in the concrete analyses offered in *Policing the Crisis* itself that the theory is most fully elaborated.

Making *Policing the Crisis*

Produced over five years, between 1973 and 1978 *Policing the Crisis* was a product of the 'Subcultures' research group at the Centre. This group was engaged in extensive analysis of 'youth subcultures' – mods, rockers, skinheads – both as they understood themselves (made evident through ethnographic studies) and as represented in media and various institutions and state apparatuses.[24] Hall's interest in subcultures can be traced back to the late-1950s when he identified, in the 'mod' and 'Teddy Boy' subcultures of London, distinct shifts in the conditions of class-consciousness.[25] Other than Hall, the members of the Subcultures Group were graduate students, nominally conducting research for their doctoral theses. Chas Critcher was involved in a 'neighbourhood action group' at 40 Hall Road, Handsworth, Birmingham, offering

> Not only help but the potential to organise and have access to an understanding of how and why Handsworth was like it was. This was more easily expressed when later we rented a small shop. The large window display was used to analyse local issues: the power utilities, Social Security, housing, police brutality.[26]

Such community action groups had emerged in the late 1960s and early 1970s, often consisting of graduate student volunteers. The rapid increase in social services that were highly bureaucratic in delivery, and driven toward professionalism, generated a barrier to those communities they were supposed to serve. Community action was a means, not to 'bridge' the space between state and community, but to mobilise the community politically, to demand rights, resources and outcomes.[27] Critcher brought the CCCS's attention to bear upon the topic of 'mugging'. Three young men from Handsworth, of Afro-Caribbean and Asian heritage, had been sentenced for a 'mugging gone wrong' – one boy, Paul Storey, for twenty years. The sentences were devastating for the boys, for their parents, and generated shockwaves in the community with which Critcher worked. The Subcultures Group sought to understand what had happened.

As *Policing the Crisis* repeatedly states, the book is both about 'mugging – a particular form of street crime, associated with small gangs of young men who violently rob their victims, often for very little gain – and also *not* about 'mugging', in that the authors were not interested in making sense of 'mugging' as the product of individual motivations and actions, or in terms of given norms of crime, morality or the consequences for victims. Instead, 'mugging' was read as an overdetermined 'moment', produced out of a range of social institutional, political and ideological conditions – primarily newspapers, the justice system, policing itself, political and cultural ideologies, and the labour market. In the end, after five years of research, the authors had come to understand 'mugging' as symptomatic of British society experiencing a 'conjunctural crisis', with profound transformations in ideology, politics and economy.

If *Policing the Crisis* is 'not about' the street crime of 'mugging', it certainly isn't about 'urbanism'. Nevertheless, within it we can identify a sharp critique of urban environments and inhabitation. In his 2013 second edition preface, Hall argues that they had to 'contextualise' mugging to understand it, progressively 'widening the frame' from the crime itself, to the media representation of it, to the police, the judiciary, and up on through finally to political economy itself. I argue that *Policing the Crisis* does such work for an understanding of the urban too.

While the term 'urban' is used frequently throughout *Policing the Crisis*, it becomes a specific concept, more or less subject to analysis, in at least six places. In each instance, the urban is registered at a quite different analytical level and, as such, it does very different kinds of work. At one level, the urban operates wholly ideologically – it is constructed within specific discursive domains and articulated with other ideological elements (crime, social or national identity, family and kinship ideals, and so on). At another level, the urban is read as a field within which particular techniques and technologies are deployed – particularly of policing. Finally, the urban operates as a material condition for social reproduction – a means for the contradictory, but successful, division of labour in society to enable the reproduction of capital, achieved by the operations of state apparatuses, both coercive and consensual. It is also at this level that the authors hint at, and ultimately retreat from, a claim for an autonomous fraction of the working class resistant to the logic of capitalist reproduction. In the summary that follows, I provide a sense of both the content of the urban presented in the text and the analytical status of that presentation as this occurs at the three distinct levels.

Ideologies of urban change

We are first introduced to an urban condition when the authors search in British print media for the origin of the term 'mugging' – a word they show at the beginning of the book lacks any empirical specificity but which had, by 1973, come to be mobilised by news media, leading figures in the British police establishment, judges and politicians, in a 'moral panic'. They find its original use in a number of feature articles, written between 1968 and 1969, about the 'urban crisis' in the United States. Correspondents in the British press were relaying first-hand accounts of 'muggings' in thick descriptions about major metropolitan centres across America, that included radical disinvestment in social programmes, infrastructural decay, 'white flight' to the suburbs, and the formation of 'Black ghettos'. As *Policing the Crisis* states, the 'mugging' label mobilised a 'whole referential context, with all its associated meanings and connotations'.[28] This 'fitted well into a whole "structure of attention" in the British media', because of the 'special relationship' forged between Britain and America in the postwar settlement.[29] Though conditioned by 'selective exaggeration', the narrative was one of 'prophecy' and 'parallel'. Thus, the urban crisis of the United States was overtly framed as a peculiar, extravagant and sensational case quite unlike anything happening in Britain. But the narrative smuggled in a suggestion that this spectacular crisis of urban life in America was a portent of a future condition, and at the same time, explanations for that urban crisis that originated in the United States – particularly the framework produced in the Nixon–Agnew 'silent majority', racialised, law and order campaign – were imported wholesale.[30]

As the authors make clear, this was an analysis of an ideological image or representation – the fidelity to any real, material conditions in America was beside the point. What mattered was how the representation of urban crisis, saturated with racialised images of infrastructural decay, violence, crime and social unrest, and the reconfiguration of the urban core and suburban enclave was articulated in an already existing ideological field in Britain. In a later chapter of the book, the authors adumbrate an ideological grid in which social phenomena, such as 'crime', are located and constructed to make them intelligible and to achieve some kind of social consensus. This grid, which is shown to contain distinct class inflections, includes: 'social respectability'; 'work'; 'social discipline'; 'family'; 'nation'; and 'the law'. A seventh element is the 'city', which is, the authors write:

> Above all the concrete embodiment of the achievements of industrial civilisation, both in terms of its embodiment of wealth and as the concentration of the sources of wealth, but also in its history – the conquest of the threats of the city in the nineteenth century: the threats of disease, insanitariness, crime and political unrest.[31]

As such, the 'city' is the ideological bellwether of social development or degeneration. This is registered or inflected differently for bourgeois and working-class communities. The authors infer that for the bourgeois crime statistics, the personal experience of burglaries, accounts of shoplifting, are enough to trigger anxieties about the decay of the 'ideal city'. But, they argue, for working-class communities, the city is not experienced at these simultaneously distanced and personalised (mass/individual) registers. 'The working-class experience of the city is more segmented', they write, 'it is carried in specific and concrete *local* ties and connections ... It is where people live, talk, play, shop and sometimes work – it is their "bit" of the city, to which people are concretely and directly attached.'[32] As such, working-class ideologies of the city are less sensitive to either the abstract impersonal or individual experience of crime of the middle-class, but are highly sensitive to material and social transformations that disrupt patterns and organisations of urban life. These patterns were already weakened if not wholly decomposed by the early-1960s as a result of

> urban redevelopment, changes in the local economies, in the structure of skills and occupations, increased geographical and educational mobility, relative prosperity supported by the postwar recovery boom, and a spectacularised 'religion of affluence'.[33]

These changes resulted in a pervasive sense of cultural 'loss', of 'unsettledness' or 'social anxiety'. It was into this condition that the national and local press inserted the image of American urban crises and a wave of 'street' crime. When the authors begin to look closely at the reporting of 'mugging' in the national and local press, they are able to identify how this ideological framing is already given in advance. Time and again they find in 'the environment' of urban decay, racialised (in many instances orientalised) images, invoked as if these provided an explanation:

> It is estimated that 70% of Handsworth's population are coloured and the area poses Birmingham with its biggest ghetto problem ... Handsworth once housed wealthy industrialists living in well-swept tree-lined streets. The streets are now littered and the children play on demolition sites.[34]

The authors write: 'It is striking that both the *Express* and the *Mail* should have led with such similar evocations of urban decay. It is an image of the city in decline: powerfully descriptive yet without explanatory dimensions.'[35] When the authors critically examine the local, rather than national press, they are able to identify the 'work' that this ideology does: 'explanation' is replaced by an 'ambiguously fused ... visual image' which enables the evacuation of 'structural and cultural determinations' which might otherwise 'occupy the space between environment and crime' – 'urban decay' *stood in for* the breakdown of traditional family and social structures; a chain linking a violent crime, a dramatic judicial response and slum conditions was forged and itself assumed the status of explanation.

This is an analysis of 'displacement' – in which material contradictions, generative of social anxiety are transferred or attached to images, events, narratives, or phenomena, often of a prior ideological origin – and 'condensation', in which disparate phenomena are compressed into an ideological image that replaces the need for explanation. The importance of this ideological development for the authors is that it provided fertile ground for a *hegemonic* political project of 'authoritarian populism' – that is, the contradictory project that fuses consensus with coercive dominance, which Hall would later go on to coin as ... Thatcherism.

Urban practices – policing

The *Policing the Crisis* authors identified, at the ideological level, a chronology in which the connotative and contextual weight of the 'mugging' label (including the specific features of urban crises) arrived historically *prior* to any acts that might be described as such. Similarly, they demonstrate how new techniques and technologies within coercive state apparatuses, the policing of urban infrastructures – particularly public spaces and transport – produced, rather than resulted from, criminal acts. In other words, the authors found that an 'anti-mugging' police campaign, 'long predate[ed] any official judicial or media expression of public anxiety' about mugging.[36] This campaign had a number of features which we can define in terms of *technology*, *practice* and *policy*.

To deal with the technology of urban policing first, the authors – relying on M.E. Cain's *Society and the Policeman's Role* and Tony Bunyan's *History and Practice of the Political Police in Britain* – note the qualitative distinction between the 'traditional bobby on the beat' and the new, technologically augmented 'specialised' crime fighter ideal. The police crime fighter relied on new technologies of telecommunications, computerised surveillance, the car, and increasingly, various forms of arms. With a robust communication infrastructure, the police could be fragmented into specialised units, targeting specific features of the urban environment, rapidly mobilised and continuously controlled from a command centre.

These technological changes supported wider transformations of urban policing policy. The authors trace the changing structural and political role of the police to the mid-1960s in a process of concentration – reducing the number of police forces from one hundred and twenty-five in 1955, to forty-three. At the same time there emerged a number of special crime 'squads' – including the Metropolitan Regional Crime Squad, the Special Patrol Group, and later the Transport Police Special Squad, which became colloquially known as the 'Anti-Mugging Squad'. Their distinct quality was that they could focus (unlike a general police force) on only one crime, they were increasingly mobilised in the policing of urban public space.

The Special Patrol Groups – and the Anti-Mugging Squads – also had their own chain of command, their own operating procedures, and their own communication network: they were a 'force within a force' established and encouraged by the Home Office to operate in a gap between civilian policing and the military, dealing with 'militant industrial disputes; increasing political protest; possible racial riots; threats from abroad'.[37] This is, the authors argue, a *pre-emptive* model of policing – not designed to respond to disruptions to law and order, but to identify and disable *before* any act is committed.

Finally, there are the actual practices of policing. In this regard the authors note that the Anti-Mugging Squads, and the wider police force, concentrated their attention on young black men and focused on particular areas of transport and public space, that is, areas with high migrant populations. Using the work of sociologist John Lambert and journalist Derek Humphry, the authors of *Policing the Crisis* affirm the view that professional police practices are structured in dominance by wider ideologies, which, as already discussed, included highly racialised and compressed readings of urban environments as well as communities themselves.

The result of the technology, policy and practices of policing was the criminalisation of urban black youth simply *occupying* or *using* public space and transport infrastructure, perfectly illustrated on 16 March 1972 with the arrest of four young Caribbean men who became known as the 'Oval Four'. The London Transport Special Squad, led by Detective Sergeant Ridgewell, arrested and charged these men for 'attempted theft'. One of the four was sentenced to Borstal, the other three to two years' imprisonment. The case became a scandal; DS Ridgewell admitted, in relation to another case, to applying techniques of racial profiling he'd learned while working for the Rhodesian police force.[38]

Urban politics

The final level of analysis at which the urban is explored operates through these two given levels – the level of ideology and the level of the state apparatuses – to the economic. However, unlike major contemporaneous works of urbanism in the period (such as David Harvey's *Social Justice and the City* and later *The Limits to Capital*, or Manuel Castells' *The Urban Question*), *Policing the Crisis* is neither concerned with the production of surplus value within the construction of the urban; nor with the realisation of surplus value in profit, interest and rent in and through urban real estate.[39] Rather, its authors are interested in the *reproduction* of the *working class*, and more specifically, the reproduction of a specific *fraction* of the working class, that can be super-exploited in specific industries, in the context of relatively 'full-employment'. This requires the formation of a reserve army of labour that can put downward pressure on wages in distinct sectors. In effect, and as the authors state clearly in the text, this requires the 'fusion' of capitalist social relations with racialised social relations – what today, we would refer to as 'racial capitalism'.

One mechanism the authors suggest that enables the maintenance of this reserve army of labour is the condition of migrancy itself. The authors point to the insertion of 'black labour' (here they use the term to refer to Asian, African and Caribbean communities) in specific sectors of 'engineering, foundry work, textiles, the building trade, transport, the service industry and low-paid health services'.[40] Beyond these broad categories, the authors note that black labour was disproportionately employed in the 'advanced' industries of international capital – precisely because it was possible to maintain high levels of unemployment within migrant, racialised communities. As the authors state:

> What has principally governed the 'flow' of black labour is the underlying rhythms and requirements of British capital. But what has *regulated* the flow is, of course, legislative (i.e. political) action. And what has prepared the ground for this use of black labour as a fluid and endlessly 'variable' factor in British industry is the growth of racism (ideology).[41]

The position in the labour market is only one factor that the authors examine in a section of the book titled 'the structures of "secondariness"': other factors include reduced educational opportunities, political disenfranchisement – if not in law in practice – and crucially for urban analyses, housing. The authors point to the high concentration of immigrants racialised as black in inner-city areas reliant on 'relatively cheap housing, tenable in a multi-occupancy fashion', which rapidly deteriorates through the late 1960s and early 1970s resulting in a worsening housing situation for young black men and women and 'the growing phenomenon of "drifting on to the streets", sleeping rough and of "homelessness" and squatting'.[42]

All of this has consequences for urban conditions. The authors point to a process of 'colonisation' of the metropolitan city, in a 'double-sense', as they put it. At one end, both consensual and coercive state apparatuses are mobilised to 'socialise' and police racialised populations in urban ghettos. The latter is encompassed in the advancement of police technologies, policies and practices. The non-coercive, 'consensual' side of colonisation refers to the development programmes initiated for the 'inner city'. The authors cite 'the ill-fated Community Development Projects', and the targeting of 'inner rings' for 'extraordinary economic support' under the Labour Minister for the Environment David Shore as examples of the flip side of increased surveillance and 'tough' policing – what would later, in a different historical conjuncture, get articulated by New Labour as 'tough on crime, tough on the causes of crime'. But the authors point to the extent to which these programmes were self-evidently not designed to eliminate the root causes of the terrible structural and environmental conditions suffered by black communities, precisely because 'race as a structural feature of each sector in this complex process of social reproduction serves to "reproduce" that working class in a racially stratified and internally antagonistic form'.[43]

At the other end of the 'colonisation', the authors observe the formation of the 'colonised' with a specific class-consciousness, one that is refracted through racialised subjectivity, and mobilised in specific reproductive practices, as well as political action. In dialogue with the *Race Today* collective – and particularly Darcus Howe – the authors describe the emergence of a particular form of political resistance within 'colony life' (at first, as that emerges literally within colonial conditions in the Caribbean, later as that appears within the metropole). Initially a 'defensive reaction' against coercive conditions, a 'West Indian consciousness' is described that becomes increasingly visible, and materially viable:

> Neighbourhoods, cafés and pubs, the growth of the revivalist churches, mid-day Sunday hymn-singing and mass baptisms in the local swimming baths, the spilling-out of Caribbean fruit and vegetables from the Indian shops, the shebeen and the Saturday night blues party, the construction of the sound systems, the black record shops selling blues, ska and soul – the birth of the 'native quarter' at the heart of the English city.[44]

This sustains a figure championed by the *Race Today* collective: the 'hustler', the young black men who might engage in petty crime, but who are substantially sustained within the informal economies and networks of the street culture of 'colony life', and who promote a *political* class-consciousness, and *economically* refuse *work*. This last suggestion enabled the *Policing the Crisis* authors to suggest that the analyses of the *Race Today* collective of the street hustler were at least close to 'that elaborated by a major current in contemporary Italian Marxist theory', that is *Operaismo*. They write:

> … it can be seen at once how this analysis can be extended to illuminate the specific position of black labour (and other migrant 'labours') in the 'advanced' sectors of modern British industry; but also how forms of 'direct resistance' – like the refusal to work – can assume a quite different meaning and strategic position, as forms of class struggle, not of a marginal but of pivotal sections of the working class.[45]

In the end, the authors retreat from fully endorsing such a position. The emphasis that the authors place on the struggles of the racialised black working class of Britain is on their *political* and *ideological* rather than *economic* valence: 'they are, from this position, less significant at the economic level: [their struggle] still clearly "corporate" in character – pursued within, rather than against, the whole "logic of capital".'[46] Indeed, the conclusion of the book is bleaker still – the colonisation of the metropolitan city enables a continuous fragmentation of the working class in which capital inserts itself, while an authoritarian populism emerges that is stubbornly committed to segregating urban space racialised through policing, surveillance, and 'community programmes'.

Still, I want to conclude by emphasising the extent to which the 'urban' is analysed in the *Policing the Crisis* text as a material, and economic, condition for the reproduction of particular class fractions, and for the purposes of the 'logic of capital' precisely because it is this point – which in fact arrives at the culmination of the text – that was so frequently missed in critical assessments of the work. All too often, and even by those who were very close to the CCCS, the 'conjunctural analysis' proposed by the authors was interpreted by Marxist critics as 'analyses of the contingent, and wholly superstructural', rather than analysis of the relatively autonomous economic, political, ideological and cultural forces which are *structured in dominance* by capital. For urban and architectural historians, the two questions this chapter began with remain: but *Policing the Crisis* opens up a space to examine how design and planning practice was not 'independent' or operative 'outside' of this conjuncture, but *overdetermined* by the conjunctural crisis it delimits.

Notes

1 Stuart Hall, Chas Critcher, Tony Jefferson, John Clarke, Brian Roberts, *Policing the Crisis: Mugging, the State, and Law and Order,* second edition (Basingstoke and New York: Palgrave Macmillan, 2013).
2 Adrian Forty, 'Appendix: Outcomes from the Liverpool Workshop 2012', in Mark Swenarton, Tom Avermaete and Dirk van den Heuvel, (eds.) *Architecture and the Welfare State* (London: Routledge, 2015), 321–3.
3 Forty, 'Appendix'.
4 Simon Gunn, 'The Rise and Fall of British Urban Modernism: Planning Bradford, circa 1945–1970', *Journal of British Studies*, vol. 49, no. 4 (2010), 865.
5 Ibid., 865.
6 See James Rhodes and Laurence Brown, 'The Rise and Fall of the "Inner City": Race, Space and Urban Policy in Postwar England', *Journal of Ethnic and Migration Studies*, 45:17 (2019), 3243–59.
7 Kieran Connell and Matthew Hilton, 'The Working Practices of Birmingham's Centre for Contemporary Cultural Studies', *Social History*, 40.3 (2015), 287–311; Stuart Hall, 'The Emergence of Cultural Studies and the Crisis of the Humanities', *October*, 53 (1990), 11–23.
8 Richard Hoggart, *The Uses of Literacy: Aspects of Working Class Life with Special Reference to Publications and Entertainments* (Harmondsworth: Penguin, 1958).
9 Michael Young and Peter Willmott, *Family and Kinship in East London,* revised edition (Harmondsworth: Penguin, 1962).
10 See Richard Hoggart, 'Schools of English and Contemporary Society: Inaugural Lecture, University of Birmingham, 1963', in Richard Hoggart, *Speaking to Each Other, Volume Two: About Literature* (Harmondsworth: Penguin, 1973), 231–43.
11 Stuart Hall with Bill Schwarz, *Familiar Stranger: A Life Between Two Islands* (London: Penguin, 2017), 3–60; Stuart Hall, 'At Home and Not at Home: In Conversation with Les Back', in Stuart Hall, *Essential Essays, Volume 2: Identity and Diaspora*, edited by David Morley (Durham, NC: Duke University Press, 2019), 263–300.
12 See for example, George Lamming, *The Pleasures of Exile*, with introductions by Richard Drayton and Bill Schwarz (London: Pluto Press, 2005); Sam Selvon, *The Lonely Londoners* (London: Penguin, 2006); Andrew Salkey, *Escape to an Autumn Pavement* (Leeds: Peepal Tree Press, 2009).
13 Editors, 'The Habit of Violence: Notting Hill Documents', *Universities and Left Review*, 5 (Autumn 1958), 5–6; Stuart Hall, 'Absolute Beginnings: Reflections on the Secondary Modern Generation [1959]' in Stuart Hall, *Selected Writings on Race and Difference*, edited by Paul Gilroy and Ruth Wilson Gilmore (Durham NC: Duke University Press, 2021), 23–41; Hall, 'The Young Englanders [1967]', *On Race and Difference*, 42–50.
14 Hall, 'At Home and Not at Home'.
15 Stuart Hall, 'ULR at Notting Hill', *New Left Review*, I, no. 1 (Jan/Feb 1960), 71–2.
16 Gus John, *Race in the Inner City* (Runnymede Trust, 1970); US121, Box 76, Harambee Project papers, US121, Box 76 (former reference 002/0022), Stuart Hall Archive, Cadbury Research Library, University of Birmingham. See also Kieran Connell, *Black Handsworth: Race in 1980s Britain* (Oakland, CA: University of California Press, 2019), 41–3.
17 Hall, 'The Young Englanders'.
18 See Stuart Hall, *Cultural Studies, 1983* (Durham, NC: Duke University Press, 2016), particularly 'Lecture 2' and 'Lecture 3'.
19 Stuart Hall, 'Encoding and Decoding in the Television Discourse' (1973), in Stuart Hall, *Writings on Media: History of the Present*, edited by Charlotte Brunsdon (Durham, NC: Duke University Press, 2021), 247–66
20 Louis Althusser, *For Marx*, translated by Ben Brewster (London: Allen Lane, 1969); Louis Althusser and Étienne Balibar, *Reading Capital*, translated by Ben Brewster (London: New Left Books, 1970); Antonio Gramsci, *Selections from the Prison Notebooks*, edited and translated by Quintin Hoare and Geoffrey Nowell Smith (London: Lawrence and Wishart, 1973); Karl Marx, *Grundrisse: Foundations of the Critique of Political Economy*, edited and translated by Martin Nicolaus (Harmondsworth: Penguin, 1973).
21 Gregor McLennan, 'Editor's Discussion of Part 1 Writings', in Stuart Hall, *Selected Writings on Marxism*, edited by McLennan (Durham NC: Duke University Press, 2021), 158–78.
22 Lawrence Grossberg, *Cultural Studies in the Future Tense* (Durham NC: Duke University Press, 2010), 20.

23 Hall and others, *Policing the Crisis*, xiv.

24 See Stuart Hall and Tony Jefferson (eds), *Resistance Through Rituals: Youth Subcultures in Post-war Britain*, a special issue of *Working Papers in Cultural Studies*, nos. 7–8 (Summer 1975).

25 Hall, 'A Sense of Classlessness [1958]'; Hall, 'Absolute Beginnings'.

26 See Chas Critcher, 'Action Not Words: Neighbourhood Activism and Cultural studies', in Connell and Hilton (eds) *Cultural Studies 50 Years On*, 247–56.

27 Peter Baldock, 'Why Community Action? The Historical Origins of the Radical Trend in British Community Work', *Community Development Journal*, 12:2 (April 1977), 68–74; Georgina Brewis, 'From Service to Action? Students, Volunteering and Community Action in Mid-twentieth Century Britain', *British Journal of Educational Studies*, 58:4 (December 2010), 439–49; Richard Bryant, 'Community Action', *The British Journal of Social Work*, 2:2 (Summer 1972), 205–15.

28 Hall and others, *Policing the Crisis*, 23.

29 Ibid., 24.

30 Ibid., 28.

31 Ibid., 144.

32 Ibid., 144.

33 Ibid., 156.

34 Ibid., 103, citing the *Daily Mail*, 20 March 1973.

35 Ibid., 103.

36 Ibid., 43.

37 Ibid., 49.

38 Ibid., 46.

39 Manuel Castells, *The Urban Question: A Marxist Approach*, translated by Alan Sheridan (London: Edward Arnold, 1977); David Harvey, *Social Justice and the City* (London: Edward Arnold, 1973); David Harvey, *The Limits to Capital* (Oxford: Basil Blackwell, 1982).

40 Hall and others, *Policing the Crisis*, 335.

41 Ibid., 336.

42 Ibid., 338.

43 Ibid., 340.

44 Ibid., 344.

45 Ibid., 365.

46 Ibid., 384.

Chapter 10
a so-called archive[1]

Onyeka Igwe

… *a so-called archive*
has 2 floors
is set back on a busy road
is beside a river
has vast empty rooms surrounded by windows
has small rooms stuffed to the brim
has ordered and catalogued repositories
is full of decaying and rotting films
is semi derelict
is plagued by pigeons
is cold
is humid
will rot.

Poetry has long been used as a wayfinder, from the navigational poems of sailors to the oral mapping of indigenous communities in the Pacific. I was trying to find a building, an imagined exquisite corpse of my own doing that my film, *a so-called archive* (2020), takes the audience on a tour around. I used these words to find my way.

I recently met the daughter of Kunle Akinsemoyin, co-author of seminal text *Building Lagos.*[2] This is a book which has recently recaptured the imagination as Nigerian colonial architecture undergoes a revisionist process reassessing the significance of tropical modernism. I told his daughter excitedly about the time, years ago, when I looked up his book in the British Library in the hope of finding architectural plans for a building that had become legendary. I described to her the scene: flipping through the pages hurriedly (a bad habit I have in archives), looking past sketches of Barclays' Bank, build-

Screen grab of *a so-called archive,* 2020, HD Video by Onyeka Igwe.

ings on the Marina, the suggested quarters for government offices, or renderings of the colonial classical style, to find the building. All to no avail.
I told her because the book felt rare and uncommon and when I held it in my hands, I had imagined myself a detective on a trail (a fantasy I have as a researcher). I was searching for a building that I heard mentioned years before during a conference in Berlin.

A building that I went to Lagos to find when I visited unchaperoned for the first time in 2018.
A building I had played a game of telephone to locate, being passed on to different assistants, secretaries and area chiefs before finally gaining permission to see it, the day before I left.
A building that became the protagonist in the last film I was to make about colonial archives.

The Colonial Film Unit was part of the British imperial visual propaganda programme. The unit ran from 1932 to 1955 and was headed by William Sellers, a man who promoted a particular form of colonial filmmaking known as the 'Specialised Technique'.[3] This grammar of filmmaking was founded on his belief that colonial subjects, especially Africans, could not become cine-literate because of deficiencies in both their perceived intelligence and the physiological composition of their eyes. These ideas were not discredited until the winding down of the Colonial Film Unit in the 1950s and a field visit from an anthropologist who disproved Seller's spurious assertions.[4]

After the end of the Second World War, the Colonial Film Unit diversified its output beyond explicit war propaganda. The unit made films both for a British public, in order to demonstrate the economic benefits of their investment in the British Empire, and for colonial subjects in order to instruct them into the British way of life. In expanding its scope, Colonial Film Unit outposts were established, in what was then the Gold Coast, Jamaica, India and Nigeria.

The Nigerian Film Unit was created in 1947, first by training three local men in filmmaking, then through the development of sub-units across northern and southern British-ruled territories. The sub-units were active in producing newsreels for local events and exhibiting colonial films through mobile cinemas. These mobile cinemas toured countries on vehicles, screening a selection of films made by the unit alongside a more commercial programme. This allowed for the distribution of films in both cities and more rural areas, where screenings were accompanied with live translation in local languages. In 1959, in the run up to Nigeria's independence, the activities of the Colonial Film Unit were administered by the newly formed Federal Ministry of Information which created the Federal Film Unit, widely known as simply *The Film Unit*.[5]

A hangover from the colonial administration, the Film Unit produced largely the same content of newsreels, 'pedagogical documentaries ... imperial spectacles ...' and narrative morality tales.[6] The Nigerian Film Unit was overseen by British colonial functionaries but staffed by Nigerian technicians trained primarily at the Overseas Film and Television Centre in London which acted as a hub for cinematic education across the former colonies.[7] Nigerian operatives were trained in the style and production regimes of the Colonial Film Unit, specifically in William Sellers' 'Specialised Technique' of filming reality without camera trickery or movement – only the one-to-one exact representation of life to film was permitted.

After the Biafran War, and with the institution of the Second Republic of Nigeria in 1979, there was the need for a new body for national film culture to reflect the latest iteration of Nigerian identity. The Nigerian Film Corporation was created by a Nigerian parliamentary act and the newly formed corporation included provisions for narrative filmmaking for the first time, the establishment of a national film school, the dispensing of financial assistance to Nigeria's filmmaking community, and proposed plans for a National Film, Video and Sound Archive (this was established in Jos, Plateau State). In the 1990s the films of the Nigerian Film Unit and the Federal Film Unit were transferred from Lagos to the cooler environment of the northern state which some locals called 'Little London' and thought better suited for the maintenance and preservation of a film archive. Film is usually archived in cold storage to prevent its deterioration, but the humid climate of Lagos makes these conditions hard to achieve.

From the colonial to the postcolonial period, to the national renaissance, the body making films about, and for, Nigeria changed its name, purpose and outlook – from Nigerian, to Federal, to National. At some point between 1947 and 1959 the Nigerian Film Unit found its home in a two-storey building on Ikoyi Road. Ikoyi Road is on Lagos Island, one of the islands that make up the lagoon city of Lagos, the former capital of Lagos state. It is known for the Brazilian Quarter of Lagos, where those formerly enslaved returned to Nigeria after they achieved their freedom and resettled. They brought with them craft and building skills that were used by the new colonial powers to build government offices, administrative spaces and living quarters. These returnees also built their own houses using methods learnt in Brazil that would accommodate for the tropical environment.

I went on a tour of Lagos Island's remaining colonial buildings during a 2018 visit. We began at Independence House, a *gift* from the British on the eve of

Nigerian independence. The concrete skyscraper rising erect and high above the traditional one- or two-storey buildings on the island, situated beside Tafawa Balewa Square, was previously used for Empire Day celebrations and similarly unveiled and redeveloped on the occasion of Nigerian independence in October 1960. I was told that the building was abandoned in the 1990s and had remained unused until 2019 when the second Lagos Biennial reoccupied the site. Activated by curator Folakunle Oshun's mission 'to use contemporary art to rejuvenate abandoned architectural sites and uncover their art historical significance',[8] I began to find these evacuated colonial buildings everywhere. Lying proud but empty of presence. Walking on Broad Street, the main thoroughfare through old Lagos Island, I photographed the house of a Brazilian returnee. His name was carved in the facade and his descendants looked down at me from atop the balcony.

Another Step Forward[9]

Humility

grand concourse of patriots and friends of Nigeria

high honour

mighty audience eminent men and women

august assemblage

orderly progress

the respect and collaboration of

the comity of nations.

the first indigenous Governor-General of the sovereign state of Nigeria.

vested with reserved powers

suzerains

ergo, they were in political servitude

Later, the Statute specifically defined 'Dominion' to mean Canada,

Australia, New Zealand, South Africa, Irish Free State and Newfoundland.

a small European minority had complete control of the government.

great social changes in the structure and outlook

are basic

colonial rule is authoritarian

equality of status

influenced the course of our

national history.

there is a bifurcation

as the erstwhile

I have gone to the length

a motive power for the revival of the stature of man impelling force

for the restoration of the dignity

an autonomous community

nourished with these

concepts

bequeathed to us

permeating our political fabric, degenerate

sheet-anchor of democratic institutions.

other ancillaries to these elements

kernel of the two oaths

respect for human

dignity.

challenge which Africa offers to

the world.

Until the conscience of the world has been energetically

aroused to solve this problem

a *revanche* movement

the cloven hoof of certain nations

Under no circumstance shall we accept the idea that the black race is inferior to any other race.

sacrilegious, if not heretical

cannot appreciate the equity in denying

extra-legal acts

people can be so wicked and

inhuman

a practicable

proposition and way of

life?

this innocuous but face-saving

convention?

the height of folly for us to hobnob with those

who regard the members of our race as inferior.

the crucible of political bondage in the furnace of

colonial tutelage

As we proceed

refined savagery.

rescue their kith and kin from this

social degradation.

sweep away the cobwebs of a venal past.

no Nigerian wants to know whether a wolf is a dog or a

cat or a cross between a dog and a cat!

the prize of freedom

we trekked the stony Golgotha of human life.

our lot was one of vicissitudes and

disappointments;

mutilation of facts, amorphous interpretation

Independence has come

dedicate our lives anew to the fascinating task

bitterness and rancour and recriminations.

reviving the stature

I call upon

I exhort

I appeal to

our internecine altercations.

outweigh the love of our petty selves.

no longer an expression of geography but a reality of

history. political vassalage

we lustily sang

bind the nation's wound

hate-free, fear-free and greed-free

As for me, my stiffest earthly assignment is ended

jealously guard our freedom with our lives, if need be.

look forward to the morrow

the task has been well done

I don't know the exact provenance of the building that I call the former Nigerian Film Unit and I never found it in *Building Lagos*, but I did get to go inside. On my last full day in the city, still not acclimatised to the humidity, and so revealing my not-from-hereness through the beads of sweat trickling down my face, I finally got to meet the Lagos area chairman of the Nigerian Film Corporation. We talked and he teased me about the sweating and educated me about the work of the corporation. I asked him to show me the former Nigerian Film Unit. He was surprised that I didn't want to see the corporation's new purpose-built cinema with air conditioning. I obliged him on a tour of the cinema, offices, conference rooms, and then we left the squat orange building of the Nigerian Film Corporation, through the back door and headed across the compound to see what I had come for.

The former Nigerian Film Unit is a building paused. Stopped clocks, rusty film cans, fungus-filled crevices, plant vines creeping up the walls, immovable broken Kodak machines, smashed windows and piles of cobwebbed files, are all that remain. It's as if everyone who worked there left at once because there was an alarm, an emergency. There was an emergency, but no one ever called it that at the time. The building was a carcass that I could dream into, hollowed out and in the shadow of the new beginning that it faced, a face visible to the world. It reminded me of somewhere else. Of a building I danced in, on the empty top floor of a bonded warehouse in the Cumberland Basin, of the River Avon, Bristol.

A building preserved, listed, and repurposed.
A building where I spent several freezing cold weeks auditing the film collection of the former Empire and Commonwealth Museum.
A building that had definitely been squatted and raved in.

A bond warehouse, Bristol, England

The derivation of Bristol's wealth, its grand Georgian buildings, the prestige of the Gothic cathedral, Wills Memorial building atop Park Street, the prominence of the Society of Merchant Venturers throughout the city and the name Colston emblazoned on roads, music halls, streets and rooms was unknown to me during the three years that I lived in the city. I was young, busy making and unmaking myself at university, preoccupied with new discoveries, enveloped in the darkest bass forward music and the twilight of a once pioneering club scene. In 2007, I was more likely to be found on underpasses, bike paths and docked ships that in any of the institutions commemorating the bicentenary of the ending of the Slave Trade. But I should have known. I should have known that: 'Bristol was a processor of slave-produced goods, a supplier of goods to West African slave traders, the provider of slaves and goods to plantations, as well as the home of planters and planters' agents (and many more who grew rich from the trade).'[10] Is that somehow my responsibility, as a black person, to know, or at least notice that the street I lived off in my second year, Whiteladies Road, intersects Blackboy Hill and ask why?[11]
The architecture of the city tells these stories. Years after graduation, I returned to Bristol looking for the remains of a museum that I walked past every time I exited Bristol Temple Meads station, returning to the city at the beginning of each of those nine terms, but that I had never noticed. The Empire and Commonwealth Museum had its beginnings in the 1980s when 'Union Jack'

Hayward, a rich businessman and John Letts, founder of the pressure group National Heritage, dreamed up the idea for a museum to display the history of the British Empire. It was a project of nationalist British patriotism, Hayward once said: 'If I had my way, I'd form my own party far more right-wing than Margaret Thatcher. I'd bring back the National Service, the Scaffold, the cat o' nine tails, the Empire – places like Sierra Leone and Nigeria were so much better off under British rule than they are now.'[12] The Board of Trustees for what was then known as the British Empire Museum was made up of former colonial administrators and district governors.

In 1989, a 90-year lease was obtained to house the museum in Sir Isambard Kingdom Brunel's old train depot in Bristol, a former centre of the triangular trade of enslaved people. It took almost another twenty years for the museum to open, somewhat diluted from Hayward's and Letts's original vision by community consultation, resulting in the compromise moniker British Empire and Commonwealth Museum (BECM). Most of the collecting for the museum was done in the 1990s through newspaper notices calling for Imperial oral histories, during these interviews researchers would enquire about any materials and deposits largely of family photographs, 8mm and 16mm films. In 2002, the museum took on the archive from the then closing Commonwealth Institute which bolstered BECM's holdings from Aubrey Williams paintings to more traditional objects befitting an anthropological cum historical institution, and officially opened its doors.

> The British Empire lasted almost 500 years and encompassed India, Africa and North America.
> You can experience the full and exciting story of it here at the museum.
> Brunel's passenger shed holds over 900 people, one of the biggest indoor event spaces in the South West and is home to the museum's permanent exhibition, displays and is also where we host events.
> And at the back of the passenger shed, facing the left is the nightmare room.
> The galleries on the first floor display a mass of information.
> The temporary exhibitions, which make history fascinating and easy to learn, are in Brunel's drawing room.

> Our first-class library, a treasure trove for academics, is situated on the mezzanine.
> Here, at the back of Brunel's famed archways are where you will find Images of Empire - our film and sound collections.
> And underneath my feet lie the original tunnels of Brunel's Old train depot where the museum's vast archives are kept.[13]

However, the museum was never economically viable as a private institution without regular guaranteed access to public funds. It closed in March 2009 after the *Breaking the Chains* exhibition to mark the bicentenary of the 1807 Act that abolished the British Transatlantic Slave Trade, a rumoured relocation to London and allegations of the unauthorised sale of objects from its own collection.[14] The Bristol Archives, a council funded municipal archive, acquired the photographic, film and sound archives from the defunct British Empire and Commonwealth Museum years after its closure. They were awarded funding over three years to catalogue and digitise over 500,000 photographs and 2,000 films. This material is now housed in the two bonded warehouses which Bristol Archives occupies on the floating docks of the Cumberland Basin.
One of Bristol's heralded benefactors is the Wills family, who were integral to the establishment of the city's university which carries their name on many buildings. The Wills's patriarch, Henry Overton Wills, opened a tobacco shop in 1786 as part of a developing tobacco industry in Bristol. Further shops, factories and warehouses were built over the centuries by this family dynasty. The tobacco industry's place in Bristol was connected to the city's role as a node in the triangular trade; goods were transported to West Africa in exchange for the enslaved, who were transported to the West Indies and North America, and then goods like sugar and tobacco were brought back to England via ports like Liverpool and Bristol. By the mid eighteenth century, the Bristol port declined in prominence, as trading became more directly localised in the Caribbean and the slave trade was officially abolished in 1807. However, a floating harbour was built from the diverted River Avon in 1809 which serviced shipbuilding as well as trade routes that began to include the burgeoning railways. A century later, in the Cumberland Basin a floating harbour directly joined

Isambard Kingdom Brunel's Temple Meads railway station to three bonded warehouses, constructed to hold imported tobacco before taxes were applied: A Bond in 1905, B Bond in 1909, and C Bond in 1919.[15] Bonded warehouses were legalised spaces of interregnum, officially not part of the country, despite being on sovereign territory. The declining tobacco industry and the introduction of VAT in 1973 shifted the requirements of these large nine-storey red-brick buildings. All three were listed by Historic England in the 1980s and two, A and B Bond, were sequestered by Bristol City Council who use them as storage space for their archives. C Bond is a Yellow Storage facility.

I visited the A Bond warehouse for the first time in 2018 with a friend who was studying to be a media archivist. She was concerned about the state of the hastily acquired British Empire and Commonwealth Collection and I was curious to see what it contained. Hoping to obtain an access rarely offered to researchers, we volunteered to assist the paper archivists in digitising their film collection. However, its unorganised and faltering state meant that we had to audit the collection before we could begin crudely transferring it to a digital copy. We methodically inspected the acetate for signs of deterioration – sniffing out any wafts of vinegar, noting observations in a spreadsheet. In the second week we got to see the films animated by light and the rudimentary cogs of the Steenbeck projector and recorded this with a 4K compatible camcorder.

My accomplice and I noticed that A Bond warehouse reminded us of buildings in which we had found community, lived in and loved each other over the preceding years. Squats - monuments of our friendship. If you looked carefully, you could see the souvenirs of A Bond's previous life strewn throughout its vastness. We reminisced, casting ourselves backwards to the acid 1990s we were too young to have known first-hand, imagining ourselves dancing at dawn on the top floor of this building roofed by glass. And so, we did, we acted out these desires for ourselves, creeping unnoticed up the lateral staircase to the long-lauded and aforementioned glass-roofed top floor to dance for each other in display, enjoyment and to free ourselves from the shackles of the stereotypes our eyes had been flushed with by the BECM collection. We channelled and communed with the dancing Othered bodies constructed by the colonial gaze.

Screen grab of *a so-called archive*, 2020, HD Video by Onyeka Igwe.

These two buildings, these two encounters separated by time and geography, these two locations in the nations that have contributed to the making of me, are conjoined in the imaginary of *a so-called archive.* While I was in Bristol in 2017, volunteering at the archive, I watched Powell and Pressburger's *Black Narcissus*, in the too-cramped micro-plex, Cube Cinema. Upon leaving and grabbing aimlessly at words to try and name our shared experience, my friend uttered the word 'metonym', another revelation. I had never heard that word before but in the fusing of the former Nigerian Film Unit with A Bond warehouse, and the stories I have told about both, 'metonym' approaches a description of what they can tell us of the enduring colonial entanglements between Nigeria and UK. That these buildings tell us both about architecture and spatiality but more so about what colonialism, archives and collective memory mean, in both countries respectively. They tell us too of what has been wrought on the people and places of those countries, the fictions that have been established through the construction of these storage palaces of material wealth, and they still reside in their very walls.

Gifts From Britain[16]

SCENE 1 INT: Café Kino, Bristol

F/X ZENANI waits at a table and NNENA walks into the café

NNENA Only 15 minutes late!

ZENANI Well, I was here 15 minutes early, so technically it's 30 …

NNENA Ah, that's your problem, why would you ever be early or me?

F/X NNENA SITS DOWN

ZENANI Yeah, I know I am just stressed and bombed it down through the underpass. I really needed to speak to you.

NNENA And it had to be in person? So dramatic!

ZENANI Kinda, I mean I don't know what I am doing but felt like the right thing to do, like what proper journalists do … So, yeah, I think I've got this huge story to pitch to the Epigram.

NNENA About that museum by the station?

ZENANI Yeah, remember they had that slavery exhibition and we heard the director give a talk about how the museum came about?

Cut to:

SCENE 2 INT: Barnard's Inn Hall, Gresham College, excerpt from Dr. Gareth Griffiths speech

'… to create a museum to examine the history of the British Empire and this is the resultant mission statement which shows that our responsibility at the moment is to serve, to explore and to

study cultural heritage associated with the former empire and today's commonwealth and to examine its legacy …'

SCENE 3 INT: Café Kino, Bristol

NNENA (Kisses teeth), oh yah, I remember that I got into that dumb argument with Simon afterwards, who was playing devil's advocate as usual …

ZENANI (interrupting) yeah yeah, so I stumbled into something yesterday. I'd just come out from a meeting at Kebele and went to the Sweet Mart to pick some things up. Was minding my business and I overheard this guy on the phone, wasn't paying too much attention but he was older, looked pretty agitated and was standing in the corner deep in his conversation.

Cut to:

SCENE 3 Aisle in Bristol Sweet Mart

F/X ZENANI walks down an aisle and sees GEORGE chatting on the phone at the other end. ZENANI stops by the aubergines and eavesdrops.

GEORGE … we're supposed to be closed and moving to London, but I am not sure that's going to happen anymore …

F/X ZENANI moves closer and picks up some celery, George listens to the person he's talking to on the phone.

GEORGE … Did I tell you about where we keep the spillover?

F/X George pauses to listen

GEORGE It's a gold mine - all unique. Some donated, borrowed, collected. It's hard to keep track sometimes. There are so many rumours and I try and keep out of it. (inaudible) Can you imagine?

Cut to:

SCENE 4 INT Café Kino, Bristol

F/X ZENANI and NNENA sit at a table by the window, each with a drink.

NNENA So you are telling me you just stood there playing around with some vegetables listening to this guy on the phone?

ZENANI yeah … he wasn't paying me no mind. After he got off the phone, I followed him to the checkout. I wanted to talk to him but didn't know what to say, then he was chatting all friendly with the guy at the till and I figured he was a regular or something. So, I carried on shopping, went back to the checkout guy, and described this tall older white guy who had been in earlier and that had dropped a book. The checkout guy was like …

Cut to:

SCENE 5 INT: Checkout Bristol Sweet Mart

F/X Till ringing, conveyor belt

WORKER Oh yeah, that's George, he's in here all the time. Leave it and I'll give it to him next time.

Cut to:

SCENE 6 INT: Café Kino, Bristol

ZENANI ... I had to give up a bloody uni library book, so I'm gonna get a huge fine but whatever. I looked up staff at that museum and there was luckily only one George. Googled him and got an email and possibly some other people to contact about him.

NNENA Look at you! A proper reporter now! Can't believe you did all that. So, what exactly do you need from me? We gonna do a stakeout outside his house? (laughs)

ZENANI Well, I need to get an interview with him.

NNENA To say what though? Run it by me again – what is the actual story?

ZENANI I wanna know what's in that room he mentioned! I was looking online at the museum's archive prospectus to see what kind of stuff they collect cos I haven't actually been there

F/X ZENANI gets out her laptop and scrolls through a website.

ZENANI ... and take a look at what's officially in their holdings.

F/X Audio scrubbing down a list of items, audio excerpts in the pauses.

NNENA The Honourable East India Company's ship Dunira passing Funchal Bay on the Island of Madeira (painting)

F/X PAUSE

373, 374 Dudley (audio recording)

F/X PAUSE

Sir Gwain's farewell (16mm film)

F/X PAUSE

Count Your Blessings (16mm film)

F/X PAUSE

Maori carved lintel (object)

F/X PAUSE

So you think there's more 'treasure' in this special room?

ZENANI I think so, for sure, what else could be? That's why I wanna talk to this George guy so I can confirm my ideas, so that it's not just all speculation.

NNENA This is all sounds kinda fucked though, you know. Like wasn't there a hoo-ha about this museum from the get-go, about who started it? Why do they even have half this stuff? Shouldn't you write about that, like why this museum that is supposed to be educating this city about Empire in that 'so it will never happen again history bollocks' is *actually* acting in exactly the same way, kinda? Hoarding all this stuff from all over. Actually, I wanna know how they got it all?

F/X ZENANI pours sugar into her coffee, stirs and lifts to her mouth.

ZENANI Nah, the real story is what's in that room! Seemed to me, it was pretty special stuff and if I could break that … maybe it's bigger than our student paper.

Music Out

Notes

1 Parts of this chapter appeared in Onyeka Igwe, 'Looking for Lost Archives' 06 *Non-Fiction 06: Inscriptions* 2. (2024).

2 Kunle Akinsemoyin and Alan Vaughan-Richards, *Building Lagos* (Jersey: Pengrail, 1977).

3 William Sellers, 'Film for Primitive Peoples : A New Technique', *Documentary News Letter* (London, 1940).

4 Brian Larkin, *Signal and Noise: Media, Infrastructure, and Urban Culture in Nigeria* (Durham, Duke University Press 2008) .

5 Telephone conversation with Emmanuel Haruna, 13 December 2018.

6 Françoise Balogun, *The Cinema in Nigeria (Enugu:* Delta Publications, 1987).

7 Larkin, *Signal and Noise.*

8 'LB 2019 – Lagos Biennial'. Accessed 30 September 2024. https://lagos-biennial.org/lb-2019/.

9 Text is from Nnamdi Azikiwe, *Respect for Human Dignity; An Inaugural Address* (Enugu: Union Publishing Company 1960) and performed by three voice actors according to the rhythm of this formatting in *a so-called archive* (2020).

10 Caine Lewin-Turner, 'Blood on the Bricks: More Than Colston?' (Bristol Museums Collection, 17 November 2022 <https://collections.bristolmuseums.org.uk/stories/transatlantic-traffic-enslaved-africans/blood-on-the-bricks-more-than-colston/> accessed 28 June 2024).

11 Despite this connection sparking outrage and public consternation leading to the renaming of Blackboy Hill, there is no known connection to the slave trade. Tristan Cork, 'What Is the Truth about Blackboy Hill and Whiteladies Road?' Bristol Live, 13 June 2020. https://www.bristolpost.co.uk/news/bristol-news/what-truth-blackboy-hill-whiteladies-4218076.

12 Sathnam.Sanghera, 'Sir Jack Hayward' , *The Financial Times,* 15 November 2003.

13 Adapted from British Empire and Commonwealth video tour 2003 and used as narration throughout *a so-called archive* (2020).

14 Rob Sharp, 'Museum Chief Sacked as Theft Inquiry Begins', *The Independent* (18 March 2011).

15 Andor Gomme, Michael Jenner and Bryan Little, *Bristol, An Architectural History* (London, Lund Humphries 1979), 341.

16 Radio play script that features in *a so-called archive* (2020).

Biographies of Contributors

Nick Beech is Associate Professor in the School of Social Policy and Society, University of Birmingham, and research lead for the Stuart Hall Archive Project. He has published on and continues to research the history of the New Left and cultural studies in relation to architecture and urban history, and contributed to the 'Translating Ferro / Transforming Knowledges of Architecture, Design and Labour' research project (2020–2024).

Alistair Cartwright is Leverhulme Early Career Research Fellow at the School of Architecture, University of Liverpool. He was previously a postdoctoral fellow at the Paul Mellon Centre and Development Manager at the architectural education charity Open City. His work sits at the intersection of architecture and social history, having published on topics such as the history of rent tribunals and subdivision in multiple occupancy homes. Expanding on a longstanding interest in the social afterlives of built spaces, his current research examines the architecture and political-ecology of post-disaster reconstruction in Mauritius during the transition from British colony to independence.

Luisa Lorenza Corna is a Lecturer at UWE Bristol. Her research focuses on materialist politics and the arts, as well as the influence of feminist epistemologies on art theory. She has recently edited and translated, with Jamila Mascat, the first anthology of Carla Lonzi's writings (*Feminism in Revolt*). Currently, she is in the final stages of editing a book on architect Giancarlo De Carlo's pedagogical writings for MIT Press. Simultaneously, she is working on her first monograph, tentatively titled *Fugitive Lives*, which explores the theme of departing the art/architectural world from the perspective of the critic.

Mark Crinson is Emeritus Professor of Architectural History at Birkbeck (University of London) and a Fellow of the British Academy. His recent books include *Rebuilding Babel: Modern Architecture and Internationalism* (2017), *Alison and Peter Smithson* (2018), *The Architecture of Art History – A Historiography* (co-authored with Richard J. Williams, 2018), and *Shock City: Image and Architecture in Industrial Manchester* (2022). He is currently writing a book on *Heathrow's Genius Loci: Architecture, Landscape and Infrastructure in Peri-Urban London.*

Onyeka Igwe is an artist, filmmaker and researcher. Her work asks the question: how do we live together? Onyeka's practice figures sensorial, spatial and counter-hegemonic ways of knowing. She has had solo/duo shows at Peer, London (2024), Bonington Gallery, Nottingham (2024), MoMA PS1, New York (2023), High Line, New York (2022), Mercer Union, Toronto (2021), Jerwood Arts, London (2019) and Trinity Square Video, London (2018). She participated in the group show 'Nigeria Imaginary' in the national pavilion of Nigeria at the 60th Venice Biennial. Onyeka has a book, *June Givanni Pan-African Cinema Archive* forthcoming in 2025. She is an Associate Professor at Ruskin School of Art, and (with Rachael Rakes and Laura Huertas Millán) she is part of a curatorial and research initiative on alternative and anti-ethnographies.

Silke Kapp is Professor of Architecture and Urbanism at the Federal University of Minas Gerais (UFMG) and a founder member of the research group MOM Morar de Outras Maneiras/ Living in Other Ways (http://www.mom.arq.ufmg.br). Her research focuses on critical theory and experimental practices, particularly in collaboration with marginalised socio-spatial groups. Publications include *Canteiros da Utopia* (2020), *Moradia e Outras Margens* (2021, with Ana Baltazar), and *Teoria Crítica da Arquitetura* (2024). From 2020 to 2024 Silke was Co-Investigator for the project 'Translating Ferro / Transforming Knowledges of Architecture, Design and Labour', coordinating the translation of Sérgio Ferro's work.

Katie Lloyd Thomas is Professor of Theory and History of Architecture at Newcastle University and a founder member of the feminist collective *taking place* (www.takingplace.org.uk). Her research is concerned with materiality, labour and technology and with their intersections with feminist theory and practice. Publications include *Building Materials: Material Theory and the Architectural Specification* (Bloomsbury, 2021) and with Tilo Amhoff and Nick Beech *Industries of Architecture* (Routledge Critiques, 2015). From 2020 to 2024 Katie was Principal Investigator (UK) for the project 'Translating Ferro / Transforming Knowledges of Architecture, Design and Labour'.

Rujana Rebernjak is a design historian interested in researching, teaching and disseminating knowledge about architecture and design in Eastern Europe under socialism. Her work focuses on postwar Yugoslavia and explores the relationship between the socialist system of workers' self-management and its materialisation through objects, spaces and technologies. She has written about Yugoslav factories as cybernetic machines, exhibitions as forms of public debate around self-management, and theories of design practice as a form of self-management. She teaches design history and theory at the London College of Communication, University of the Arts London.

Nicholas Thoburn is Professor of Sociology at the University of Manchester. His research interests are in architecture and social housing, material cultures of publishing, and social and political theory. He is author of three books, *Brutalism as Found: Housing, Form, and Crisis at Robin Hood Gardens* (2022), *Anti-Book: On the Art and Politics of Radical Publishing* (2016), and *Deleuze, Marx and Politics* (2003).

Tom Wilkinson is a historian specialising in modern architecture and German visual culture. He is currently a Research Associate at Karlsruhe Institute of Technology and has previously been a Lecturer at the Courtauld Institute and at Birkbeck (University of London) and a Leverhulme Early Career Fellow at the Warburg Institute. He has a PhD from University College London. His most recent book, *Emergency Money: Notgeld in the Image Economy of the German Inflation, 1914–1923*, was published by MIT in 2024. He regularly writes for the *Architectural Review* and is co-director of New Architecture Writers, a programme for young people of colour.

Claire Zimmerman has recently worked on architecture in nineteenth- and twentieth-century industrialising environments. Publications include *Albert Kahn Inc: Architecture, Labor, and Industry, 1905–1961* (MIT Press, 2025), *Architecture against Democracy: Histories of the Nationalist International* (co-edited with Reinhold Martin, Minnesota 2024), and *Detroit-Moscow-Detroit: An Architecture for Industrialization* (co-edited with J.-L. Cohen and C. Crawford, MIT Press, 2023). 'The Costs of Architecture' is a themed issue of *Grey Room* (number 71, 2018) co-edited with Lucia Allais and Zeynep Çelik Alexander, focused on building costs and their importance in histories of the built environment. Zimmerman directs the PhD programme in Architecture, Landscape, and Design at the University of Toronto.

Picture Credits

Archive Milan Prelog, Institute za Povijest Umjetnosti, Zagreb – pp91, 107
Bentley Historical Library/ Albert Kahn Associates – p68
DLA Marbach – p35
Fondazione Elvira Badaracco, Milan – p175
The Henry Ford – cover, pp28, 78, 79, 82
Kois Miah – pp88, 119
Onyeka Igwe – pp194, 217, 229
Public domain – pp8, 50, 91, 107, 138, 141, 145, 178
RIBA Archives – p58
RIBA Library – p59
Smithson Family Collection – pp121, 122
Wikimedia Commons – pp21, 155
Yale Center for British Art/public domain – pp152, 164, 165